"Whenever I read anything written by Robert Smith, I am never disappointed. His ability to treat a text within its context and yet make penetrating personal application to today's world is almost uncanny. True to form, his latest book, *Joshua*, is an example of a master expositor at work. Readers will find these sermons a satisfying combination of solid exposition, captivating illustrations, and practical applications. The sermon titles in these 22 chapters alone are worth the price of the book. Robert Smith's *Joshua* will become a regular go-to volume for those who preach or teach the sixth book of the Old Testament."

David L. Allen, founder of *PreachingCoach*, Distinguished Visiting Professor of Practical Theology, and dean of the Adrian Rodgers Center for Biblical Preaching, Mid-America Baptist Theological Seminary

"With delight I commend this commentary from one of my favorite preachers as he provides exposition from his favorite book. The many insights gained from Robert Smith's years of preaching from the book of Joshua are ours to reap and sow again in the hearts of God's people as we are blessed from this work designed to be pastorally sensitive, exegetically insightful, and Christ-centered. The only demerit of these written messages is that we cannot hear them delivered from the lips of this master preacher who has been such a faithful colleague and friend with his resolute determination to be a true servant of the Word."

Bryan Chapell, pastor, Stated Clerk of the Presbyterian Church in America, and author of *Christ-Centered Preaching*.

"The Old Testament book of Joshua is a treasury of powerful preaching possibilities, and this tremendous commentary by Robert Smith Jr. will prove to be one of the essential resources preachers will want on hand as they prepare to proclaim God's truth from Joshua. Robert Smith is one of today's most engaging and effective preachers, and his insights will offer a significant foundation on which to stand as we prepare for preaching and teaching this inspired story of God leading his people into a land of promise. It is a book I plan to use in my own study, and I would encourage every proclaimer of God's Word to do the same."

Michael Duduit, executive editor of *Preaching* magazine and dean of Clamp Divinity School of Anderson University, Anderson, South Carolina

"An enormously helpful guide for preachers that provides a careful reading of the biblical text, a deep understanding of its place in God's unfolding plan, and wise insights into present-day application drawn from a lifetime of ministry. Smith's love for the book of Joshua shines through!"

Dr. Tim MacBride, dean of Bible and theology, Morling College, Sydney, Australia.

"Adept skills in exposition are essential tools for successfully navigating the terrain of divine Scripture in a way that honors the original intent of the text. Dr. Robert Smith's *Christ-Centered Exposition Commentary: Exalting Jesus in Joshua* is an invaluable resource that takes the reader on a masterful journey through the book of Joshua while expertly highlighting pictures of Christ in the Old Testament. Staying true to his posture of exegetical precision, Dr. Smith provides a commentary that will empower readers to simultaneously see the redemptive history in the text while maintaining the integrity of its historical accuracy."

Dr. Craig L. Oliver Sr., pastor of Elizabeth Baptist Church, Atlanta, Georgia

"In the spirit of the old Black spiritual, 'You can have 'dis ole world but give me Jesus,' legendary and beloved homiletical sage Robert Smith Jr. gives us Jesus through every page of this commentary. Through his Christological reading of Joshua, he demonstrates how the whole counsel of God leads us to Jesus Christ, while offering practical wisdom for traveling on a Christ-centered homiletical highway. This book is more than a commentary; it is a literary loving altar of worship in the throne room of God. All who read will be ushered into the presence of the living, incarnate Word."

Luke A. Powery, dean of Duke University Chapel, associate professor of homiletics and African and African American studies, Duke University

"Robert Smith is one of the most beloved preachers of our day, and one of the most faithful exponents of the Word I've ever known. Joshua just so happens to be his favorite book of the Bible. What a treat, then, to have a preachers' commentary from him on this book that does so much to shape our knowledge of and love for the gospel of Jesus Christ. Dr. Smith expounds Joshua in a Christological manner, emphasizing its crucial place in the history of redemption. He presents 'preaching that teaches and teaching that preaches,' helping expositors to demonstrate its utter practicality for daily Christian living in the twenty-first century. I recommend this treasure trove wholeheartedly."

Douglas A. Sweeney, dean and professor of divinity, Beeson Divinity School

"Robert Smith Jr. is a premiere preacher, Bible commentator, and Christ-centered expositor. This work is filled with rich and insightful lessons from the book of Joshua. I thought I knew the book of Joshua until I read this book. I am ready for a new sermon series on Joshua forthwith."

Frank A. Thomas, director, PhD Program in African American preaching and sacred rhetoric, Christian Theological Seminary

"When Dr. Robert Smith Jr. preaches, he paints a picture for the listener. Through vivid explanation, he brings you to the time, place, and context of the biblical text. Once you are fully immersed, he uses hymns, personal experience, or historical examples interwoven with the exposition of the text to bring a new and rich understanding of the truths found in the passage. In this commentary on Joshua, Dr. Smith brings the gifts utilized in his oratory to the printed page. The sermon in each chapter is prefaced with the 'Big Ten' elements, providing the reader with an outline for understanding themes, New Testament connections, and the behavioral response to the passage. Preachers, teachers, and students of the Word will benefit from Dr. Smith's research and application as he uses the text of Joshua to point us to the 'greater Joshua'—Jesus."

Jeanna Westmoreland, Ed.D., Samford University, Birmingham, Alabama

CHRIST-CENTERED

Exposition

AUTHOR **Robert Smith Jr.**

SERIES EDITORS **David Platt, Daniel L. Akin, and Tony Merida**

CHRIST-CENTERED
Exposition

EXALTING JESUS IN

JOSHUA

HOLMAN®
REFERENCE
NASHVILLE, TENNESSEE

SERIES DEDICATION

Dedicated to Adrian Rogers and John Piper. They have taught us to love the gospel of Jesus Christ, to preach the Bible as the inerrant Word of God, to pastor the church for which our Savior died, and to have a passion to see all nations gladly worship the Lamb.

—David Platt, Tony Merida, and Danny Akin
March 2013

AUTHOR'S DEDICATION

To my parents, Deacon Robert Smith Sr. and Deaconess Ozella Smith, on whose shoulders I stand and to whose testimonies I give voice.

TABLE OF CONTENTS

ACKNOWLEDGMENTS

The title of my first published work, coedited with Dr. Timothy George, reflects the investment in this work—it's been *A Mighty Long Journey!* Nearly fifty years ago I began teaching and preaching from the book of Joshua, my favorite book of the Bible. I preached through Joshua during my nearly twenty-year pastorate at New Mission Baptist Church of Cincinnati, Ohio. I also preached through Joshua during my seven-year tenure as preacher in residence at the historic Allen Temple AME Church of Cincinnati, Ohio. I have shared the material from this volume locally, statewide at the Arkansas Baptist Evangelism Conference, with numerous denominational congregations, and nationally at the National Baptist Convention, Inc. USA, and at various theological schools including Trinity Evangelical Divinity School in Deerfield, Illinois, Houston Baptist University in Houston, Texas, and Western Theological Seminary in Portland, Oregon. I am grateful for the opportunity to develop my thoughts about Joshua internationally, as well, in Glasgow, Scotland, and London, England.

To my efficient and proficient administrative assistant, Carlea Jordan, who served as my theological conversation partner as well as typist and research assistant throughout this project, thank you. I am also grateful for persons who assisted in typing and other clerical tasks: Allison Davis, Michelle Gray, Jacqueline Helm, and Traci Harper. Many thanks to my son in the ministry, Pastor Freddie T. Piphus, who provided a well-appointed and comfortable office in which I could study, write, and pray with freedom. Thanks to Dr. Dave Stabnow, who made editing a joy rather than a chore. Thank you, Dr. Wanda Taylor-Smith, my sweet wife, for giving me sacred space and extending grace to me to finish this sacred assignment. My utmost praise and deepest gratitude go to the triune God who has been faithful to me throughout my entire life. "He who calls you is faithful; he will do it" (1 Thess 5:24). God be praised!

Soli deo gloria
Robert Smith Jr.
Cincinnati, Ohio

SERIES INTRODUCTION

Augustine said, "Where Scripture speaks, God speaks." The editors of the Christ-Centered Exposition Commentary series believe that where God speaks, the pastor must speak. God speaks through his written Word. We must speak from that Word. We believe the Bible is God breathed, authoritative, inerrant, sufficient, understandable, necessary, and timeless. We also affirm that the Bible is a Christ-centered book; that is, it contains a unified story of redemptive history of which Jesus is the hero. Because of this Christ-centered trajectory that runs from Genesis 1 through Revelation 22, we believe the Bible has a corresponding global-missions thrust. From beginning to end, we see God's mission as one of making worshipers of Christ from every tribe and tongue worked out through this redemptive drama in Scripture. To that end we must preach the Word.

In addition to these distinct convictions, the Christ-Centered Exposition Commentary series has some distinguishing characteristics. First, this series seeks to display exegetical accuracy. What the Bible says is what we want to say. While not every volume in the series will be a verse-by-verse commentary, we nevertheless desire to handle the text carefully and explain it rightly. Those who teach and preach bear the heavy responsibility of saying what God has said in his Word and declaring what God has done in Christ. We desire to handle God's Word faithfully, knowing that we must give an account for how we have fulfilled this holy calling (Jas 3:1).

Second, the Christ-Centered Exposition Commentary series has pastors in view. While we hope others will read this series, such as parents, teachers, small-group leaders, and student ministers, we desire to provide a commentary busy pastors will use for weekly preparation of biblically faithful and gospel-saturated sermons. This series is not academic in nature. Our aim is to present a readable and pastoral style of commentaries. We believe this aim will serve the church of the Lord Jesus Christ.

Third, we want the Christ-Centered Exposition Commentary series to be known for the inclusion of helpful illustrations and theologically driven applications. Many commentaries offer no help in illustrations, and few offer any kind of help in application. Often those that do offer illustrative material and application unfortunately give little serious attention to the text. While giving ourselves primarily to explanation, we also hope to serve readers by providing inspiring and illuminating illustrations coupled with timely and timeless application.

Finally, as the name suggests, the editors seek to exalt Jesus from every book of the Bible. In saying this, we are not commending wild allegory or fanciful typology. We certainly believe we must be constrained to the meaning intended by the divine Author himself, the Holy Spirit of God. However, we also believe the Bible has a messianic focus, and our hope is that the individual authors will exalt Christ from particular texts. Luke 24:25-27,44-47 and John 5:39,46 inform both our hermeneutics and our homiletics. Not every author will do this the same way or have the same degree of Christ-centered emphasis. That is fine with us. We believe faithful exposition that is Christ centered is not monolithic. We do believe, however, that we must read the whole Bible as Christian Scripture. Therefore, our aim is both to honor the historical particularity of each biblical passage and to highlight its intrinsic connection to the Redeemer.

The editors are indebted to the contributors of each volume. The reader will detect a unique style from each writer, and we celebrate these unique gifts and traits. While distinctive in their approaches, the authors share a common characteristic in that they are pastoral theologians. They love the church, and they regularly preach and teach God's Word to God's people. Further, many of these contributors are younger voices. We think these new, fresh voices can serve the church well, especially among a rising generation that has the task of proclaiming the Word of Christ and the Christ of the Word to the lost world.

We hope and pray this series will serve the body of Christ well in these ways until our Savior returns in glory. If it does, we will have succeeded in our assignment.

David Platt
Daniel L. Akin
Tony Merida
Series Editors
February 2013

Joshua

Introduction

For years I have said to the students of my preaching classes at Beeson Divinity School, "For every New Testament doctrine, there is an Old Testament picture." The doctrinal teaching of inheritance gazed upon in the New Testament letters of Ephesians and Hebrews is glimpsed in the Old Testament book of Joshua. Jesus is the hero of both the Old Testament and the New Testament. He said to the Jews, "You pore over the Scriptures because you think you have eternal life in them, and yet they testify about me" (John 5:39). On the Emmaus road Jesus told the discouraged and doubtful disciples about his being resurrected from the dead: "Wasn't it necessary for the Messiah to suffer these things and enter into his glory?" (Luke 24:26). From this question Jesus began with the Pentateuch and proceeded to connect with the prophetic literature as well as the Psalms, or Writings, in expounding to them the things concerning himself. All Scripture must be linked to Christ, who not only gives believers an eternal inheritance (1 Pet 1:4) but *is* the believer's inheritance. The Bible is a HIMBOOK and must be seen and understood through the lens of Christ. It was Christ who, "beginning with Moses and all the Prophets, . . . interpreted for them the things concerning himself in all the Scriptures" (Luke 24:27; see also v. 44).

While vacationing in Myrtle Beach, South Carolina, I was walking on the beach and noticed a man with a small bucket, shovel, and a metal detector. He was using the metal detector across the surface of the beach. I asked why he was doing this. He replied, "I am searching for metal objects—things like rings, bracelets, necklaces, and watches that fall from those who walk and run on the beach, escaping their notice." These elements become quickly buried in the sand below. He told me his metal detector would emit a ticking sound when it was in the area of buried metal. When the sound grew stronger, he would start digging and bring valuable commodities to the surface. This volume will serve as a Christological detector for locating valuable insights about Christ illustratively, typologically, conceptually, narratively, and metaphorically.

It is all about him. Jude 24 records, "Now to *him* who is able to protect you from stumbling." Ephesians 3:20 states, "Now to *him* who is able to do above and beyond all that we ask or think." It's about Christ. Charles Haddon Spurgeon is considered by some to have said, "I take my text and make a beeline to the cross."[1] This attribution may not be correct, but it does represent Spurgeon's conviction that the Bible is about *him.* It is a HIMBOOK.

During Jesus's conversation with his two disciples on the Emmaus road, after a bit, he exposited the Hebrew Bible to them. He revealed how the volume bears witness to his essence and his eventual bodily presence on earth in the incarnation. Never does the Bible foreshadow Jesus more than in the book of Joshua, for the book of Joshua aligns itself with Jesus in its **revelation.** Joshua received the following:

A New Name

Joshua's original name was Hoshea (Num 13:8,16; Deut 32:44), which means "salvation." He was a minister to Moses. Moses reconfigured his name to "Joshua," which means "Yahweh is salvation." The Hebrew name *Joshua* is a form of the Hebrew designation *Yeshua* and the Greek

---

[1] Many people have attributed this quotation to Spurgeon. This is because Lewis Drummond, in his 1992 definitive biography, *Spurgeon: The Prince of Preachers* (p. 223) attributed it to him. See also, https://www.spurgeon.org/resource-library/blog-entries/6 -quotes-spurgeon-didnt-say/, which debunks the attribution to Spurgeon.

New Testament designation *Jesus*. That is, the Greek form of "Joshua" in the New Testament is *Jesus*. The name *Jesus*, which like *Joshua* means "Yahweh is salvation" in Hebrew, carries a soteriological purpose. "You are to name him Jesus, because he will save his people from their sins" (Matt 1:21). In the New Testament, the greater Joshua, Jesus, is anticipated by the Old Testament Joshua.

Joshua's name necessitates the name of Yeshua because Joshua could only lead the Israelites into the land of promise without giving them rest, but Yeshua gives believers rest (Matt 11:28-30; Heb 4:8). As believers we have been given both rest and a new name (Rev 2:17). For a long time, African Americans have been singing, "There's a new name written down in glory and it's mine, oh yes, it's mine" (Miles, "I Was Once a Sinner"). At other times they would sing regarding the new rest, that we're going to a place where "the wicked shall cease from troubling and the weary shall be at **rest**. All of the saints of the ages are gonna sit at his feet and be blessed" (Dixon, "The Wicked Shall Cease Their Troubling"). Down here many pejorative names are given to believers. Paul was even called a fool and was accused of being mad because of his learning (Acts 26:24). But God has given believers a different name and title. We will be called servants (Matt 25:21; Rev 22:3).

A New Family

Joshua is an Ephraimite. Ephraim was one of Joseph's two sons born in Egypt of a Gentile mother, Joseph's wife. Joseph's brothers sold him, a member of their family, to foreigners, and God gave Joseph a new family. Eventually, Joseph was positioned to save his father's family from the devastating effects of famine. Jacob, Joseph's father, and his family eventually moved to Egypt because there was grain there, and Joseph was in charge of the grain. When Jacob was dying, Joseph brought his two sons, Manasseh and Ephraim, to see their grandfather, Jacob. Jacob not only gave Joseph's sons a prayerful blessing but also granted them a land inheritance through the process of adopting them. He said in Genesis 48:5, "Ephraim and Manasseh belong to me just as Reuben and Simeon do." This is formal and legal adoption. Manasseh and Ephraim's mother was a Gentile from Egypt. Therefore, they were not purely Israelite (Jewish). Rather, they would have been Gentiles unlike their Jewish father, Joseph. However, upon being adopted by their grandfather, they would have a new family identity with the legal granting of land inheritance. They were grafted into the Jewish family—the family of God. Jacob was saying to Joseph, "These are now my sons!"

Jacob, the grandfather, is thus the father by adoption. These two sons are not only given a land inheritance but are designated as tribal leaders in the place of Joseph. There are twelve tribes of Israel—Manasseh and Ephraim are two of those tribes, and Joseph is not included in this twelve-tribe configuration. This reality is a harbinger of Romans 8:14-17:

> For all those led by God's Spirit are God's sons. For you did not receive a spirit of slavery to fall back into fear. Instead, you received the Spirit of adoption, by whom we cry out, "Abba, Father!" The Spirit himself testifies together with our spirit that we are God's children, and if children, also heirs—heirs of God and coheirs with Christ.

There is intratrinitarian presence in this transaction. (1) God the Father—"We cry out, 'Abba, Father!'" (v. 15); (2) God the Son—"And coheirs with Christ" (v. 17); and (3) God the Holy Spirit—"You received the Spirit of adoption" (v. 15). We are given an inheritance in Christ.

Joshua was an Ephraimite. He has royal ancestry because Ephraim was raised in royalty in Egypt. Ephraim's father Joseph was the vice-regent in Egypt and the second in command. Joseph rode in the second chariot behind Pharaoh, who rode in the first chariot during parades and processions. Ephraim was clothed in royalty, was educated in the highest academic institutions in Egypt, and was probably assigned teachers of the greatest intellectual acumen. As believers, we are a *royal* priesthood (1 Pet 2:9). We are sealed by the Spirit until the day of redemption. We are washed in the blood of the crucified one. We are the children of the Most High God and joint heirs or coheirs with the greater Joshua, who is the Second Person of the Trinity.

Hebrews 2:11 makes note of an amazing reality: our Christ of royalty was not ashamed or embarrassed to call us brothers and sisters. Therefore, the greater Joshua, Jesus, has done what the Old Testament Joshua could not do—make us one in the family of God by virtue of his death and resurrection. The Old Testament Joshua died and is awaiting the resurrection as an Old Testament saint. The New Testament or the greater Joshua died and rose again. He will raise Joshua and all the saints from the Old Testament, New Testament, and more contemporary times from the dead.

A New Home

After Israel endured four hundred years of Egyptian bondage, the exodus occurred. Israel then spent approximately forty years wandering in the wilderness because the people of God balked at Kadesh-barnea. The

Israelites lacked faith even after seeing God bring them out of bondage, enable them to cross the Red Sea on dry land, and eradicate their pursuers. Though God had been faithful before they reached the boundaries of the promised land, the Israelites failed to trust him to give them victory over the idolatrous residents in Canaan. Ten of twelve spies came back from area reconnaissance with a discouraging report. The ten "viewed God through the difficulty. The two viewed the difficulty through a God for whom nothing was impossible" (Sanders, *Promised Land Living*, 27). Joshua was one of the two unwavering spies.

Therefore, Joshua would inherit a new home, Canaan, which Yahweh promised more than five hundred years earlier to Abraham and his descendants (Gen 15:18). Yahweh had identified the boundaries of the land—north, south, east, and west—even before Moses was born, and Joshua just takes the people over into the land. This reflects the omniscience of God who knows the boundaries of the land that is to be possessed even before Joshua and Israel possess it. God is faithful in keeping his promises and is not slack concerning them. God is not **in** time. Time is in God. God's clock keeps perfect providential time. Therefore, God **owns** time, and when he fulfills his promises, they are always fulfilled **on** time. The fulfillment comes in *kairos* time (the qualitative right time, an opportune moment, the due season) not *chronos* time (the quantitative hour, minute, and second). This truth is indelibly etched in redemptive and salvation history particularly in the birth of Christ—"When the time came to completion, God sent his Son, born of a woman, born under the law" (Gal 4:4). Jesus was born on time. He died on time: "Father, the hour has come. Glorify your Son so that the Son may glorify you" (John 17:1). He was resurrected on time: "After three days I will rise again" (Matt 27:63). And Jesus will come again on time: "Now concerning that day and hour no one knows—neither the angels of heaven nor the Son—except the Father alone" (Matt 24:36).

Christ will take his children to their new home—in that land that is fairer than day, a land where we will never grow old, a land where there will be no overcrowding or discriminatory housing—for Jesus said, "In my Father's house are many rooms" (John 14:2). The residents in the new Jerusalem will consist of people from all nations, tribes, peoples, and languages (Rev 7:9). The Old Testament Joshua could only lead the nation of Israel to a land in which they would have to expel and evict the present residents in order to possess the territory. However, the greater Joshua has gone away to prepare a place for believers, so upon their arrival the only thing that will be necessary will be to worship the triune God, for all of the hindering causes and people will be dismissed. He will make all things new in our new home.

A New Presence

The ark of the covenant symbolically represented the presence of the Lord in the midst of his people Israel. It contained three significant items of historical memorabilia: (1) the tablets of stone, which represented the word of God; (2) the pot of manna, which represented the provision of God; and (3) Aaron's rod that budded, which represented the power of God. The Lord instructed Joshua to have the priests carry the ark of the covenant to the edge of the Jordan River. As soon as the priests' feet touched the water's edge, the Jordan stopped flowing, and the Israelites crossed over into the promised land through the Jordan River and did not even get their feet wet. (This is a flashback to their crossing the Red Sea under the leadership of Moses from Egypt into the wilderness.) The waters of the Jordan River did not stop flowing until the feet of the priests carrying the ark of the covenant of the Lord touched the edge of the Jordan River on the wilderness side. The ark of the covenant was carried by the priests as the processional proceeded around the walls of Jericho for seven days. On the seventh day and the seventh revolution around the city, the people shouted, and God caused the walls to fall down flat. Once again the presence of the ark of the covenant of God represented that God was in the midst of his people, fighting for them and making the impossible possible.

Through the ark of the covenant, the Lord was expressing his presence among his people. In Revelation 21:3 eschatologically, God's nearness is not symbolized by an ark made of a box composed of acacia wood. No, he is actively present in the midst of his people—not in a box but in his own person. Hear the words of John as he ponders this truth and thinks out loud in his writing:

> *Then I heard a loud voice from the throne: Look, God's dwelling is with humanity, and he will live with them. They will be his peoples, and God himself will be with them and will be their God.* (Rev 21:3)

What a day of rejoicing that will be when the long-expected Jesus is no longer symbolized by a box nor must limit himself to reside in the presence of only some of his people at a time as he did during his thirty-three-year pilgrimage on earth as the historical Jesus. Instead, Jesus will actually be present in the midst of all his people in his glorified body with radiance that outshines the sun and glory that cannot be captured with the pen of the most astute and eloquent writers. God himself, literally, will be in the midst of his people. The God before whom angels bow. The God whom heaven and earth adore. The God who speaks and it is done—who wills and it comes to pass. The God who cannot be described yet the God who can be engaged. The God who would not permit Moses to see his glory but will be on display for all the saints to behold. John says, "They will see his face" (Rev 22:4) and live in his presence.

A New Spiritual Location

The Old Testament Joshua was the assistant to Moses the leader of Israel; he was his apprentice and understudy. Upon Moses's death, Joshua was appointed as Moses's successor. He possessed the necessary experience to lead Israel, for he had been born in Egypt and had served in various capacities under the administration of Moses for forty years. He had obtained the necessary credibility to lead Israel through his faithful witness as one of the twelve spies commissioned by Moses to participate in the espionage of the promised land. He had rapport with the Israelite community. He had secured the confidence of the people of Israel in his victorious battle against the Amalekites at Rephidim (Exod 17:13). But the most significant qualification Joshua had for leading Israel now that Moses was dead was not what he had but rather what had him, or better stated, *who* had him. It was not what he possessed; rather, it was who possessed him. With regard to a type of installation or investiture service, the biblical writer makes this important attribution regarding Joshua: "The LORD replied to Moses, 'Take Joshua son of Nun, a man who has the Spirit in him, and lay your hands on him'" (Num 27:18). The Spirit rested on Joshua.

The greater Joshua was conceived by the Spirit, filled with the Spirit without measure, and raised by the Spirit from death (Rom 8:11). Upon his ascension, the greater Joshua would send the Spirit on the day of Pentecost, not to rest on believers but rather to reside in believers and fill them for effective service (Eph 5:18). The Greek tense in this verse means "keep on being filled with the Spirit"; it is an ongoing process and reality.

I'm grateful for the book of Joshua and for its treasures. In it lies the precious gem of the gospel—Jesus, the pearl of great price. Jesus is the greater Joshua. Jesus is greater than Solomon (Matt 12:42) in wisdom, and he is also greater than the Old Testament Joshua in deliverance. He is the deliverer from the bondage of sin and holds the title deed to the heavenly kingdom. The book of Joshua is a written testimony that points to Jesus, who not only spoke the word of God but who is the Word of God. The spoken word of the Old Testament Joshua applied to those who would live in a land of significance, for the land would be the earthly place where the greater Joshua would be born—in the city of Bethlehem of Judea (Mic 5:2) as the revealed Word in the incarnation (John 1:14).

Israel's population during Joshua's leadership is over one million. Israel does not have sufficient military strength to defeat the seven nations of Canaan during the three military campaigns: central, northern, and southern. They emerged victorious and became the landlords of Canaan because the Lord fought for them. In his closing statement, Joshua told the people of Israel they were victorious because "the LORD [their] God was fighting for [them], as he promised" (Josh 23:10).

The book of Joshua must be understood by looking through the lens of redemptive historical progression. Sydney Greidanus asserts,

> It's a matter of connecting the dots—the dots that run from the periphery of the Old Testament to the center of God's revelation in Jesus Christ. . . . Christian preachers must understand an Old Testament passage in light of this progression in redemptive history. (*Preaching Christ*, 25)

Joshua learned to serve as an assistant under Moses, whose designation was "the LORD's servant" (Josh 1:1). At the end of Joshua's life, he too is called "the LORD's servant" (Josh 24:29). Joshua would lead the Israelites into Canaan. Jesus leads believers to heaven. Canaan is not heaven. Canaan stands for a victorious type of Christian experience. Canaan was God's gift to Israel as promised to Abraham (Gen 15:18). God even gave the boundaries to Abraham centuries before Israel took possession of it.

Undergirding Convictions

Roughly the first half of the book, Joshua 1–12, is devoted to the possession of the land through warfare. Roughly the second half of the book, chapters 13–24, relates the distribution of the land to the tribes. Above all else, the reading of Joshua bears witness to Jesus Christ. The central aim of this volume is to view the book of Joshua through the lens of Christology. Jesus Christ is the greater Joshua.

The following convictions undergird this work:

- That the Spirit inscripturated the Word of God (2 Tim 3:16) serves as the launching pad for pursuing Christ in every chapter of this commentary. It was Martin Luther's conviction that the canonicity of a book of the Bible and its exegesis ought to be based on "that which promotes Christ." Accordingly, this is a Christ-centered commentary.
- This commentary on Joshua, the first of the former prophetic books in the Hebrew Bible, presents preaching that teaches and teaching that preaches.
- The thematic thread that runs throughout the fabric of the book of Joshua is found in Joshua 21:45: "None of the good promises the LORD had made to the house of Israel failed. Everything was fulfilled."
- This commentary on Joshua consults the whole counsel of God. Since Christ is the end of the Law and the Prophets and fulfills both, the commentary will examine the larger context as it relates to its Christological concentration.
- The truths embedded in this commentary are practical for contemporary living. Twenty-first-century Christians are seemingly ignorant of what it means to claim our spiritual inheritance.

The Big Ten

Canonicity relates to the larger picture of Scripture. It seeks to show the relationship between the biblical passage in the book of Joshua under consideration with the wider corpus of Scripture, namely, the entire Bible. This is the relationship of intertextuality—how one text of Scripture finds its fuller meaning in another text of Scripture outside the immediate book, whether from the Old or New Testament. This volume will seek to encourage putting the overwhelming emphasis on living at the interpretive *address* of the passage in Joshua before visiting the *zip code* of the wider text of Scripture in which the Joshua passage will find its fuller meaning in redemptive history, especially in the life of Christ. The following **Big Ten** areas will introduce the sermon in each chapter. Immediately following the sermon in each chapter is a section called **Reflections**. This section will expose some of the Big Ten

elements highlighted in the sermons more fully. The Reflections section
is designed to motivate preachers and teachers to be more intentional
and thorough in preaching Christ-centered sermons.

1. **Text:** The literary foundation on which the textual historical
   narrative is based. The book of Joshua is a historical narrative.
   Therefore, the messages to be preached and/or taught from
   Joshua lend themselves more to illustrations and not just propo-
   sitions, moves and not simply structures, stories and not merely
   syllogisms. *Readers are challenged to read each passage to be preached
   fifty times*, not necessarily in one sitting. However, the passage
   being preached needs to be read fifty times to elicit participation of the five senses in the investigation of the total passage.
2. **Title:** The brief description that announces, summarizes, and
   popularizes what each message in the chapters is all about.
3. **New Testament Companion:** The New Testament is concealed
   within the Old Testament. The Old Testament is revealed in the
   New Testament. The book of Joshua will be interpreted in light
   of the New Testament. The thread of the book of Joshua will be
   woven into the fabric of the New Testament through a process
   of intertextuality.
4. **Fallen Condition Focus:** In the words of its conceptual origina-
   tor, Dr. Bryan Chapell, the fallen condition focus is "the mutual
   human condition that contemporary believers share with those
   to or about whom the text was written that requires the grace of
   the passage for God's people to glorify and enjoy him" (*Christ-
   Centered Preaching*, 50).
5. **The Whole Counsel of God:** This overarching and broad concept unites and ties together every passage of Scripture so that
   it relates to the overall plan and comprehensive purpose of
   God revealed in the Scriptures by the Holy Spirt in order to
   magnify Christ.
6. **The Christological Highway to Jesus:** This element represents
   the heart and centerpiece of the Big Ten. Jesus said about himself, "You pore over the Scriptures because you think you have
   eternal life in them, and yet they testify about me" (John 5:39).
   Christ is the destination of salvation history. The Bible is the
   road map that leads to Jesus. Ultimately, the Bible is about the
   Man of salvation who carries out and fulfills the plan of salvation.

7. **Intratrinitarian Presence:** This element is based on the coalescence and distillation of Jonathan Edwards's intratrinarian thought expressed throughout the breadth of his writings: "God has forever known himself in a sweet and holy society as Father, Son, and Holy Spirit" (in Smith, *Oasis of God*, 94).

8. **Proposition:** The proposition is that concise, clear, and singular sentence based on a Joshua text that summarizes the entirety of the text and carries with it a behavioral action and an eschatological projection.

9. **Behavioral Response:** The response of the contemporary believer based on *what* the text means. The response also answers the *so what* of the text: What difference does this text make in my life? Finally, it answers the *now what* of the text: What am I to do now?

10. **Future Condition Focus (Sermonic Eschatonics):** Each textual message will be examined in light of *sub specie eternatatis*, or under the light of eternity. This component provides a sense of purpose and hope as it relates to the pervasive pessimistic presence that is often attributed to various historical narrative episodes (i.e., texts describing the total wiping out of cities like Ai and Jericho where everyone is killed, including babies).

The Man Joshua

The book of Joshua bears the name of the essential character, Joshua, the son of Nun. Joshua is a real historical personality (Acts 7:45) who by divine appointment is intended to secure and sustain Abraham's seed and to lead the Israelites into the land of promise—Canaan. He is from the tribe of Ephraim. Ephraim was the youngest son of Joseph and would receive a territorial plot through Joseph's line. First Chronicles 7:20-29 provides the family tree of Joshua. He was a contemporary of fellow spy Caleb, who is believed to have been born around 1484 BC. Both were born into slavery in Egypt. Joshua lived to be 110 years of age (Josh 24:29; Judg 2:8). Therefore, apparently, he lived forty years in Egypt, forty years in the wilderness, and thirty years in the promised land. It appears that Joshua's last thirty years were spent in this way: seven years leading Israel to conquer Canaan and about twenty-three years in retirement in his territorial allotment at Timnath–Serah in Ephraim.

Joshua had two formal titles: he was Moses's minister or assistant (Num 11:28; Josh 1:1); however, by the time of his death, Joshua is referred to as "the LORD's servant" (Josh 24:29; Judg 2:8). This was the esteemed title afforded Moses (Deut 34:5; Josh 1:1,13,15). Jesus Christ would be referred to as the Suffering Servant of the Lord (Isa 49–53). The Joshua account is replete with God speaking to Joshua just as he had spoken to Moses, except that God spoke to Moses "directly" (Num 12:8; lit. "mouth to mouth").

The central theme of the book of Joshua is found in Joshua 23:14:

> You know with all your heart and all your soul that none of the good promises the LORD your God made to you has failed. Everything was fulfilled for you; not one promise has failed.

Pockets of the land of Canaan remained unconquered, however, and the residents in those territories continued to live in those areas (e.g., 10:1-5,33; 13:1-7). Only Jesus the greater Joshua, after all, will bring the church into the full possession of their inheritance and rest (Heb 3:18-19; 4:1,8). In Christ, all of God's promises find their fulfillment.

> For the Son of God, Jesus Christ, whom we proclaimed among you— Silvanus, Timothy, and I—did not become "Yes and no." On the contrary, in him it is always "Yes." For every one of God's promises is "Yes" in him. Therefore, through him we also say "Amen" to the glory of God. (2 Cor 1:19-20)

In the eschaton, Jesus, who conquered the grave at his resurrection and ascended to heaven, will return for the people of his church to give us our eternal inheritance in a better country (Heb 11:16), the new Jerusalem (Rev 21). There God's people, saved through faith in Jesus Christ, will have eschatological rest (Heb 4:8-11).

Joshua is suitable for an expositional sermon or for a teaching series. Thematically, Joshua is a historical narrative. It reflects the components of the antagonist, protagonist, plot, resolution, and fulfillment. As the Word of God, it is alive and profitable for believers today.

A New Beginning

JOSHUA 1:1-9

Main Idea: Christ, our new beginning, brings us out of the wilderness of sin through the power of the Spirit to do the work of the kingdom of God.

I. **What Are We Going to Do?**
   A. The punctuation of time
   B. The "now" of time
II. **God Promises.**
   A. Land
   B. Success
   C. Presence
III. **Delight in the Lord.**
IV. **Fear Not.**

The Big Ten

Text: Joshua 1:1-9

Title: A New Beginning

New Testament Companion: Matthew 6:25-34

Fallen Condition Focus: The great enemy of faith is fear. Fear causes the believer to approach the challenges of Christian service with a sense of reduced confidence. Therefore, the Lord said to Joshua, "Do not be afraid, . . . for the LORD your God is with you wherever you go" (Josh 1:9).

The Whole Counsel of God: Jesus, the Son of God, the greater Joshua, did what the law of Moses could not do—deliver humanity from the bondage of sin and provide believers with rest (Heb 4:8) and freedom—for "where the Spirit of the Lord is, there is freedom" (2 Cor 3:17).

The Christological Highway to Jesus: Jesus, the greater Joshua of the New Testament, does what the Old Testament Joshua could not do—gives believers eternal rest (Heb 4:8).

15

Intratrinitarian Presence: God will never leave the believer. The death, burial, resurrection, and ascension of the Son made it possible for the Spirit of God to dwell within men and women who believe.

Proposition: Christ, our new beginning, brings us out of the wilderness of sin through the power of the Spirit to do the work of the kingdom of God.

Behavioral Response: Face every calling and trial with the strength and courage that comes from the Spirit and obedience to God's Word, for God will never leave you or abandon you.

Future Condition Focus (Sermonic Eschatonics): The closeness we have with God through the Spirit is only a down payment of what we will experience in the new creation—the place without fear, pain, or worry where believers will dwell with the triune God forever.

Introduction

When I pastored the New Mission Missionary Baptist Church of Cincinnati, Ohio, a congregation I served for nearly twenty years, the Seay family sang, "How Far Am I from Canaan?" I imagine Joshua and the Israelites, in the midst of their grief, introspectively asked the same question. After forty years of wandering and noting the growing absence of those who had dared complain during the journey, it is likely the Israelites did not pose the question as a complaint but in anxious anticipation of the fulfillment of God's promise to their ancestors. There is the temptation to be fearful and to doubt God, as the Israelites did at Kadesh-barnea. Joshua 1:1-9 is a critical moment for the Israelites.

The children of Israel are poised and positioned to cross over the Jordan River into Canaan land. They could feel the watery spray of the Jordan River as they stood on its banks and cast a wishful eye. They had crossed the Red Sea forty years prior under Moses and were standing in tiptoe-anticipation awaiting the journey to the river's other side, to the promised land. There must have been great anxiety among the Israelite congregation as they experienced the changing of the guard in leadership. Could they attempt to cross over into the promised land without their former leader, Moses?

Sacred history requires reflecting on the past, embracing the future, and holding both in simultaneity as one lives in the present. Two relevant words have a similar phonetic sound. They are *amnesia*, which means "to forget," and *anamnesis*, which means "to remember." (This is the same word Jesus used when he said to the disciples gathered around the Lord's Supper table, "Do this in remembrance of me"; Luke 22:19.) The book of Joshua is bookended by Deuteronomy and Judges. Deuteronomy refers to the importance of *remembering not to forget*. There Moses gives the law the second time (this time orally). Moses is rehearsing what God has said to the Israelites so that they will be prepared to live obediently and knowledgeably when they enter the promised land. The book of Judges reminds the Israelites *not to forget to remember*. However, Judges 2:10 relates the sad saga of the Israelites forgetting to remember, for it says, "After them another generation rose up who did not know the LORD or the works he had done for Israel." Joshua is the book in the middle that admonishes the Israelites to *remember to remember*.

Christ, our new beginning, brings us out of the wilderness of sin through the power of the Spirit to do the work of the kingdom of God. The people of God have a propensity, a proclivity, a tendency to forget. This necessitates God's saying the same thing to us over and over again. This may be due to our being hard of hearing or experiencing amnesia. James Weldon Johnson wrote of the propensity to forget from where one has come in his "Lift Every Voice and Sing." Another musicologist, Jennie E. Hussey, lifts up this tendency to forget when she reminds hearers to remember the cost of the crown at Calvary ("Lead Me to Calvary"). Similarly, the philosopher George Santayana admonished us to remember when he wrote, "He who forgets the past is condemned to repeat it" (*Life of Reason*, 5).

What Are We Going to Do?

This first chapter of Joshua begins with a cataclysmic announcement that had a catastrophic effect on the nation of Israel. God said to Joshua, "Moses my servant is dead" (v. 2). This announcement sent tsunami waves across the surface of the nation of Israel. Their great lawgiver who had served them for forty years was dead. Their liberator and mediator was dead. The one God had used to work miracles in their midst was dead. The lingering question in the mind of this nation was, Now that Moses is dead, what are we going to do?

The United States of America has experienced similar dilemmas when crises have occurred within our nation:

- On April 14, 1865, President Abraham Lincoln was shot at Ford's Theatre in Washington, D.C., and died the next day.
- On April 12, 1945, four-time elected President Franklin Delano Roosevelt died.
- On November 22, 1963, President John F. Kennedy was assassinated in Dallas, Texas.
- On April 4, 1968, Dr. Martin Luther King Jr. was assassinated in Memphis, Tennessee.

Each time, our nation faced the question, What are we going to do now? Similarly, I was confronted with this question over three decades ago when my wife, Gayle Walker Smith, died unexpectedly in a hospital at age thirty-nine, leaving me with our children to raise. What was I going to do? Like the Israelites, I had to believe God had the answer. In the words of Howard Thurman, the great African-American prophet, in his reference to Jeremiah 8:22, "God took Jeremiah's question mark of, 'Is there no balm in Gilead? Is there no physician there?,' and turned it into an exclamation point!" Many can attest, as I do, that there is a balm in Gilead that can make the wounded whole! This passage teaches that God buries his workers, but never his work, for the text says, "Moses my servant is dead; now you, Joshua, take these people over into the land that I have promised them." He always has a plan.

No believer is indispensable or nonexpendable. God does not need us; we need him! Therefore, we should assume a posture of humility and gratitude when we carry out God's calling on our lives. In Numbers 27:22-23 Moses had been wondering who would replace him once he had completed his earthly assignment. God informed him that his replacement was none other than his understudy and servant, Joshua. Moses was to have Joshua stand in the presence of Eleazar, the high priest, and before the nation of Israel who would witness the commissioning scene. Moses was then to lay his hands on Joshua as a symbol of transferring his authority to Joshua. In chapter 1 God is activating and executing what was only symbolically performed previously. "Moses my servant is dead."

The Punctuation of Time

Neither the Old nor New Testament in the original languages (Hebrew and Aramaic in the Old Testament and Greek in the New Testament) contained punctuation marks. There was just straight text. There were no periods, semicolons, commas, question marks, ellipses, exclamation points, etcetera. There were just letters. However, our versions of Scripture contain punctuation marks. Oftentimes these marks provide an interpretation of a particular text and furnish a theology for the believer to live by. For example, the first clause in verse 2 ends with a period: "Moses my servant is dead." The period is certainly the most proper and needed punctuation mark following the word *dead*. Just as death is a terminating point, the period is a punctuation point of finality and conclusion. In many English versions a period follows the word *dead* in verse 2. However, the King James Version does not put a period after *dead*; instead, it places a semicolon there. The period is a mark suggesting *termination*; the semicolon is a mark intimating *continuation*. Too many believers live their lives with a period, a theology of *termination*, instead of with a semicolon, a theology of *continuation*. When faced with serious surgical decisions, when confronted with a relational rift, when struggling with financial loss, when discouraged by ecclesiastical division, when treading on the verge of dropping out of school, one will either live with a theology of the period—*termination*—or a theology of the semicolon—*continuation*. God would have his children live lives based on a theology of the semicolon—*continuation*.

Scripture often vocalizes a theology of the semicolon—*continuation*. In Genesis 50:20 Joseph said to his brothers, "You planned evil against me;"—you must place a semicolon here—"God planned it for good to bring about the present result—the survival of many people." In Psalm 30:5 David said, "Weeping may stay overnight; *but* there is joy in the morning."[2] In Psalm 34:19 the psalmist says, "One who is righteous has many adversities; *but* the LORD rescues him from them all." In Habakkuk 3:17-18 the prophet says, "Though the fig tree does not bud and there is no fruit on the vines; though the olive crop fails and the fields produce no food; though the flocks disappear from the pen and there are no herds in the stalls; *yet* I will celebrate in the LORD; I will rejoice in the God of my salvation!" Jesus said in John 16:33, "You will have suffering in this world; be courageous! I have conquered the world." Paul states in Romans 6:23 that "the wages of sin is death; *but* the gift of God is eternal life in Christ Jesus our Lord."

---

[2] Punctuation changed and emphasis added in this and the following examples to illustrate the point.

A semicolon is a combination of two punctuation marks, a period and a comma. However, there is space between the period and the comma. The period is necessary because it serves as a reference reminder of our past, what God has brought us from and how God has brought us out. We must not eliminate the period. All of us are products of our pasts; however, we must not be prisoners to our pasts. The past is a necessary place to visit; however, it is a disastrous place to live. The apostle Paul said in Philippians 3:13-14,

> Brothers and sisters, I do not consider myself to have taken hold of it. But one thing I do: Forgetting what is behind and reaching forward to what is ahead, I pursue as my goal the prize promised by God's heavenly call in Christ Jesus.

The "Now" of Time

The word that follows the death of Moses is the word *now*. This is a word of urgency. The children of Israel had spent four hundred years in bondage in Egypt followed by forty years of wilderness wandering and thirty days of mourning the death of Moses, as seen in Deuteronomy 34:8. *Now* is the appropriate word. *Now* is the time. Too much time has been wasted. In the spirit of the Latin concept, *carpe diem*—"seize the day"—the children of Israel needed to go beyond Canaan's edge and cross over into the promised land.

Too much time has been wasted by many believers. As a young boy I heard the saints and sages in our little church sing about their unwillingness to waste days and their dedication to run the race set before them. We must ask ourselves perpetually, "How long will we procrastinate? How long will we delay? *Now* is the time!"

God Promises

Land

God tells Joshua to take the Israelites across the Jordan to possess the land that he is about to give to them; in fact, he had already given it to them. This seems rather confusing because God is saying that he's about to give when he has already given. *I am giving* relates to the future while *I have given* relates to the past. On the surface, the Almighty seems to be making a contradictory statement. However, what God is saying is he had promised and ceded this land over five hundred years ago to Abraham and his descendants (Gen 15:18). However, it would not be theirs until they possessed their possession. God said, "I have given you every place where the sole of your foot treads" (Josh 1:3).

This is an instance of "divine-human instrumentality": we do what we're responsible for doing, and God will do the rest. The children of Israel are to march around the Jericho walls one time for six days and seven times on the seventh day. Then they are to blow the shofar and shout, and the Lord will pull the Jericho walls down. They must do their part first, and God will do the rest. Jesus tells men at the Bethany cemetery to roll back the stone where Lazarus was buried, and when Jesus calls Lazarus back to life, the Lord instructs them to loose Lazarus and let him go. This too is divine-human instrumentality. We have no right to presume on God. Augustine is commonly credited with saying, "Pray as though everything depended on God. Work as though everything depended on you." Of course, everything is dependent on God in our prayers and in our working; however, Augustine encourages believers to do their part in expectation of God doing his part.

God gives Joshua the boundaries of the land. These are the same territorial boundaries he had given Abraham over five hundred years earlier—in the north, Lebanon; in the west, the Mediterranean Sea; in the east, the desert; and in the south, Egypt. Only an omniscient God who knows the end before the beginning begins could accomplish through his people what he had promised to his servant Abraham hundreds of years prior.

Success

God assures Joshua that no one would be able to stand against him successfully. This anticipates the rhetorical question that Paul asks in Romans 8:31: "If God is for us, who is against us?" This statement does not deny the reality of opposition, but it does promise ineffective and failing attempts of the enemy to overthrow Israel and its new leader, Joshua. The caveat is, as long as Joshua and Israel are obedient to the ways and will of God, then they will experience incessant and uninterrupted victory.

Presence

The Lord assures Joshua of success because he promises his presence: "I will be with you, just as I was with Moses" (Josh 1:5). God would validate and certify that Joshua was his appointed replacement for Moses. Joshua would not have to prove himself. In Joshua 3:7 and 4:14 God both exalts Joshua and gives his divine approbation of him as his chosen leader before the people. God was with Moses at the Red Sea and opened up the sea for the nation to cross over into the wilderness on dry ground. God would be with Joshua at the Jordan River and open up the Jordan River for the nation to cross over into the promised land on dry ground. God was with Moses at the burning bush and told him to take off the shoes from his feet, for he was standing on holy ground. God would be with Joshua outside the city of Jericho and would send the captain of his heavenly army to tell Joshua to take off the shoes from his feet, for he was standing on holy ground.

The Lord promised his consistent presence to Joshua: "I will not leave you or abandon you" (Josh 1:5). This anticipates the Hebrew writer penning the same words in Hebrews 13:5. It also anticipates the coming of Jesus, our Immanuel (meaning "God with us"). In verses 6, 7, and 9 there is the trifold encouragement, "Be strong and courageous." When the Lord says something twice it is urgent. For instance, when he calls Moses's name twice, "Moses, Moses! . . . Remove the sandals from your feet, for the place where you are standing is holy ground," this is an urgent command (Exod 3:4-5). When he says, "Saul, Saul, why are you persecuting me?" (Acts 9:4), this is an urgent question. However, when God says something three times it is even more crucial that we heed his voice. So in verses 6, 7, and 9 the Lord says, "Be strong and courageous."

Why would he say, "Be strong"? Because he knew that innately, intrinsically, and naturally we are not strong, nor are we creatures of valor or courage. The word *be* carries with it the reality of an imperative, not an option. This is a command. We ought to be strong and courageous because of the promise in verse 5: "I will not leave you or abandon you." The Swiss theologian Karl Barth often quoted Karle Wilson Baker, who defined *courage* as "Fear That has said its prayers" ("Courage" in Monroe, *Poetry*). We do not need to fake courage and valor. We can confess our fear and find strength to move to faith because we know God will never leave us or abandon us.

In Mark 9 a father stands between powerless disciples and a powerful Savior. His son was demon assaulted and attacked. The devil had been trying to kill the boy through potential drowning and burning. When the father went to the nine disciples at the bottom of the Mount of Transfiguration and requested that they exorcise the demon from his son, he met disappointment. The disciples were unable to do so. When Jesus and the inner circle of disciples (Peter, James, and John) descended from the top of the Mount of Transfiguration to the valley, the father requested that Jesus do what the disciples were not able to do—exorcise the demon from his son. The father also made an honest confession: "I do believe; help my unbelief!" (Mark 9:24). The Lord is looking for authentic faith and not feigned faith. It's all right to confess our fears, our anxieties, and our angst to God and wait on him to embolden us so that we become strong and have good courage.

God keeps his promise and assures Joshua that he will give each tribe a land inheritance based on the promise he made to the patriarchs Abraham, Isaac, and Jacob. And, once again, God says to Joshua the leader, "Be strong and courageous." His strength and courage are directly tied to his obedience to God's law, the instructions he gave through Moses. His obedience is not to be selective obedience. Joshua is to observe all that is written in God's law. No deviation or detouring is allowed: "Do not turn from it to the right or the left" (v. 7). Joshua is to be so focused as he centrally concentrates on God's word that he is not distracted by anything going on around him. This should remind us of Jesus's statement in Luke 9:62: "No one who puts his hand to the plow and looks back is fit for the kingdom of God." It is a call for concentration. It is a call to be singularly focused. It is a call to refuse to be attracted to anything that will distract one from God's way, will, and word.

Delight in the Lord

The word *prosperity* in many Christian circles has been misused and abused. In some ecclesiastical spheres, prosperity is considered normative for the Christian. This is the prosperity gospel and the health-and-wealth religion that attracts many gullible and would-be believers. Many leaders of this movement would say if an individual is a true believer, then that person will be exempt from poverty and sickness. The person ostensibly would be guaranteed success. However, it is possible to be a successful failure, as the barn-building man was in Luke 12:13-21. Jesus would say to him in the midst of his prosperity, "You fool! This very night your life is demanded of you. And the things you have prepared—whose will they be?"

In verse 8, the Lord is talking about true prosperity, that is, richness in one's relationship with God, which cannot be calculated in dollars and cents. It is the prosperity and the success alluded to in Jeremiah 29:11;

"I know the plans I have for you—plans for your well-being, not for disaster, to give you a future and a hope." The assumption that Joshua will "prosper and succeed" wherever he goes is contingent on Joshua's going where God leads him. Joshua is to focus on the word of God's instruction without being distracted by the world and is to be assured that God will not leave or abandon him as he consistently obeys God.

In verse 8 Joshua is not to allow the book of instruction to depart from his mouth. He is to constantly rehearse the word out loud. This constant verbalizing of the word will enable him to hear anew old truths for his day. *Meditate* is a word that suggests pondering, internalizing, and contemplating. A poignant image of this word is that of a cow chewing its cud over and over again until it extracts all the nutrients from the grass or the feed. The cow tosses the substance over and over again in its mouth, swallows, and then brings it up for further chewing. This is the essence of Psalm 1:2: "His delight is in the LORD's instruction, and he meditates on it day and night." The word of God is not to be an emergency ration for a crisis moment. It is to be a constant source of nutrition for one's mind: "Give us today our *daily* bread" (Matt 6:11; emphasis added).

The Jews practiced meditation. They read the Torah aloud. The Shema in Deuteronomy 6:4-9 admonishes parents to speak to their children about the Torah upon rising from the bed, to talk about it as they walk along the way, to share its truths as they return home and when they retire at the end of the day. The word was to be pronounced and announced. It was more than a silent meditation; it was a verbally expressed meditation. The day-and-night prose represents the totality of both one's day and one's entire life. This could also suggest that the word is to be meditated on not only in the nighttime of crisis but during the daytime of pleasant existence, when the storms have passed over and the clouds disappear from the sky.

Fear Not

Once again, prosperity and success are inextricably connected with obedience. The opposite is also true: disobedience will bring about failure and a lack of prosperity. We are reminded of the imperatives in verses 6-9. The commands are not optional. "Haven't I commanded you?" This is a rhetorical question. The answer, of course, is yes! God had commanded Joshua to be strong and courageous, and he had given the command three times (vv. 6,7,9). "Do not be afraid." This is a "fear not" command.

It has been said that there are 365 "fear nots" in the Bible. If that is true, there is a "fear not" for every day of the year. The first "fear not" in the Bible is found in Genesis 15:1 where God says to Abram, "Do not be afraid, Abram. I am your shield; your reward will be very great." God does not say, "I am *going to provide* a shield" for Abram. Rather, God says he *is* Abram's shield.

A shield is a military defense implement to prevent the enemy's weaponry from injuring or destroying the one carrying it. A shield is designed to *prevent*. God prevents his children from being destroyed but not always from being injured. Whatever God permits to happen to us, he has a purpose to promote. Joseph's brothers are permitted to sell Joseph into slavery; however, God promoted his better purpose in enabling Joseph to move from being a slave in Egypt to being the vice-regent of Egypt. Elsewhere, Satan recognized that he could not injure Job unless God granted him permission. Satan said that God had a hedge around Job, thus putting Job under divine protective custody. Satan said to God, "If you were to remove the hedge, I could cause him to curse you to your face." God permitted Satan to afflict Job because he had a divine purpose to promote. In the end, Job would hold on to his integrity and would be blessed with twice as much as he had lost. So God has the believer's *front*. We have no need to fear.

We have no need to fear because God also has the believer's *back*. Psalm 23:4 says, "Even when I go through the darkest valley, I fear no danger, for you are with me; your rod and your staff—they comfort me." And in verse 6 David concludes this psalm by saying, "Only goodness and faithful love will pursue me all the days of my life, and I will dwell in the house of the LORD as long as I live." We have no reason to fear (v. 4) because God has positioned goodness and faithful love to follow behind us (v. 6). God has our backs to protect us, all the way home. When we stand before God in the eternal state and hear him pronounce us blameless, faultless, guiltless, and sinless, it will only be because goodness and faithful love have come behind us to clean up our past sins, mistakes, disobedience, and waywardness so that we will stand before God spotless because we are washed in the blood of the Lamb.

Finally, we have no reason to fear because God has the keys of authority. In Revelation 1:17-18 the apostle John sees our glorified Lord. He falls at his feet as if he were a dead man. The Lord Jesus says to him, "Don't be afraid. . . . I was dead, but look—I am alive forever and ever, and I hold the keys of death and Hades." We have no need to fear because Christ has the keys—even to Satan's house, hell. Keys represent authority. Satan does not even have the keys to his own house. So, why should we fear? God has our front and our back, and he has the keys!

Satan has many tools that he uses to confront Christians to bring them to defeat. One of his most effective tools is discouragement. In light of all that God has promised in this passage—namely himself— then the appropriate encouragement to ourselves through soliloquy, our own self-conversation is, "God is faithful."

This passage ends with the unparalleled promise of God's presence: "The LORD your God is with you wherever you go." It is the Mount Everest of all the "I am" statements Jesus will make in the Gospels (Matt 28:20). "I AM" was the name God used to identify himself to Moses in Exodus 3:14. Moses essentially asked God, "Who should I say sent me when I stand before Pharaoh or lead the Israelites?" And God said, "Tell them, 'I AM WHO I AM sent me to you.'" "I AM WHO I AM" is an unusual designation. Richard Lischer says this designation does not include an adjective, only a noun (I) and a verb (AM) (*End of Words*, 8). Lischer posits when it comes to God an adjective is not needed because you have the best noun available. An adjective is designed to modify or describe the noun. But what adjective would one use to describe God? No adjective is sufficient to modify or describe our Creator. Therefore, God is the great "I AM." This name designation carries the idea of God being "the self-existent one." God is the eternal now. God exists in a state of eternal "is-ness." God is the God who was, who is, and who is to come. In reality God never *was* and God never *will be*. God always *is*. As believers, our "am-ness" is based on God's "am-ness." In 1 Corinthians 15:10—"By the grace of God I am what I am"—Paul did not attribute his "am-ness" to his own industry and worth. He attributed it to God. It was purely by God's grace.

Reflections

Fallen Condition Focus

Times are filled with great transitions (particularly in 2020 with the coronavirus pandemic), which evoke fear for many—even believers as they face an uncertain future. We must learn to face what is facing us, knowing God has a plan for his fallen creation. Jesus is the greater Moses promised to be raised up by God: "The LORD your God will raise up for you a prophet like me from among your own brothers. You must listen to him" (Deut 18:15). Fourteen hundred years later, on the Mount of Transfiguration, Moses appeared along with Elijah and witnessed Jesus being transfigured in the presence of Peter, James, and John. Moses and Elijah represented the Law and Prophets respectively. However, in speaking out of the cloud, the Lord God said, "This is my Son, the Chosen One; listen to him!" (Luke 9:35). Jesus is God's last word to the world (Heb 1:1-2).

The Christological Highway to Jesus

God dwelt among his people as Immanuel and delivered us from sin (Matt 1:21). The **Spirit** is given to empower us to do ministry. Joshua son of Nun anticipates Jesus, the Son of God. The name *Jesus*, which like *Joshua* means "Yahweh is salvation" in Hebrew, carries a soteriological or salvation purpose: "And you are to name him Jesus, because he will save his people from their sins" (Matt 1:21). Only Jesus, the greater Joshua, will bring rest to the people of God (Heb 3:18-19; 4:8-10).

The Spirit of Yeshua exposes the rebellion and resistance in our hearts as Christ invites us into his rest: "Come to me, all of you who are weary and burdened, and I will give you rest" (Matt 11:28-30). Saint Augustine said, "Thou hast made us for thyself and our souls cannot find rest until they rest in thee" (*Confessions*, 3).

Future Condition Focus

The Lord God assures Joshua of his presence: "I will be with you, just as I was with Moses" (Josh 1:5). The pericope in verse 9 once again ends with this assurance: "For the LORD your God is with you wherever you go." Jesus assured all those who followed him, "And remember, I am with you always, to the end of the age" (Matt 28:20). He is our Immanuel, God with us. One day we will be physically with God, who has been with us during our earthly pilgrimage: "Look, God's dwelling is with humanity, and he will live with them. They will be his peoples, and God himself will be with them and will be their God" (Rev 21:3).

Intratrinitarian Presence

In Old Testament times the Holy Spirit rested upon some of the people of God. This was true with Joshua: "The LORD replied to Moses, 'Take Joshua son of Nun, a man who has the Spirit in him'" (Num 27:18). Since the day of Pentecost, the Holy Spirit has been dwelling in the believer.

Reflect and Discuss

1. How does Joshua's name help us understand Jesus's purpose on earth?
2. How is Israel's new beginning with Joshua similar or dissimilar to believers' new beginning in Christ?
3. Where has God placed semicolons in your life and you reacted as if they were periods?
4. When is it difficult to obey God with the expectation of God keeping his word to be with you? What do you do when you doubt he will come through?
5. In what ways is Jesus the new and better Joshua?
6. How can Karl Barth's understanding of courage as "Fear That has said its prayers" help believers act courageously?
7. Describe a time when you prayed along with the father in Mark 9:24, "I do believe; help my unbelief!"
8. How can believers differentiate authentic faith and feigned faith in the church today? What does Scripture teach about our role in identifying the difference?
9. How can believers explain the difference between the prosperity gospel and God's desire that believers prosper even as our souls prosper (3 John 2)?
10. In what ways can believers remember not to forget and remember to remember when combating fear's temptation to make us selectively obedient?

The Order of Liberty

JOSHUA 1:10-18

Main Idea: The Spirit of God provokes believers to remember their commitment to Christ, who will give them rest as they obey God's commands.

I. **Carefully Prepare to Keep the Commitment.**
    A. Prepare the leaders.
    B. Prepare the people.
    C. Prepare provisions.
II. **Review God's Divine Plan.**
    A. For the two and a half tribes to work together in harmony
    B. For the Jews and Gentiles to live in harmony with no wall of partition
III. **Rest in the Promised Land Points to the Believer's Rest in Christ.**
    A. Know God's commands.
    B. Obey God's commands.
    C. Find rest for your soul.

The Big Ten

Text: Joshua 1:10-18
Title: The Order of Liberty
New Testament Companion: Romans 6:23
Fallen Condition Focus: The people had not obeyed the law of Moses in all things and would not obey Joshua in all things, though they had promised to be obedient to both (Josh 1:17). Prevalent sin means lasting rest will not be available for humanity until believers rest in Christ.
The Whole Counsel of God: When Adam and Eve introduced sin into the bloodline of humanity, God had to sacrifice an animal to provide a covering for them (Gen 3:21). One thing dying for another prefigured our Kinsman Redeemer who went to war with sin and died in our stead (Titus 2:14). We must go to war for our spiritual siblings (Gal 6:2; 1 John 3:16-18)

The Christological Highway to Jesus: Christ, the Son of God, sends the Holy Spirit to bring to our remembrance his Word so that through Word and Spirit believers are enabled to walk in obedience to the Word.

Proposition: The Spirit of God provokes believers to remember their commitment to Christ, who will give them rest as they obey God's commands.

Intratrinitarian Presence: The people's desire is that the Lord God be with Joshua as he had been with Moses. The Spirit of the Lord would rest on Joshua (Num 27:18), prefiguring the indwelling Holy Spirit later promised to believers by the greater Joshua, Jesus the Christ (John 14:15-17).

Behavioral Response: Moses made clear no one can rest until they have taken the land. These two and a half tribes stood on the shore of the Jordan, not knowing when they would ever return to their homes and families on the east side of the Jordan in the land of Gilead. No matter the cost, believers must live as one in fulfillment of Jesus's prayer (John 17:21) and love one another (John 13:34-35).

Future Condition Focus (Sermonic Eschatonics): God will grant rest to those who are faithful to their covenant with God through the blood of Jesus the Christ.

Carefully Prepare to Keep the Commitment

Prepare the Leaders

In 1:1-9 God has spoken to his chosen servant and new leader, Joshua. Now Joshua, in verses 10-18, speaks to the officers of the people. The officers will in turn take the orders to the people. God's orders follow God's chain of command. God speaks directly to Joshua, the leader. Joshua the leader now speaks to the officers, just as Moses had done in the years he led the Israelite congregation. This is a reflection of the eulogy God gave in verse 2: "Moses my servant is dead." Now Joshua is the leader, and it is his recount of God's commands that the officers take to the other people of God.

The trajectory is from God to people and not from people to people. Even today, God prepares his leader just as he had prepared Joshua to lead, and then he leads his leader to lead leaders. God is a God of order. God's ways begin with sovereignty and descend to humanity. When I was a little boy, I would hear the elders say, "God sits high, and he looks low." In today's society, we are familiar with the order that begins with us and ends with us. We have forgotten Maltbie Babcock's reminder that "this is my Father's world." Joshua takes the words he has heard from God in verse 10 and gives the orders to the officers of the people; there is no disconnect between what he has heard God say and what he says to the officers.

Joshua's history indicates that he obediently followed the leadership of the Lord, being "a man who has the Spirit in him" (Num 27:18). Like the other faithful spy, Caleb, Joshua wholeheartedly followed the Lord (Num 22:12). He did not ask God for a logical explanation of how they were going to cross the Jordan River, which was at flood stage (Josh 1:11; 3:15). Joshua was probably in his forties back when he and the congregation of Israel stood at the edge of the Red Sea without a ship to carry them over to the other side. He witnessed the whole congregation walking through the Red Sea on dry ground—while the watery walls stood at attention—as they made their way to the other side into the wilderness. Joshua thus knew that God specializes in making the impossible possible. That display of God's command and nature's obedience anticipated the miracle on the Sea of Galilee fifteen hundred years later, when Jesus would speak to the wind and the water, "Silence! Be still!" and the winds would go back to the four corners of the earth, and the waves would lie down like gentle lambs (Mark 4:35-41).

The officers in turn were to communicate the orders to the people without modification. The people did not resist God's plan. This is God's way of leadership for the church today.

Joshua is the new Moses, yet he is uniquely Joshua. After the transference of leadership, Joshua must take the reins handed to and crafted for him by the God of all creation, and he must confidently lead the Israelites into the promised land. God admonished Joshua to fearlessly lead in accordance with what he had seen and heard. The presence of the Lord was with Moses at the burning bush just as his presence was with Joshua outside the city of Jericho. Both Moses and Joshua heard the same divine imperative: "Remove the sandals from your feet, for the place where you are standing is holy." Joshua had to trust that the same God who led Moses would lead him as he stood before the leaders of the people and delivered the word of the Lord. One day we will see our Lord face-to-face, *panim 'el panim* (1 John 3:2). Until then, we must know he will fight for us.

Prepare the People

Though the people said they had obeyed Moses in all things (Josh 1:17), they had not. When Moses had stayed at the invitation-only Mountaintop Conference for longer than the people thought a conference should last, the Israelites had Aaron craft a golden calf that they worshiped as their god (Exod 32:19). Aaron's apparent fear of the people caused him to lead the people into a great sin against Yahweh in spite of Moses's teaching and in spite of all the things they had witnessed from God's hand. Now Joshua has to lead this shortsighted group into the land of promise and corral them to stay together until they conquer the land as they had promised Moses. God's leaders must not rely on the people of God for victory. Like Moses and Joshua, God's leaders must trust and look to the author and finisher of their faith for direction and protection that leads to eternal rest. Israel will not take the land; God will give it to them as he promised Abraham (Gen 12:1-3).

Prepare Provisions

The people will be on the move soon according to God's commands, and they are to prepare provisions for themselves. Within three days the Israelite congregation will cross the Jordan River and go over to the promised land, which the Lord had promised their forefathers and had already given to them. Joshua is to lead the people as they cross to take possession of the promise. God allocated three days for their preparation. The period of three days is significant throughout Scripture. In Genesis 22:3-4 it takes Abraham, Isaac, and the servants three days to reach Mount Moriah from Beersheba, where Abraham lived. Jonah was in the belly of the fish for three days and three nights (Jonah 1:17). However, the most important three-day period is the sign of Jonah— the three days between the crucifixion and resurrection of Jesus. These three days in verse 11 are a period of preparation.

Review God's Divine Plan

For the Two and a Half Tribes to Work Together in Harmony

The Reubenites, Gadites, and the half tribe of eastern Manasseh will speak to the leader, Joshua, to make sure he knows about their permanent residence on the east side of the Jordan. In verse 13 they remind him of what Moses had commanded: these two and a half tribes would be permitted to stay on the east side of the Jordan with their families and livestock and set up permanent residence there without having to move to the west side of the Jordan. Forefather Reuben was the oldest of the twelve sons of Jacob, Gad was another son of Jacob, and Manasseh was the oldest son of Joseph. The full tribes of Reuben and Gad have been permitted by Moses to live on the east side of the Jordan. One-half of the tribe of Manasseh may reside on the east side of the Jordan, too, and the other half will set up permanent residence on the west side.

These two and a half tribes remember the words of Moses stipulating that their wives, children, and livestock could remain on the east side of the Jordan, but the armed men of these two and a half tribes are obligated to participate in the battle on the west side and fight with the other nine and a half tribes until the nation of Israel had taken full possession of the promised land. They do not know how long this will be. They are just to fight until the land has been conquered. This means that the fighting men of these two and a half tribes will be away from their wives and children until the land is conquered.

Much like military action today, soldiers in ancient times often were involved in combat in distant lands and without a furlough for many years. The word *until* is significant, then. They are to be faithful and active *until* the land is conquered. Upon carrying out their assignment and after Joshua has distributed lots to the nine and a half tribes on the west side of the Jordan, then and only then will these two and a half tribes be allowed to return to their families on the east side of the Jordan.

These two and a half tribes represent borderline believers. They are Israelites for sure, but they do not want to live in the promised land proper; they want to live on its border. History will show that when the northern kingdom is invaded by the Assyrians, these two and a half tribes are the first ones to be taken because they are geographically closer to Assyria than the tribes that were situated west of the Jordan. It is dangerous to live on the border. Too many people are so close to getting into the promised land, yet so far away.

For the Jews and Gentiles to Live in Harmony with No Wall of Partition

This occurrence, particularly with half of the tribe of Manasseh living on the east side of the Jordan and the other half living on the west side of the Jordan, is reminiscent of the post-World War II division in Germany between the east and the west. The Berlin Wall separated the east from the west. Children who had friends on the west side visited them that day as the wall went up, only to find they could not return to the east afterward. Relatives and friends could see one another through its barbed wire but could not touch. They could toss notes over the dividing wall but could not hug one another. One day President Ronald Reagan spoke to that area's leader with profound authority: "Mr. Gorbachev, tear down this wall!"

Because he desires unity among his true people, a greater word is uttered by our Lord through an inspired writer. Paul writes in Ephesians 2:14 that the dividing partition that separated Jew from Gentile has been torn down. The dismantling is so significant that we as believers reflect on the time when Jesus died on the cross and the veil in the temple was torn from top to bottom, which enabled us to enter into the holy of holies and approach God for our salvation without the intercession of a priest. The wall has been torn down. Paul declares in Galatians 3:28, "There is no Jew or Greek, slave or free, male and female; since you are all one in Christ Jesus." Jesus paid our entrance fees.

Rest in the Promised Land Points to the Believers' Rest in Christ

Know God's Commands

At one time all of us lived on the border; however, we were not able to get into the promised land of salvation. Our works were not sufficient, our sacrifices not worthy, and we were bankrupt as relates to merit. But the grace of God moved us from separation from Christ to integration in Christ. The Spirit of God provokes believers to remember their commitment to Christ who will give them rest as they obey God's commands.

Obey God's Commands

In response to Moses's command, these two and a half tribes said to Joshua, "Everything you have commanded us we will do, and everywhere you send us we will go" (v. 16). There is a direct connection between their promise to Joshua and God's command to Joshua in 1:7:

> *Above all, be strong and very courageous to observe carefully [do] the whole instruction my servant Moses commanded you. Do not turn*

from it to the right or the left, so that you will have success wherever
you go. (emphasis added)

Find Rest for Your Soul

Joshua was able to lead the children of Israel from the wilderness into
the promised land. However, he was not able to give them rest. Jesus,
whose name in Hebrew is "Yeshua"—meaning the same as "Joshua" in
Hebrew ("Deliverer" or "Yahweh is salvation")—was able to do what the
Old Testament Joshua was not able to do: give the people of God rest
(Heb 4:4). Hear him say in Matthew 11:28-30,

> *Come to me, all of you who are weary and burdened, and I will give*
> *you rest. Take up my yoke and learn from me, because I am lowly and*
> *humble in heart, and you will find rest for your souls. For my yoke is*
> *easy and my burden is light.*

In Joshua 1:16-17, the people promise to obey. The greater Joshua
would equate obedience with love in John 14:15 when he said, "If you
love me, you will keep my commands." Just as Joshua was to hear God's
voice and convey the message faithfully to the people, so the preachers
and teachers of God must preach and teach with fidelity the message of
the holy Trinity. Jesus sent the Holy Spirit, the Comforter, to empower
New Testament believers to do what Old Testament believers pledged to
do but did not have the power to achieve. The answer to their tendency
is the greater Joshua, Jesus, who has the power to save and sustain.

The Lord instantaneously gave the land of Canaan to the Israelites
in his words to Abram; he even told Abram the boundaries of the land
centuries prior to the leadership of Joshua (Gen 15:18). Now, over the
next seven years, Israel must participate in appropriating what God had
promised and predelivered. Three times the Lord tells Joshua to be
strong and courageous (1:6,7,9). Of course, Joshua's strength will be
found in the Lord and not in himself. The key to continuous victory was
Joshua and Israel's continuous obedience to and faith in the word of
God. God would work on Israel's behalf, and their leader would observe
and obey God's precepts from the book of the law of Moses. This was to
be done by strictly following the law of Moses and stepping not to the
right or the left of it.

This passage serves as a paradigm of how to depend on God
and allow the Spirit of God to empower us to be victorious in living

as believers in the Son of the one true God. Joshua 1:8 and Psalm 1:2 make a proper connection regarding the permanent posture toward the Word: "You are to meditate on it day and night." This meditation is inwardly processed but spoken and heard outwardly. As the rabbis still audibly verbalize the Scriptures at the Wailing Wall in Jerusalem, so Joshua was to constantly repeat God's word to himself, his leaders, and the congregation. Joshua was to speak the promises God made to Israel back to God himself. God is a God of order. Out of the chaotic waters of creation, God brought clarity by separating the water from the land. Likewise, the Spirit of God provokes believers to remember their commitment to Christ, who will give them rest as they obey God's commands.

Reflections

The Whole Counsel of God

Geographically, the eastern two and a half tribes and the western nine and a half tribes are divided by the Jordan River; however, they are united in purpose: the conquest of the land of the seven nations of Canaan in fulfillment of God's promise to Abraham (Gen 12:1-3; 15:18). We are to be the church of an undivided Christ and not reflect a Christ of a divided church: "For we were all baptized by one Spirit into one body—whether Jews or Greeks, whether slaves or free—and we were all given one Spirit to drink" (1 Cor 12:13).

The Christological Highway to Jesus

The rest that the Lord God is giving the Israelites in the promised land finds its full realization and expression in Jesus, who said, "Come to me, all of you who are weary and burdened, and I will give you rest. . . . For my yoke is easy and my burden is light" (Matt 11:28,30).

Behavioral Response

Individualism is opposed to God's blueprint for his people, in both the Old Testament and the New Testament. The two and a half tribes cannot fully enjoy rest on the east side until their armies have participated with the armies of the nine and a half tribes in the conquest of the promised land. All believers must take responsibility for the ministry of "one-anothering" one another.

Future Condition Focus

As the two and a half and nine and a half tribes were united during the conquest of Canaan even though they were separated by the Jordan River, in the eschaton, the dead in Christ and those alive in Christ will be united and never participate in war again. "They will beat their swords into plows and their spears into pruning knives. Nation will not take up the sword against nation, and they will never again train for war" (Isa 2:4).

Reflect and Discuss

1. In what way(s) does the two and a half tribes partnering with the nine and a half tribes to conquer the seven nations in Canaan foreshadow the divine intention for Christ's church?
2. How do the tribes of western Manasseh and eastern Manasseh anticipate the two missionary journeys of Paul and Silas in Acts 15:39-41?
3. Look at this passage through the lens of Matthew 16:24. What do you see in relation to love, loyalty, and priority? Explain.
4. As relates to spiritual warfare, what are some dangers of being a borderline Christian—that is, a Christian who lives close to the edge by having only nominal association with the local church?
5. Since Reuben was the firstborn son of Jacob and Leah, do you think there was an expectation for this tribe to exert a higher standard of leadership and commitment over the tribe of Gad and the half tribe of eastern Manasseh? Why or why not? Should the elders (those who have Christian maturity) in the local church be expected to exemplify a higher level of loyalty than others? Why or why not?
6. Since Gad is a small tribe, should less be expected from Gad in terms of leadership and loyalty? Why or why not?
7. Why do you think God allowed three days of preparation before Israel crossed the Jordan? Describe a time in your life when God gave you a time of preparation just before you experienced a spiritual breakthrough or a spiritual renewal.
8. How do you think the families of the two and a half tribes fared while waiting for their husbands and fathers who were fighting in Canaan? Do you think these eastern tribes were likely plagued by memories of the faithlessness they experienced while traveling with the entire Israelite family? Why?
9. The men of the two and a half tribes promised to heed Moses's words. Their combined sentiment was desire for the Lord be with

Joshua as he had been with Moses. How would the congregation of Israel be affected in the way that God manifested his presence with Joshua?
10. The consequence of a person from the two and a half tribes reneging on their commitment was death. How does the failure of one member of the body of Christ impact the effectiveness of the church?

Rated R for Redemption

JOSHUA 2

The Main Idea: Christ, who redeems through the power of the Spirit of God, uses unlikely persons to proclaim the message of the cross for the salvation of sinners, allowing all believers to serve together in the kingdom of God.

I. **Fallen Humanity Can Participate in God's Redemption Plan.**
    A. Rahab has a dubious designation.
    B. God redeems dubious designations.
    C. God uses unlikely persons.
    D. The mess becomes the message.
II. **Redemption Might Look Daunting.**
    A. Disobedience is disruptive.
    B. Obedience is effective.
III. **We Are Saved by Faith.**
    A. Rahab
    B. Abraham
IV. **Christ Redeems the Dubiously Designated to Be Monuments of Faith.**
    A. Welcome the dubiously designated.
    B. Christ redeems the dubiously designated.
    C. The dubiously designated proclaim the message.
    D. The dubiously designated are not demolished.
    E. The dubious designation disappears in Christ.

The Big Ten

Text: Joshua 2
Title: Rated R for Redemption
New Testament Companion: 1 Peter 1:18-19
Fallen Condition Focus: Like Rahab, all humanity is sordid, stained, sinful, and therefore worthy of being devoted to destruction. We have prostituted ourselves to various idols. Romans 6:23 gives a

candid assessment of our plight: "The wages of sin is death," and
we all deserve to die for the earned penalty we cannot pay.

The Whole Counsel of God: Just as the Spirit of God allows Rahab to
believe in Yahweh and be delivered from destruction by means of
a scarlet cord in her window, so the Spirit of God allows sinners
to be delivered from destruction by belief in Christ, the Lamb
of God (John 1:29), and be sanctified by the blood of the Lamb
(Heb 13:12).

The Christological Highway to Jesus: Christ is the only way of deliverance for those who seek redemption from eternal damnation
and the only way for the redeemed to join his unified body working for the kingdom of God.

Intratrinitarian Presence: Our God of three persons—Father, Son,
and Holy Spirit—enables diverse believers to serve as one in the
church universal.

Proposition: Christ, who redeems through the power of the Spirit
of God, uses unlikely persons to proclaim the message of the
cross for the salvation of sinners, allowing all believers to serve
together in the kingdom of God.

Behavioral Response: Believers must witness to the lost through the
power of the Holy Spirit, sharing the good news of redemption
through the blood of the Lamb and experiencing new life as
one body in Christ.

Future Condition Focus (Sermonic Eschatonics): The inclusion of
Rahab and her family into Israel anticipates the diverse yet unified church and reflects a Kodak moment of the future state of
eternity. Rahab will not be dressed in harlotry apparel in the
new Jerusalem; rather, she will be praising God in heaven in a
long white robe (Rev 7:13-14). In eternity, believers from every
nation, tribe, people, and language will mirror the multifac-
eted kingdom of God (Rev 5:9; 7:9).

Introduction

This is a great story. Yet one of the greatest obstacles to the knowledge
of the Bible is the knowledge of the Bible! One thing that keeps us
from knowing more about Scripture is what we think we already know
about it. This is often due to being so familiar with the biblical narrative

that we are lulled to sleep and miss the relevant application of living Scripture. Is it possible for us to crawl up into the thoughts of Yahweh and stay there long enough until the common becomes uncommon, the familiar becomes unfamiliar, the mundane becomes magnificent, and the simple becomes stupendous? Yes, but it takes our deliberate desire. Christ, who redeems through the power of the Spirit of God, uses unlikely persons to proclaim the message of the cross for the salvation of sinners, allowing all believers to serve together in the kingdom of God.

The Bible is a beautiful gem. Even those who have read this story many times can find that, like a diamond, it has many facets. As we turn to it anew, the new mercies we see daily can illuminate fresh revelation relevant to our current circumstances. We benefit most by assuming a childlike posture of second naivete in which we approach this story as if we are hearing it for the first time. Dwight Lyman Moody, the great nineteenth-century evangelist, famously noted, "It's not how many times you have gone through the Bible; rather, it's how many times the Bible has gone through you."

Fallen Humanity Can Participate in God's Redemption Plan

Rahab Has a Dubious Designation

As the Bible goes through us, doctrines remain the same yet can shine brilliantly in light of truths freshly gleaned. For certain, every major doctrine in the New Testament reflects an Old Testament doctrine. For instance, consider the doctrine of redemption appearing in this chapter and the corresponding picture of Rahab. She is first mentioned in Scripture with the dubious designation "Rahab the prostitute." This is clearly seen in Joshua 2:1; 6:17, 22, and 25. One would think this dubious designation would be dropped once the reader crosses from the Old Testament into the New Testament. However, in the New Testament's Hall of Faith, Rahab is still called "the prostitute" (Heb 11:31). James, who emphasizes works that follow faith, retains this dubious designation in James 2:25, writing, "In the same way, wasn't Rahab the prostitute also justified by works in receiving the messengers and sending them out by a different route?" Rahab is referred to as a prostitute both under the law in the Old Testament and under grace in the New Testament. She does not escape this dubious designation.

God Redeems Dubious Designations

Even today we often characterize people by what they were rather than by who they are and by what they've done rather than by what they're doing. But God is more interested in our present than in our past. God is more interested in where we're going than in where we've been. God is more interested in who we are than in who we were.

When it comes to discussing Scripture, though, we associate a person with their inescapable past. The name *Jacob* means "trickster," "supplanter," or "deceiver." When he wrestled with the divine presence, God changed his name to "Israel," which means "he struggled [with] God." Yet we still call him by his old name, Jacob. Naaman was the five-star Syrian general. He had a great reputation, great power, and great influence, yet he was a leper. Leprosy was an incurable disease and was a death sentence at that time. However, when he obeyed the command of Elisha to dip seven times in the Jordan River, he came out of the water with skin resembling that of a child and was healed of his leprosy. Yet we still know him as Naaman the leper. Thomas, who was willing to go to Jerusalem and die with Christ if necessary, cannot escape the dubious designation of "doubting Thomas" (John 11:16). Zacchaeus was a publican or tax collector. He was unscrupulous and dishonest. He was a traitor to his people and was despised by the Jews. However, when Christ ate at his home and changed his life, he was called a son of Abraham by Jesus (Luke 19:9). Yet we know him today as Zacchaeus the tax collector. Mary Magdalene was the first human being to see the resurrected Jesus on resurrection morning, and she was sent to deliver the resurrection message to the disciples. Yet we still identify her as the woman out of whom the Lord cast seven demons (Mark 16:9).

All of us are ex-offenders of the law of God. All of us have come short of the grace of God. All of us like sheep have gone astray. Yet God has canceled out the penalty of our yesterdays and declared us innocent today so that we might live with him in a tomorrow that will never have a concluding benediction. Whatever dubious designations we held do not need to be erased because they speak of the glory of our redemption. We are his children—former prostitutes, alcoholics, liars, thieves—redeemed by the blood of the Lamb. This is why John Newton, the ex-slave trader, could write the hymn "Amazing Grace." He recognized that he was a "once was" individual who was redeemed, as are all believers in Christ, the Redeemer. Rahab the prostitute was redeemed because her sins were forgiven, and we still talk about her today. She knew what it was like to be redeemed in spite of a dubious past. Christ who redeems through the power of the Spirit of God uses unlikely persons to proclaim the message of the cross for the salvation of sinners, allowing all believers to serve together in the kingdom of God.

God Uses Unlikely Persons

Corrie ten Boom, a Holocaust survivor of a German concentration camp, experienced what it meant not only to be forgiven but also to forgive. She recounts the time when she and her sister were in a German concentration camp during World War II. She recalled the women there being herded into a facility where they had to strip down to nothing, only to see the male guards laughing at their nude bodies. The humiliated women then took showers and put on the clothing of those who were destined to live in the concentration camp. She well remembered one particular German officer who laughed and made fun of her, her sister, and all of the women in this facility. Corrie survived the concentration camp, but her sister Betsy would die there.

Once the war was over, she began to teach and preach in Germany. Corrie was preaching in a church and looking out over the congregation, in fact, when she spotted the German soldier who had laughed at her, her sister, and all the women in the concentration camp facility as they stood there without clothing. The German soldier had become a believer. He came up to her and said, "Isn't it good to be redeemed?" He reached out his hand to shake her hand and to thank her for the message. Corrie ten Boom admitted that she did not want to shake his hand because of his cruelty to her and all the women in that facility. However, the Lord began to speak to her about forgiveness.

She was able to preach on it, but she was now challenged to live it. She made an effort to reach out and shake his hand; however, she was unable to do it. She prayed that God would enable her to do what she could not do in her own strength and related feeling a kind of electricity shoot through her shoulder blade down her arm, which released her to respond to his effort to shake hands.

She paraphrases Psalm 103:10-12:

When God forgives us, He casts our sins as far as the east is from the west. He then puts a no fishing allowed sign on the

shore which does not allow anyone to purchase a license to
fish up our sins; in fact, we are not even able to purchase a
license to fish up our own sins.[3]

There is nothing to fish up. Any old dubious designation is nothing
compared to the redeeming blood of the Messiah. Believers are all
in the same boat. Our sins are cast as far as the east is from the west.
They will never rise to condemn us again because Christ who redeems
through the power of the Spirit of God uses unlikely persons to proclaim the message of the cross for the salvation of sinners, allowing all
believers to serve together in the kingdom of God.

The Mess Becomes the Message

Darryl Strawberry, the former pro baseball player of the New York Mets,
the New York Yankees, and the Los Angeles Dodgers, shortened his
career through his drug and alcohol abuse. He fell from the top of society to the bottom of shame and ineptitude. However, one day the Lord
redeemed him, and he now preaches the gospel of redemption. The
model of his ministry is, "Make your mess your message." He understands that one cannot spell "Messiah" without the word "mess." The
Messiah has come to take us out of our messes. This is why the angel
Gabriel said to Joseph, "You are to name him Jesus, because he will save
his people from their sins" (Matt 1:21).

God is in the business of redeeming us, saving us from our messes, and
giving us a message of redemption for others. This is through no work of
our own but rather through the work of the Holy Spirit (1 Cor 12:11,13).
Therefore, we witness and share with others so that they might become
one body with us in Christ.

Redemption Might Look Daunting

Disobedience Is Disruptive

Joshua sends two spies to the city of Jericho. Jericho would seem to be
Israel's most formidable enemy. It is in central Palestine. Joshua's plan is
to divide and conquer the promised land. He will initiate a central campaign, then move to conduct a southern campaign, and finally conclude
with a northern campaign. It is a divide-and-conquer military strategy.

---

[3] This story can be found in Billy Graham's documentary film, *The Hiding Place.*

The first city on his list is Jericho, one of the oldest cities in civilization, the "city of palms." Joshua sends two spies to investigate the city.

Forty years prior, he and Caleb had been sent to the promised land on a reconnaissance mission, too. Ten other spies went with Caleb and Joshua. When the twelve came back and gave their report to Moses and the congregation, the report was a divided one. They saw the same thing but from different perspectives. Ten of the spies saw giants, which produced fear and caused them to discourage the Israelite congregation. They believed the oversized men would easily view them as grasshoppers and concluded they could not take the land from them. Joshua and Caleb, however, came back and focused their report on the grapes and not the giants. They were impressed with the size of the promised land's grapes—one bunch of grapes was so large and heavy that it took two men to carry it. They believed Israel could take the fertile land because God would take care of the giants.

The congregation rejected the minority report of Joshua and Caleb and accepted the majority report of the ten other spies. Israel balked and hesitated at Kadesh-barnea. As a result, they would participate in the longest funeral procession in history. They would march around the wilderness for nearly forty years after having spent two years at Mount Sinai receiving the law and instructions for how to live in the promised land. The entire congregation suffered because they refused to accept a report honoring the Lord. Joshua sends two spies to Jericho, not twelve. Perhaps he has learned not to assign too many persons to a mission.

Obedience Is Effective

The two spies went to a brothel managed by Rahab, the prostitute. She was Madame Rahab. They may have gone there to listen to the latest reports from those who were entering the city as well as those who lived there. A brothel was a kind of haven of unofficial news. Soon the spies are detected. Their cover is blown, and their anonymity is dispelled. They can no longer be incognito. The report gets to the king of Jericho, and he in turn sends members of the JPD (Jericho Police Department) to the brothel. Before they can arrive, Rahab the prostitute has hidden the spies and covered them up with flax. When the JPD officers interrogate her about visitors coming to her brothel, she says they had been there but had since left. She recommends the officers immediately leave and apprehend the spies before they return to their camp.

What she says is a lie. Rahab could have told the truth, which could have resulted in the extermination of these two spies, thus preventing their report from reaching Joshua and the congregation. She could have told the truth and the message still make its way to Joshua. Yet she lied, and God's purpose was carried out in spite of the lie. God is able to use a crooked stick and make a straight lick. There is no indication that God approved of the lie, justified the lie, or necessarily blessed the lie. What was at stake was his purpose. God is able to accomplish his purpose even though he may adjust or change his method. He is not committed to a specific method; rather, he is committed to an unalterable purpose. That purpose is to give the children of Israel the land he had promised to their forefathers Abraham, Isaac, and Jacob.

We Are Saved by Faith

Rahab

We must not be too hard on Rahab the prostitute, nor must we be impatient with her. Her motive was right. Her ethics were wrong. God cannot lie. Therefore, God does not approve of lying, yet he can accomplish his purpose even through unethical means. He knows his fallen creation better than we know our sinful selves.

Abraham

Abraham is the father of our faith. Yet when he felt his life was in jeopardy in Egypt, he got temporary amnesia and told the pharaoh that Sarah was not his wife; rather, she was just his sister. The text says that Sarah was beautiful. Even at the age of eighty or more she was still beautiful. Abraham felt like the pharaoh would take Sarah and put her in his harem, leaving Abraham's life expendable. But though he lied, God still took Abraham, the liar, and made him the father of our faith. Please be patient with me. God is not through with me yet, either.

Christ Redeems the Dubiously Designated to Be Monuments of Faith

Welcome the Dubiously Designated

We need to exercise great patience with one another. Christ has called us to be fishers of people. However, when young people come into our churches with clothing we may not approve, with hairstyles we might not find desirable, and with despicable language, we often try to clean the fish before we catch the fish. We're not told to be cleaners of fish but to be catchers of fish. Our task is to catch them with the gospel net and let the Lord clean the fish once they are his. The Lord will clean up their language and will teach them to dress modestly as well as to carry themselves in a Christlike manner.

Rahab the prostitute serves as a reminder that the Lord can use us in spite of our foibles and infractions because Christ who redeems through the power of the Spirit of God uses unlikely persons to proclaim the message of the cross for the salvation of sinners, allowing all believers to serve together in the kingdom of God.

Christ Redeems the Dubiously Designated

Rahab the prostitute is one of the most heroic females in Scripture; she is a heroine. She risked her life when she hid the spies. Had she been discovered, she would have been executed. Perhaps she mused, "What do I have to lose?" Regardless, she provides one of the most profound testimonies to the sovereignty of God in all of Scripture. Once the members of the JPD had left the city of Jericho, she went to the place where she hid the spies, removed the flax, and said to them, "I've scratched your back and saved your lives; now you must scratch my back and save my life and the lives of my family members." In her testimony, Rahab confessed she and the entire city of Jericho were fearful because they'd heard the track record of the God of Israel who had been fighting for his people. They had heard how God had defeated the Amorite kings, Og and Sihon. They had heard how God had opened up the Red Sea and dried up its bottom so the children of Israel crossed over on dry land. Now they were afraid, their hearts melted, and they had no courage left. She, however, confessed God as not only God in heaven but God on earth as well. What a testimony to the sovereignty of God! Where did this prostitute get this kind of faith? Romans 10:17 says, "Faith comes by hearing, and hearing by the word of God." She *believed* what she had heard not just of Israel but about God.

Rahab the prostitute said to the spies, "Since I've shown you favor, you will show me favor by sparing my family." She requested a sign or a visible pledge for this promise of sparing her family. That given, the spies told her if she divulged their whereabouts, then the promised protection would be null and void. She sent the spies on their way to rejoin Joshua and the congregation of Israel.

How did they get out of the city? Verse 5 says that the gate was shut when it was dark. How did they escape when the gate was shut? According to verse 15, Rahab let them down by rope through the window. Similarly, when the doors are shut for us, God can open a window. Rahab tells the spies to go to the mountain and to hide there for three days until the members of the JPD returned to the city of Jericho. Then they were to resume their return to their camp.

After the spies left, a cord identified Rahab's residence. Some have suggested that its color, scarlet, reflects the blood of Jesus Christ (v. 18). The blood of Christ reflects the Passover, during which a lamb was slain and the blood was smeared on the doorposts of the Israelites' homes. The Lord sent a death angel down to Egypt, and when the death angel saw the blood over the doorposts, he spared the members of the family inside those houses. Where there was no blood, the firstborn son died. This scarlet cord could represent the new covenant in Jesus's blood, as does the wine we are to drink in remembrance of him. This scarlet cord could also anticipate the marriage supper of the Lamb in fulfillment of Jesus's promise at the Last Supper: "From now on I will not drink of the fruit of the vine until the kingdom of God comes" (Luke 22:18).

The Dubiously Designated Proclaim the Message

Rahab the prostitute turns out to be an effective evangelist. In the course of a week or so, she knocks on the doors of her family members and urges them to come into her house. She promised them that when the city of Jericho was destroyed those individuals who were in her house with the scarlet cord hanging out of the window would be saved. This is reminiscent of Noah's ark—only those who came into the ark survived the flood.

Rahab is recognized in Hebrews 11:31 as being a believer. She was saved. In James 2:25 she is recognized as being justified by her works. How can this be? Is she saved by faith as in Hebrews 11:31 or saved by works as in James 2:25? Who is right, the author of James or of Hebrews? Both! She is saved by faith because she believed in the God she heard about. She is justified by her works because authentic faith is followed by authentic works. The order or sequence is most significant. Faith precedes works; works succeed faith. Salvation produces works. Works do not produce salvation. We are saved by faith alone, but faith is never alone; it is always accompanied by works.

Charles Colson, of Prison Fellowship, believed that those who need to know the love of God are often overlooked or ignored because we continue to evangelize the same persons over and over again until we finally exist in order to entertain ourselves (*Loving God*, passim). We are prone to witness to people who look like us and have the same socioeconomic status as we do. However, we are commanded by Christ to share the gospel with people regardless of their station in life, realizing we are called to be one diverse body of Christ.

The Dubiously Designated Are Not Demolished

In 6:20 we are told Joshua and the Israelites marched around the city of Jericho, and the walls eventually fell flat. Flat means flat, but with one exception here. This is not a result of an earthquake; it is a result of the power of God! What is most amazing about this reality is that in Joshua 6:22, Joshua sends the two spies who had gone to Jericho to go to Rahab the prostitute's house and bring out Rahab and all of the people who were in her house. How could this be? Joshua 2:15 says that her house was on the city wall and that she lived on the wall. This means that her house was a part of the wall. So, if the wall fell down flat, how did her house stay intact, and how did she and the members of her family who were in it survive? I believe this is an instance of *selective demolition*. Because these two spies had made an oath in the name of God that both Rahab and the residents in her house would be spared, in order for God's name not to be repudiated, God kept his word by sparing Rahab and her family. How amazing that the entire prodigious and massive wall of Jericho fell, but God selectively procured that section of a wall where Rahab's house was built and did not allow it to collapse into destruction! This makes me think that God has a way of allowing many things around us to fall, yet he protects us in keeping us from falling. We may not be able to explain why everything around us at times seems to fall while we are spared. It's a mystery. It's grace. It's inexplicable. We are undeserving, but we must not be unappreciative

The Dubious Designation Disappears in Christ

Rahab the prostitute was spared. How will she respond to such grace now that she and her family have been spared? I cannot imagine Rahab starting over and establishing a brothel again. Would she not have a new life? This would be the expected response to grace.

Surely, Rahab the prostitute had a new *life*. Certainly, Rahab the prostitute got a new *liturgy* with that. The people in Jericho were polytheistic: they worshiped idol gods. But Rahab the prostitute testified in Joshua 2:10-11 that God was the true God. Before, Rahab the prostitute heard what God had done in the wilderness in fighting for Israel by defeating the Amorite kings who opposed them. Now, Rahab the prostitute could see what God was doing in her own life and in her own midst. She has her own testimony that has now been experienced in her recent day. Before, her testimony was based on history; now it is based on his-story. Unquestionably, Rahab underscores for Christians a new ecclesiology, that is, a fuller conception of what it means to be a member of the church. Rahab was not Jewish. She was Gentile. Yet Hebrews 11:31 and James 2:25 readily admit that she is now a part of the family of God. The family of God consists of both Jew and Gentile (Gal 3:28). Undoubtedly, Rahab the prostitute symbolically represents the diversity of the end times church and is also a reminder of the mixed multitude that came out of Egypt in the exodus (Exod 12:38). Rahab the prostitute was not of the nation of Israel. However, she will forever be a part of the universal kingdom of God in which there will be people from every nation, tribe, people, and language (Rev 5:9; 7:9).

Rahab the prostitute's dubious designation disappears only when she is associated with Jesus. According to the genealogy of Jesus in Matthew 1:5-6, Rahab married Salmon. They are the parents of Boaz, and Boaz is the husband of Ruth. Boaz and Ruth are the parents of Obed. Obed is the father of Jesse. Jesse is the father of David. Out of David, eventually, comes Jesus. A former prostitute is honored to be one of the great-grandmothers of Jesus. In Christ, dubious designations are dropped, and each is given a new designation: redeemed.

Surely, the church's story is rated "R" for Redemption.

Reflections

Fallen Condition Focus

All humanity can glimpse itself in Rahab the prostitute. God does not relate to sin according to a Richter scale. For God, sin is sin. Sin is spelled s-i-n, and we all must admit the "I" is in the middle, a subtle reminder that all have sinned (Rom 3:23). Yet even after conversion there remains in believers a bent to sinning, as the song says: "Prone to wander, Lord, I feel it" (Robinson, "Come Thou Fount").

The Whole Counsel of God

Joshua 2 contains the essence of God's plan of salvation. All humanity, represented by Rahab and her family, is lost. God provides the only way for humanity to be saved. Had the spies not been sent to Jericho, Rahab and her family would have perished in Jericho's destruction. Rahab is justified by faith (Heb 11:31), and her works certify her justification (Jas 2:25). She witnesses to her family, and they take residence in her house, the only place of refuge and salvation. They were not necessarily ethical or moral. They lived in a city of idol worshipers, but they were spared because they were in the house of security, Rahab's house, with a scarlet cord hanging out the window. This scenario is echoed throughout Scripture: those who entered Noah's ark and those who were in the houses of Egypt with doorposts smeared with the blood of the Passover lamb were saved. Both instances point to Christ as the only way of salvation.

The Christological Highway to Jesus

The open window in Rahab's house was the only way of escape for the spies because the gate was shut. Likewise, Jesus is the only escape for sinful humanity: "I am the gate. If anyone enters by me, he will be saved" (John 10:9). He is the only way to salvation (John 14:6). He is the only mediator between God and humans (1 Tim 2:5).

Intratrinitarian Presence

Although the Holy Spirit is not explicitly mentioned in this passage, the Spirit is working. As Rahab heard what God had done in delivering the Israelites from Egypt through the opening of the Red Sea, and she heard about the defeat of the two kings, Sihon and Og, and their armies in the wilderness, the Holy Spirit planted faith in Rahab's heart. It is prevenient faith or enabling faith (Rom 10:17). The scarlet cord that hung outside the window at Rahab's house through which the two spies escaped could be a symbol of the blood of Christ that guarantees our deliverance from damnation: "And without the shedding of blood there is no forgiveness" (Heb 9:22).

Behavioral Response

Like Rahab who was spared by grace, we are called to live in a way that promotes the purpose of God. Rahab doubtlessly abandoned the institution of prostitution and lived among the Israelites where she would be exposed to their liturgy or worship, and she began to worship the one true God (Josh 6:25). Rahab's inclusion anticipates the diversity of the church as she presages Paul's inspired words: "There is no Jew or Greek, slave or free, male and female; since you are all one in Christ Jesus" (Gal 3:28). Finally, Rahab forecasts the inclusivity of eschatology (last things). She is from a non-Israelite people yet becomes a great grandmother of Jesus (Matt 1:5). She will be part of that "vast multitude from every nation, tribe, people, and language, which no one could number, standing before the throne and before the Lamb" (Rev 7:9). Rahab serves as an example to present-day believers regarding our response as grace recipients. We ought to have a new liturgy because we are a part of a new community of faith (ecclesiology) and will be a part of the kingdom of heaven (eschatology).

Reflect and Discuss

1. How should God's forgiveness of you affect the way you forgive others?
2. Describe seemingly random events in your life that were later revealed to be God's determined events.
3. What can you learn from moments in Scripture when God accomplished his purpose in spite of an ethical failing (like a lie) by his vessel?
4. How should the implied evangelism of Rahab influence believers' willingness to share the Word of God?
5. What does it mean to melt in fear? Melt in reverence?
6. How might the patriarchal society in which Rahab lived influence our view of her profession and her love for family? How can this impact our interactions with overt sinners?
7. How can we use a dubious past to help us evangelize those who know us well?
8. What does Rahab's inclusion in Jesus's genealogy imply regarding God's thoughts toward his creation? How is this reflected in his plan for redemption?

9. How can believers minister God's love to those whose scarlet cord is a perpetual companion?
10. How should Christ's redemption of you shape your view of those who do not look like, believe like, talk like, or think like you? How does it impact your views?

Following the Leader

JOSHUA 3

Main Point: The only way to achieve redemptive success before God is by following Christ, our leader and Lord, through the power of the Holy Spirit.

I. **God's Instructions**
    A. Misguided by the majority
    B. Guided by God's Word
    C. Empowered by the Spirit
II. **God Is a God of Order.**
III. **The Ark of the Covenant**
    A. The ark represents the presence of God with his people.
    B. Deity and dust must be separated so dust can see God.
    C. The presence of God makes the difference among creatures of clay.
IV. **The Stones and Redemption**

The Big Ten

Text: Joshua 3
Title: Following the Leader
New Testament Companion: John 14:6-18
Fallen Condition Focus: Just as there needed to be a distance of about a mile and a half between deity (the ark of the covenant) and humanity (the children of Israel), sinful human beings cannot commune with a holy God without a mediator.
The Whole Counsel of God: Just as there was a great distance between the ark of God and the Israelites, there also exists an immeasurable distance between a holy God and sinful humanity. Humanity could not come to God, so God came to humanity in the incarnation in the person of Jesus, the Son of God, our mediator. The Son of God sent the Spirit of God to be our sanctifier in conforming us to his image.

The Christological Highway to Jesus: Jesus Christ is the new and better ark of the covenant, God in flesh who dwelt among us. In knowing Christ, we hear God's proclamation and experience God's provision and power.

Intratrinitarian Presence: God is holy, and holiness cannot have a relationship with sin. The Son has made the way for us to come to the Father, and Jesus and the Father have sent the Spirit to dwell within us.

Proposition: The only way to achieve redemptive success before God is by following Christ, our leader and Lord, through the power of the Holy Spirit.

Behavioral Response: As the Israelites followed the presence of God when they crossed the Jordan, so must we follow God's Word as we make decisions and encounter obstacles.

Future Condition Focus (Sermonic Eschatonics): In the new creation, we will not have to keep our distance from holiness as the Israelites did with the ark. We will live with God forever, and he will be our light (Rev 22:5).

God's Instructions

The Jordan crossing, like so many other miraculous biblical events, reminds us that God is living and active in our world. He did not write the story of time, wind the clock of destiny, and stand back to watch things unfurl. He cares about his creation.

Misguided by the Majority

The old adage, "Better late than never," could apply to the Israelite community of over a million people crossing the Jordan River in Joshua 3–4. Earlier Moses wrote in Deuteronomy 1:2, "It is an eleven-day journey from Horeb to Kadesh-barnea by way of Mount Seir." After the Passover, the Israelites had been expelled from Egypt by the reigning pharaoh to go worship their God. They stood still at the Red Sea and saw the salvation, the deliverance of the Lord. The pharaoh, his charioteers, and his foot soldiers were in hot pursuit behind them, and the raging Red Sea was in front of them. The Lord opened up the Red Sea to the extent that its bottom became a superhighway, and the waters stood up at attention like retaining walls as the children of Israel crossed over without getting their feet wet.

They spent about a year at the Sinai/Horeb mountain range receiving laws, precepts, and instructions for how to live once they arrived in the promised land. But then they came to a place of great pain and regret—Kadesh-barnea. Kadesh-barnea is the place of the "desert of wandering." Moses sent twelve spies to inspect, look over, and examine the land of Canaan. God had already promised Abram that his posterity would inhabit the land. The only question to be answered was, When? The majority report of the ten tribal representatives was, "It is a great land, but we are outmatched and undersized because the giants in the land make us look like grasshoppers. We cannot be successful in combat against them." The minority report was given by the two tribal representatives Joshua and Caleb. They looked beyond the giants and focused on God. As a result they marveled not at giants but at the grapes of Eschol. They thus said Israel should go up at once, knowing that with God helping them, they would succeed. The Israelite congregation rejected the minority report and accepted the majority report. In essence, they were not rejecting the report of Joshua and Caleb; they were rejecting the promise of the God who cannot lie. As a result of the congregational unbelief, Israel had to wander in the wilderness for thirty-eight years.

Guided by God's Word

Chapters 3 and 4 of Joshua share an inextricable relationship—they cannot be divided. They are not independent of each other; rather, they are interdependently related to each other. It is now time for the Israelites to finally cross over the Jordan and begin to possess the land God promised them through Abraham a half millennium ago. This people group had waited four hundred years in slavery in Egypt. They had spent forty years more wandering in the wilderness. They had mourned for thirty days over the death of Moses (Deut 34:8). They were now ready to cross over. However, before they crossed over, God, who is a God of order, provided them with instructions. The instructions represent his word. They will be guided by his word and empowered by his Spirit.

Empowered by the Spirit

Spirit and Word cannot be separated. Too many local congregations take pride in being *Word churches*, but they reject the Spirit and become

Holy Spirit *shy*. Other churches boast about being Spirit churches, but they are unwilling to be informed and led by the Word of God. A church that is a so-called "Spirit church" absent of the Word is a church with inspiration without information; a church that boasts of being a "Word church" and rejects the Spirit is a church with information without inspiration; there must be both.

Even though the word *Spirit* is not explicitly mentioned in these two chapters, the Spirit is active. God cannot be trichotomized; he is a trinitarian God and never acts outside of his trinitarian nature. As Jonathan Edwards stated in the breadth of the corpus of his writings, "God has forever known himself in a sweet and holy society as Father, Son and Holy Spirit." Even though the Spirit is not mentioned in these two chapters, he is actively involved in leading the children of Israel from the wilderness to the promised land.

By comparison, the book of Esther has ten chapters, and the name *God* is not mentioned one time in the entire book. Does this mean God is absent from the book? Absolutely not! God is in the shadows, keeping watch above his own, protecting and preventing the Jews under Persian authority from being exterminated. God takes care of his people. A few years earlier, God had preserved a remnant who returned to Jerusalem and the promised land to rebuild the temple, restore the walls, and renew spirituality and worship in the city of Jerusalem. Ultimately, because of this remnant God spared, Jesus Christ himself would come through its loins.

God once again starts with the leader as he prepares to do his great work. The only way to achieve success before God is by following Christ, our leader and Lord, through the power of the Holy Spirit.

God Is a God of Order

In Joshua 3:1, Joshua rises up early in the morning, and he and all the children of Israel prepare to camp on the bank of the Jordan River before they cross over. The officers or leaders are prepared to relay to the people the instructions they had received from Joshua, who had received them from the Lord. This is the thread that runs throughout the fabric of the entire book of Joshua: God gives his directions to Joshua, who in turn shares them with the leaders, and they deliver them to the people. Authority comes down from God to the leader. After three days, these officers share specific instructions with the congregation (v. 3).

The Ark of the Covenant

The Ark Represents the Presence of God with His People

This chapter is replete with the mentioning of the significance of the ark of the covenant. Everything begins and ends, it seems, with the ark of the covenant.

The ark was a box of acacia wood that was overlaid with gold; in fact, gold lined the inside of the box as well as its lid. There were carved angelic beings known as cherubim that faced each other and lifted up their wings toward heaven in a posture of giving glory to God. This box represented the presence of God in the midst of his people.

The time had come for them to cross the Jordan River. This would not necessarily be an easy task. How could it be? Over a million people would have to cross over. There would be senior men and women, young married couples with small children, mothers carrying babies in their arms and nursing them, teenagers, and military personnel along with their livestock. How long would it take for over a million people to cross the Jordan? Additionally, according to 3:15, they were to cross the Jordan while that river was overflowing the banks of the promised land. It was at flood stage. So God wanted them to cross over not during the normal water level of the Jordan River but rather when the river was overflowing its banks.

That's just like God. Why didn't God allow them to cross over during times when the Jordan River had receded and its level had been greatly reduced? Why didn't he send them when places along the edge of the Jordan River were shallow? Why would God put Israel in such a position to cross over at a time when it was humanly impossible?

We must remember that the ark of the covenant represented the presence of God in the midst of his people. It contained two tablets of stone, the jar of manna, and Aaron's staff that budded—symbols of proclamation, provision, and power. God specializes in doing things that seem to be impossible, and he will do what no other power can do! Also, in verse 3 the priests and the Levites are instructed to take the lead as the congregation marches toward the edge of the Jordan River.

Deity and Dust Must Be Separated so Dust Can See God

The priests are to carry the ark of the covenant on their shoulders without touching it. The book of Exodus instructs them to take poles and insert them through rings on either side of the ark so that the ark is carried on their shoulders without their shoulders touching the ark (Exod 27:7). The ark represented deity—God—and the priests as well as the entire congregation represented dust. Deity and dust must keep a distance from each other. Deity is holy, and fallen humanity or dust is unholy. The only way to achieve redemptive success before God is by following Christ, our leader and Lord, through the power of the Holy Spirit.

The congregation is instructed to let there be a space of about two thousand cubits between them and the ark (v. 4). A cubit is about eighteen inches. Therefore, this is a space of about three thousand feet. The purpose of this distance is so that the entire congregation can have an undisturbed and clear view of the ark of the covenant and follow it wherever it goes. Here God is teaching his people to keep their eyes on him and not to be distracted by anyone or anything. No one but the priests is to come near the ark because God is absolutely holy. Everyone is to observe the direction the ark goes and to follow it. The reminder is that they have not passed this way before. This is an admission that God is the ultimate Leader and that we are to follow him. He knows the way; we do not. As Job says in Job 23:10, "[God] knows the way I have taken; when he has tested me, I will emerge as pure gold." We have not passed this way before; therefore, we must follow the Way who knows the way. This anticipates the words of Jesus in John 14:6: "I am the way, the truth, and the life. No one comes to the Father except through me."

The Presence of God Makes the Difference among Creatures of Clay

Joshua instructs the people to sanctify themselves, informing them that tomorrow the Lord will do great wonders in their midst. Sanctification is a process in which the people of God are set apart and cleansed in order for God to perform his work through them. They are to be set apart from anything that would distract from holiness. If they are to experience the movement of God in their midst, they must prepare themselves for God to move.

Joshua tells the priests to take up the ark of the covenant and cross over before the people. The priests obey. The Lord specifically tells Joshua that he will credentialize him on this day, reminding him of what he had already promised in Joshua 1:5: "I will be with you, just as I was with Moses." As God was with Moses at the Red Sea and opened up the sea for the children of Israel to cross over into the wilderness, so now God will be with Joshua and open up the Jordan River for the children of Israel to cross over into the promised land. The Lord assured Joshua that he would begin to exalt Joshua in the sight of all Israel so that the Israelite nation would know that he was divinely appointed to replace Moses. This would give the people great confidence in their leader, knowing that God was with him. This is a definite word of encouragement to Joshua in that he will not have to vindicate or prove himself to the people; God will exalt him. This is a much-needed word to contemporary believers. We spend too much time trying to impress people so that they become believers in our ministries and our work. God desires to exalt us so that people will see his work in us.

Once again God directs Joshua to command the priests who carry the ark of the covenant to approach the edge of the waters of the Jordan River and to put their feet in it (v. 13). Simultaneously, the placing of the feet on the river's edge will signal God's holding back the flowing waters of the Jordan, thus causing these waters to stand up in a heap and at attention while the children of Israel cross over on dry ground into the promised land. In fact, the priests who bear the ark of the covenant are to go on to the middle of the Jordan River in the path of the waters standing at attention. (Behind this miracle is the hand of God holding back the waters.) The priests bearing the ark serve as traffic personnel, like school crossing guards impacting traffic while young children cross the street.

The key to this entire episode is not the priests or their feet touching the edge of the Jordan River, however. The real key is that they're holding the ark of the covenant, which represents the presence of God in the midst of his people. The priests could have stood at the edge of the Jordan River without the ark of the covenant and with their feet touching the water's edge and the Jordan River would have kept on flowing. The ark of the covenant made the difference. We may preach, sing, and serve in the ministry of the church in myriad ways, but without God's presence in our midst and in our lives, we will not see the effective proclamation of the Word of God, the provision of God, or the power of God. We will simply be going through the motions.

God was providing for Joshua and the children of Israel a preview of coming attractions. They knew they would face enemies that seemed to be formidable and cities that appeared to be impregnable. They knew Canaan was inhabited by seven peoples—the Canaanites, Hethites,

Hivites, Perizzites, Girgashites, Amorites, and Jebusites. The miracle that took place at the Jordan River demonstrated that if God could hold back the river until all Israel had crossed over, then God could defeat this sevenfold nation of Canaan.

The Stones and Redemption

The children of Israel would cross over into the promised land. Joshua would select one man from each one of the twelve tribes to go to the middle of the Jordan River, where the priests carrying the ark of the covenant were standing, and to pick up a large stone and bring it to the Canaan side of the promised land. These twelve stones would be properly placed to form a memorial. This suggests that not only did the nine and a half tribes place a stone on the memorial, but the other two and a half tribes did as well. The nine and a half tribes would include nine full tribes of Israel and the half-tribe of Manasseh that would live on the west side of the Jordan. The tribes of Reuben, Gad, and the other half-tribe of Manasseh would live on the east side of the Jordan.

Some believe that the two and a half tribes who would live on the east side of the Jordan did not have men selected by Joshua to pick up a large stone and place it in order to contribute to this memorial altar. Rather, they think other tribes were selected like Ephraim, who was not a son of Jacob but a son of Joseph, to place the additional stones. Frankly, there's a great deal of controversy about the selection process. However, the critical thing to note is the question that must be answered by that generation and ours: What do these stones mean? These were not pebbles; they were probably large boulders. They were to be carried on the shoulders of the twelve men who were selected. Obviously, twelve represented the number of the twelve tribes of Israel. So this memorial is symbolic of the unification of the entire nation of Israel.

When the twelve men gathered the stones and carried them to the Canaan side of the promised land, the priests bearing the ark of the covenant resumed their journey across the bottom of the Jordan River, and as soon as their feet touched the ground on the Canaan side, God removed his hand that had been holding back the waters of the Jordan, and the watery wall that was once standing at attention collapsed and flowed downstream. Simultaneity is an act of sovereignty. As soon as the priests' feet touched the edge of the Jordan River on the wilderness side, the waters stopped flowing. However, as soon as the priests' feet bearing the ark of the covenant came out of the Jordan River and touched the dry land of Canaan, the waters resumed their flow. This is not luck. It is not an abracadabra, open-sesame form of tricky illusion. This is the sovereign hand of God at work. God is never acting before time or after time; he is always on time.

Similarly, the only way to achieve redemptive success before God is by following Christ, our leader and Lord, through the power of the Holy Spirit at his time, which is always on time. The critical thing is the question surrounding the stones, a question that must be answered by that generation and ours today: What do these stones mean?

Reflections

The Christological Highway to Jesus

The ark of the covenant is emblematic of Christ, for it represents God in the midst of his people in relation to a *box*. In the incarnation, the Word would be made flesh and dwell in the midst of his people in relation to a *body*. God's presence in a body made Christ's death eligible. A box could not bleed, die, or be resurrected—or for that matter, be tempted to sin. In the incarnation, God in Christ could identify with us and, more importantly, take upon himself our sin for us (2 Cor 5:21). So, in Christ we not only have God's presence; we also have his person.

Behavioral Response

Just as God, not Joshua, established Joshua's credibility before the Israelites (Josh 3:7; 4:14), contemporary leaders must not use human methods and tactics to solidify their leadership presence. They must remember this: "'not by strength or by might, but by my Spirit,' says the LORD of Armies" (Zech 4:6).

Intratrinitarian Presence

As the Israelites followed the ark and were given instructions by God for crossing over the Jordan River, so the Holy Spirit leads believers to follow God so that their greater Joshua is ultimately exalted.

Fallen Condition Focus

The priests were to carry the ark with poles that were inserted within the rings of the ark. No part of their bodies was to touch the ark. Because of our sin, we could not reach out to God; therefore, as he did to Isaiah in the temple, God had to reach out and touch us. Isaiah testified, "He touched my mouth with [a cleansing coal] and said: Now that this has touched your lips, your iniquity is removed and your sin is atoned for" (Isa 6:7).

The Whole Counsel of God

The Jordan River is a place of departure. The Israelites departed from nearly forty years of wilderness wandering to the promised land through the Jordan River (Josh 3:17), Elijah departed from earth to heaven at the Jordan River (2 Kgs 2:6,12), and Jesus came up immediately from the Jordan River at his baptism (Matt 3:16). Figuratively, one day believers will cross the Jordan River of time into the Jubilee of eternity.

Reflect and Discuss

1. Why is it important and relevant to sanctify or consecrate yourself?
2. Reflect on a personal experience you have had with the Word of God. How were you able to reconcile God's direction with your life as a member of the family of God?
3. Explain the proclivity to question the provision of God in light of his ability to be trusted to keep his word.
4. Where have you experienced the power of God?
5. How is Jesus the new and better ark of the covenant?
6. Reflect on the thought that deity and fallen dust must keep a distance from each other. How often do you consider God's holiness?
7. In your life right now, are there any "flooded rivers" you are waiting to cross?
8. Do you agree that God is always on time? Why or why not?
9. How do the events of Joshua 3 relate to those of Exodus 14?
10. What does it mean that God is "the living God" (v. 10)?

Stones with a Story

JOSHUA 4

Main Idea: God saves us through faith in the Son and sends us the Spirit who raised Jesus from the dead in the subsequent rolling away of the stone so that we may declare his excellencies to a world that does not know him.

I. **Unify in Purpose.**
    A. Each tribe is significant.
    B. United in worship
II. **Tell the Story.**
    A. Build with the stones.
    B. Build on the Stone.
    C. Build in community.
III. **Obey the Word.**
IV. **The Reproach Is Rolled Away.**
    A. At Gilgal
    B. At Calvary
V. **The Presence Is Manifested.**
    A. Ark of the covenant—wood
    B. Ark of the covenant—deity and dust

The Big Ten

Text: Joshua 4
Title: Stones with a Story
New Testament Companion: 1 Peter 2:1-10
Fallen Condition Focus: Believers have a proclivity to forget God and all his benefits (Ps 103:2) and need reminders to continue to tell their stories of redemption.
The Whole Counsel of God: The story of the stones in Joshua 4 anticipates the greater story of Christ, the Son of God, who was crucified and buried in a tomb of stone and three days later raised by the Spirit of God, who empowers believers to tell the story of the empty tomb.

The Christological Highway to Jesus: Christ, our chosen and honored cornerstone (1 Pet 2:6), was placed inside Joseph of Arimathea's tomb. On the third day, Christ was raised by the power of the Holy Spirit of God. The angels rolled back the stone as a testimony to the resurrection of Christ: "He is not here. For he has risen, just as he said" (Matt 28:6).

Intratrinitarian Presence: One can only proclaim the good news of God after having been brought to the Father through the Son by the Spirit.

Proposition: God saves us through faith in the Son and sends us the Spirit who raised Jesus from the dead in the subsequent rolling away of the stone so that we may declare his excellencies to a world that does not know him.

Behavioral Response: We are to tell future generations of God's power and faithfulness. We are to let those we encounter know that the Lord is mighty. The Holy Spirit brings Christ's redemptive narrative to our remembrance so we can proclaim him daily and avoid having the stones cry out due to our silence (Luke 19:40).

Future Condition Focus (Sermonic Eschatonics): Believers are "living stones, a spiritual house" (1 Pet 2:5). That spiritual house will one day be complete, and God's people will live with him forever in a house with "many rooms" (John 14:2).

Unify in Purpose

Something happens when the bonds of a family are shaken, especially after a traumatic or dynamic event. Family members look to one another, realizing they have suffered the same debilitating blow (or are soaring on the same high cloud) and are now united together in purpose, in memory. In Joshua 4, we look in on the story of a people united under the hand of God, under the leadership of Joshua, and in the wake of a miracle. This moment must be memorialized forever.

In chapter 4 we see a nation unified in its purpose and not distinguished by the size of its individual tribes. There are no big I's and little yous. The selection of a man from every tribe is significant. It tells the story that they are all in this together. The stone altar being built is special. These stones are not held together by mortar or fashioned by tools.

God forbade tool work on his handiwork in Exodus 20:25. He spoke to Moses and said, "If you make a stone altar for me, do not build it out of cut stones. If you use your chisel on it, you will defile it." Using tools suggested the forming of an idol that would be worshiped, and God had explained to Moses that he is Israel's God and they are to worship no other gods.

Each Tribe Is Significant

In this story, we see God's love and impartiality for all his children. Some tribes were larger than others. Some tribes, like Ephraim and Manasseh, had a sense of greater entitlement. But regardless of size, historical prestige, or significance, each tribe was represented by a man who carried a stone and used it to join the stones carried by representatives of other tribes to form one memorial.

United in Worship

In the church of God, no one is more important than anyone else. There are many members of the body of Christ who have different gifts, but all are important and carry out their God-given callings through the power of the Spirit. "The eye cannot say to the hand, 'I don't need you!' Or again, the head can't say to the feet, 'I don't need you!'" (1 Cor 12:21). We all need one another.

Tell the Story

Build with the Stones

In Deuteronomy 6 God admonished fathers to teach their children when they arose from bed, when they walked along the way and returned to the house, and when they lay in bed at the close of the day. They would have ample opportunities, then, to teach their children the significance of these stones. The Israelites were to tell the story, and these stones were stones with a story.

Build on the Stone

If these stones could come to life and talk, they would tell their own story. This anticipates what Jesus will say to the religious leaders who object to the vocal excitement and physical demonstration of the people's joy upon Jesus's triumphant entry into the city of Jerusalem. The religious leaders said to Jesus, "Teacher, rebuke your disciples." Restrain them from all of this vocal celebration (Luke 19:39). In other words, they were asking Jesus to make the disciples hush. Jesus's response was, "If they were to keep silent, the stones would cry out" (Luke 19:40), which might alternatively be translated, "If it were possible for these disciples to remain silent, then rocks would protest and walk a picket line with a loud chant." Congregations sing in some churches that rocks must not cry out for us. We have to tell the story, our unified story. Elie Wiesel, a Jewish Holocaust survivor and Nobel Peace Prize winner, was asked how the Jewish people could retain the history of the Holocaust. Elie Wiesel explained that he believed in the power of retelling the story. This story is for all of God's people.

Build in Community

These stones provided the children of Israel an enduring catalyst to tell the story. They would be able to tell their children and grandchildren that these were the stones taken out of a flooded Jordan River and placed on the Canaan side because God had held back the waters until the nation crossed over.

Every believer ought to have a memorial to call to mind the story of God's work in the world that needs to be passed along. Memorials do not necessarily need to be physical memorials. They could be memorials invoked by memory. They could be stories of dire situations the Lord has brought them through, tragedies that the Lord has brought them out of, impossibilities the Lord has made possible, and dilemmas the Lord made into deliveries of good things pressed down and running over. We must never forget to tell this kind of story. Had it not been for the Lord on our side, where would we be?

All believers see different parts of the same story. You can't tell in total what the Lord has done for me, and I can't tell like you can what the Lord has done for you. This is a reason we live in community and worship together. We build one another's faith as we share our stories of God's goodness, mercy, and grace. We must never forget to do so, for telling parts of the story helps us remember our dependence on the Lord of all the earth and our interdependence on one another as prayed for by Jesus the Christ. Only his power allows our progress; only his goodness enables the grace we receive. We must tell the story!

Obey the Word

In Joshua 4:12, the tribes of Reuben, Gad, and the half tribe of eastern Manasseh kept their word to Moses and to Joshua. They crossed over the Jordan River into the promised land ready to fight, and they resolved to stay until the nation of Israel had gained the victory. They knew they would not live on the west side, but because they had promised to fight until the nation of Israel had conquered the west side, they would participate in realizing the promise God gave to their fathers and then go back across the Jordan River to rejoin their families on the east side. They knew they could not enjoy the blessings of God in fullness until they obeyed the word of the Lord. They were committed to the greater cause, which involved helping the nation of Israel achieve its purpose in conquering the land. This was God's agenda based on the promise he had made to their forefather Abraham over five hundred years earlier.

Believers must be willing to place their agendas beneath the agenda of what is best for the people of God. Egos and narcissism (self-infatuation, self-love) must be crucified so that our interests are lost in the will of God.

The Reproach Is Rolled Away

At Gilgal

About forty thousand men of war crossed over and prepared themselves for battle in the plains of Jericho. In 4:14 God does exactly what he said he would do in 3:7—he exalts Joshua in the sight of all Israel. As a result, the children of Israel had reverence and respect for Joshua like they had for Moses.

In 4:19 Joshua and the children of Israel camped in Gilgal not far from the city of Jericho. The word *Gilgal* means "roll." Gilgal was Joshua's headquarters like Capernaum was Jesus's headquarters. Gilgal reminded the Israelites that the reproach, the embarrassment, and the shame of their four-hundred-year servitude in Egypt had been rolled away. Some of them could remember slavery in Egypt. Some, after all, had been child slaves in Egypt. Others certainly knew the stories. Who could forget Pharaoh's genocide attempt when he tried to exterminate their nation by having the Hebrew boys drowned in the Nile? Some could remember having to make bricks without straw. They could remember building the royal cities and the extravagant palaces in Egypt with no pay and no gratification. Perhaps they still could hear the sound of the whips on their parents' bare backs.

At Calvary

"Egypt" was synonymous with shame—seemingly invited by Israel's own disobedience to God. However, "Gilgal" implies the reproach or the shame has been rolled away. There is a distinction between shame and guilt. Shame is associated with who you are, and guilt is related to what you have done. Guilt is a good reaction for the believer who has a healthy conscience. When believers sin, the Holy Spirit convicts them. This is good, for it causes the believer to repent of his or her sin. Shame is not good for believers because it embraces lies about who we are. Believers should not be victimized by shame, for we are the children of God. We have been adopted into the family of God. We are born of God. We have a new name, a new role, and a new home. We should not be people of shame, for we are no longer who we were; we are who we are. Sanctification or Christian maturing is really the process of manifesting who we are in Christ. As Martin Luther, the great Reformer, famously put it, "We only advance by going backwards." As we advance in Christ, we do so by remembering. When we sin, we must always return to the fact that we have been baptized—not simply baptized in water but baptized in Christ.

When Satan tries to accuse us because of sinful acts we have committed yet repented, we must tell him that we have been baptized. We have been washed in the blood of the Lamb. We must tell him and ourselves that nothing can separate us from the love of God that is in Christ Jesus. We must tell ourselves that even though we may be prodigal sons and daughters, we can go back home to the Father's house, not as hired servants but as sons and daughters. As one songwriter has so aptly put it, "I'll tell Him, I'm a wretch undone, without his sovereign grace" (Jones, "The Successful Resolve"). God saves us through faith in the Son and sends us the Spirit who raised Jesus from the dead in the subsequent rolling away of the stone so that we may declare his excellencies to a world that does not know him.

The purpose of this astounding miracle is found in Joshua 4:24. The Jordan River crossing, likewise, was not simply to establish and exalt a man as the new leader of the Israelites. It was not an overt opportunity for God to be omnipotently ostentatious. Rather, each miracle happened so all the people of the earth could know that the hand of the Lord is mighty and his children are to fear him forever. That is the purpose of every believer. The Westminster Confession asked a question, "What is the chief duty of man?" The answer is, "To glorify God and to enjoy him forever." This is our mission. This is why we live. And this is the story we unite to regularly tell anew and in eternity.

The Presence Is Manifested

Ark of the Covenant—Wood

God manifested his presence in the midst of the children of Israel through a wooden box known as the ark of the covenant.

Ark of the Covenant—Deity and Dust

This anticipates fourteen hundred years later when Yeshua, Jesus Christ the Son of God, will manifest his presence, not in the form of a wooden box but in the form of a human body. John puts it this way in John 1:14: "The Word became flesh and dwelt among us. We observed his glory, the glory as the one and only Son from the Father, full of grace and truth." Jesus is the ark of God. Jesus is the parable of God. Jesus is the human face of God. Jesus said to Philip in John 14:9, "The one who has seen me has seen the Father."

One day in the eschaton when time will fall exhausted at the feet of eternity, when the new Jerusalem will come down from God out of heaven, a voice will announce, "Look, God's dwelling is with humanity, and he will live with them. They will be his peoples, and God himself will be with them and will be their God." The word *dwelling* in Revelation 21:3 is the same Greek word employed in John 1:14 for "dwelt," which we could translate as "tabernacled." God saves us through faith in the Son and sends us the Spirit who raised Jesus from the dead in the subsequent rolling away of the stone so that we may declare his excellencies to a world that does not know him. In eternity future God will tabernacle with us throughout ceaseless ages. He will be in our midst and will wipe away all tears from our eyes. Until that day comes, we must continue to tell the story!

Reflections

The Christological Highway to Jesus

The question, What do these stones mean to you?, directs the believer to hermeneutically explain the meaning of redemptive metaphors: What does baptism mean? What does the Lord's Supper mean? What does the cross mean? Ultimately the stones question points to the one that was rolled away to reveal an empty tomb, and to Christ, the stone the builders rejected, who is the chosen and honored cornerstone.

Behavioral Response

We are to live our lives not as monuments that give us notoriety but rather as memorials that magnify Christ for what he has done for us. We are to be living epistles of the Lord, known and read by all people (2 Cor 3:2).

Reflect and Discuss

1. Is God's instruction in Deuteronomy 6:6-7 relevant to today's believers? Why?
2. How well do you think your life and choices point young believers to Christ? Explain.
3. How confident would you have been about retrieving stones from the Jordan River's bed? How confident are you now about carrying out God's commands?
4. What is the purpose of the additional stone memorial Joshua set up in the middle of the river?
5. Describe the "memorial stones" in your life. How do they remind you of God's faithfulness?
6. How does it help you to consider the impact of your actions painted on the canvas of faith of your church community that are collectively being painted for God's glory?
7. Why do you think the command to remember is so prevalent in Scripture?
8. How do the memorial stones of Joshua 4 compare and contrast with the sacraments of baptism and the Lord's Supper?
9. What is the significance of the meaning of the name *Gilgal*? Describe an experience of reproach being rolled away in your life. How lasting were its effects?
10. What are you doing to show the peoples of the earth that the hand of the Lord is mighty?

Have You Been to Gilgal?

JOSHUA 4:19-24; 5:9

Main Point: Just as the reproach of shame is rolled away at *Gilgal*, so the reproach of sin is rolled away at *Golgotha* through the death of Christ, raised by the Spirit of God so that we may worship him anew in *glory*.

I. **Gilgal Is a Place of Preparation.**
II. **Gilgal Is a Place of Remembrance.**
III. **Gilgal Is a Place of Removal.**
    A. Children of Israel
    B. Christians
    C. Christ
IV. **Gilgal Is a Place of Rest.**

The Big Ten

Text: Joshua 4:19-24; 5:9
Title: Have You Been to Gilgal?
New Testament Companion: Luke 24:1-2
Fallen Condition Focus: Believers have the propensity and proclivity to live with shame though Jesus has rolled both guilt and shame away by his blood upon his resurrection from the dead. Believers have sinned, and the wages of sin is death, but we do not live with the shame because Jesus rolled our sins away and has given us a new identity. Our conviction of guilt reminds us to be quick to repent as ones who have been purchased with the cost of Jesus's blood.
The Whole Counsel of God: In eternity past, in the mind of God, Christ died to forgive our sin and dismiss our shame (Rev 13:8). In history, Christ demonstrated in time at the cross what he had declared in eternity. In eternity future, believers will worship the Lamb who was slain from the foundation of the world without sin and shame (Rev 15:3).

The Christological Highway to Jesus: Just as the Old Testament Joshua led Israel through the Jordan River to Gilgal, the place where the reproach was rolled away, so the New Testament Joshua, Jesus (Yeshua), leads the believer toward the promised land of salvation at the cross through the fountain that was opened in his side from which emerged blood and water. The memorial stones at Gilgal anticipate the elements of bread and wine, which are emblems of remembrance of Christ's death.

Proposition: Just as the reproach of shame is rolled away at *Gilgal*, so the reproach of sin is rolled away at *Golgotha* through the death of Christ, raised by the Spirit of God so that we may worship him anew in *glory*.

Intratrinitarian Presence: The Father has sent the Holy Spirit to bring to our remembrance the salvific substance of the things the Savior has taught us (John 14:26).

Behavioral Response: Believers must live in the reality of the Trinitarian activity by giving glory to God in the already of time in preparation for the not yet of eternity.

Future Condition Focus (Sermonic Eschatonics): The Westminster Confession asks, "What is the chief duty of man?" We exist to glorify God and enjoy him forever. Therefore, our ultimate purpose is to live for and glorify God, according to his purpose, in the stone that the builders rejected, Christ (Ps 118:22-23), who has become the chosen and honored cornerstone.

Introduction

Just as the reproach of shame was rolled away at *Gilgal*, so the reproach of sin is rolled away at *Golgotha* through the death of Christ, raised by the Spirit of God that we may worship him anew in *glory*. The children of Israel were to remember God and his law. God knew they were prone to amnesia, so God said to them in Deuteronomy 6:6-7, "When your children lie down at night or when they get up, talk to them about my words and talk to them about me. When they sit at home or when they walk along the path, talk to them about the God of the law and talk to them about the law of God. When you are sitting, think about it. Write and store my words in phylacteries and put them on your wrists and on the foreheads of your bodies. Write my Word on the gates and the doorposts of your residences, because I don't want you to forget my Word" (author's paraphrase).

Joshua is sandwiched between Deuteronomy and Judges. In Deuteronomy the Israelites are told to remember not to forget the law of God and the God of the law. In Judges they are to recall the law so they put it in action and live it out. However, in Judges they forget to remember. The Bible says in Judges 2:10-11 that a generation arose that did not know the Lord. They did not know what he had done for his people. They thus did evil in the eyes of the Lord, and they served the Baals. They forgot to remember. But Joshua 24:31 says that the people of Israel served the Lord during Joshua's lifetime and during the lifetime of those elders who survived Joshua. They remembered to remember. God calls us today to remember his law and to remember him because there is within us this inherent proclivity—a propensity or tendency—to forget God. James Weldon Johnson reminds us in "Lift Ev'ry Voice and Sing" not to forget the God who remembered us when we were weary. God constantly reminds us to remember. Sometimes he uses symbols to remind us to remember the law of God and to remember the God of the law.

Gilgal Is a Place of Preparation

It had been a long time coming. The Israelites had finally come to the edge of Canaan on the wilderness side and were ready to cross over. It was as if they could sing the song "On Jordan's Stormy Banks" as they stood remembering their forty-year journey. They had waited for four hundred years in slavery while in Egypt serving under a Pharaoh who did not know Joseph or his children. They were made to make brick without straw. Their backs looked like freshly plowed new ground from the whips of their slave taskmasters. It had been years of watching their boys thrown into the rivers of Egypt in an effort to wipe out the Hebrew male population, which, of course, would exterminate the Hebrew population altogether. For four hundred years they waited and spent forty years in the wilderness in the longest funeral procession in history. Those of military age twenty and older dropped dead every day as they continued to march around in the wilderness because they balked and hesitated at Kadesh-barnea. When God said step, they stopped, and when God said stop, they stepped. They were discomfited by the giants in that particular land. They continued moving but making no progress. They waited. They waited thirty days to mourn Moses's death (Deut

34:8). They waited. Finally, God would say in effect, "The days of mourning for Moses are over. Moses my servant is dead. Now Joshua, you take and lead these people over the Jordan River to a land that I'm about to give to them. In fact, I've already given it to them. I've even provided the boundaries five hundred years ago in Genesis 15:18 to Abram. This is the land that's yours as long as you take and possess your possession. Wherever your feet are placed, that will be your land."

Moses the worker died. Yet God buries his workers but not his work. No wonder Shakespeare reminds us that all of life is a stage and we're just actors. We must remind ourselves of that. We are not indispensable. We are expendable. We come here to do our work, and when our work is finished, God has a replacement system. Someone will step into our places. In the meantime, we must do our jobs well. The Lord says in essence to Joshua, "As I was with Moses, so will I be with you. I was with Moses at the Red Sea, and I opened up the Red Sea and caused the walls to stand up at attention as retaining walls. I dried up the bottom, and the people walked through as if it were a superhighway. They didn't have mud between their toes. They had dust around their ankles. I will be with you at the Jordan River. I will cause the walls to stand up and hold back the waters of the Jordan from flowing down south from up north. You will lead the people over to the promised land."

Because God said, "I will be with you, just as I was with Moses" (1:5), the people will understand that Joshua is his chosen one. God was with Moses at the burning bush. There he put an amplification system in the burning bush and spoke to Moses saying, "Moses, don't come any farther! Take off the shoes from your feet, for the ground you're standing on is holy ground." God was with Joshua outside the fortress city of Jericho in Joshua 5:13-15. Both Moses and Joshua got to hear the voice of the captain of the Lord's armies, which may be a Christophany, perhaps even a theophany. They each heard, "Remove the sandals from your feet, for the place where you are standing is holy," and Joshua heard, "I will be with you, just as I was with Moses."

The congregation gets a great report from the two spies who had participated in the espionage campaign. They scouted Jericho. Joshua was wise. He didn't send twelve spies like Moses did. He sent two. They come back and say the people's hearts are melting and running like water, and we are going to take the city because God has said we will. The people know this because of what God did with Og and Sihon, the Amorite kings. Now they come to the edge of the promised land.

It's been a long time coming, but they're there. Israel is at the Jordan River. God says to the priests, "Take the ark of the covenant and take it down to the water's edge of the Jordan River and hold it there" (see 3:8). The ark of the covenant represents the presence of God in the midst of his people. In that ark are three items of historical significance. There is the jar of manna, which represents the provision of God because God from heaven's kitchen baked bread for forty straight years to feed them. Then there's Aaron's rod that budded without the benefit of photosynthesis, without roots, without rain, without soil, without cultivation, and without fertilization. It just instantaneously blossomed, bloomed, and produced almonds, which represented the power of God. Then there were the two tablets of stone on which were written God's words. The ark is lined with gold, and on the outside of its acacia wood is gold. Its lid, representing the mercy seat, is gold, too. "Take that and stand at the river's edge."

The Bible says there were to be three thousand cubits between the first non-priest and the ark (3:4). A cubit is eighteen inches; that works out to about half a mile or one kilometer. Why that kind of distance? First, God is holy. There must be separation between mere humanity and divinity, between deity and post-fall dust. It was also because they needed to be able to see where the ark, which represented the presence of God in the midst of his people, was going. They must not be distracted and sidetracked by anything peripheral. They must keep their eyes on the ark of the covenant. When the soles of the priests' feet touched the river's edge, God dammed up the water and held it in suspension up north. In these conditions, the children of Israel began their march across.

Now the priests are standing in the middle of the Jordan. They are acting like school-crossing guards. As long as they hold the ark and stand there, the waters stand up. They don't collapse and drown the people. This, for some of them, inspires déjà vu. Forty years prior they, as children, had crossed the Red Sea, and now it was time to cross a body of water again. This time it's the Jordan River. For all of them, it must be a moment in which they understand God's plan, promise, and faithfulness. This crossing could not happen unless God supernaturally intended it. God is supralogical, able to defy logic. Thus, there are some things in my life and in your life that can only be explained by and attributed to God. This cannot be explored scientifically or fully grasped with enough education. All you can do is take the stance of the psalmist in Psalm 124:1: "If the LORD had not been on our side . . .?"

Your intelligence can't explain it. Your heritage can't explain it. The only reason I am here today is because of what God did.

God wanted the people of Israel to know that he was confirming and ratifying and certifying Joshua as his chosen leader. He says, essentially, "Tomorrow I'm going to exalt you in the eyes of all the people so that you will not have to vindicate yourself. I will do it" (see 3:7). In 4:14 God actually executed what he said he was going to do. The people understood that no one voted Joshua into his position. No one elected him. God chose him. Brothers and sisters, if you have a call of certitude, if you know God has called you and placed you, then you can be comfortable that God will vindicate you. You will not have to prove yourself. You will not have to grandstand and talk about your greatness. If God has called you, he will vindicate you, and he'll keep you there until his work is done no matter what is against you.

Now they're crossing over. When the last Israelite gets to the Canaan side, Joshua has twelve men who've been selected, one out of each tribe, to go to the middle area where the priests stood holding the ark of the covenant of God, to each pick up a boulder, and to put them on their shoulders and carry them to the other side to form a monument of remembrance. When that's done, the priests come out. When they get to the other side and get out of the river, God releases the water from up north, and it comes down and flows again. It flows and floods the bank because this is harvest time when the flooded waters of Jordan overflowed the land of Canaan. The place where this took place is called Gilgal. And just as the reproach of shame was rolled away at Gilgal, so the reproach of sin is rolled away at Golgotha through the death of Christ, raised by the Spirit of God, that we may worship him anew in glory. Gilgal is a place of preparation.

Joshua 12:24 states that Joshua defeated thirty-one kings. The only loss, of course, was at Ai because of sin. Every military battle was planned in Gilgal. They would go out, execute their plan, come back, and plan again. Gilgal was the equivalent of the New Testament Capernaum for Jesus. It was the headquarters. It was a place of preparation for him and his disciples.

Are we getting what we can get out of our places of preparation? The success of our ministries might just lie in what we do at our Gilgals. Will we look back and regret that we never put in the dedicated time for studying and for the discipline called preaching? Our Gilgals are a launching pad for us. This is where God is preparing us for what God is preparing us for! It is a place for God to equip us to edify others when we go to minister to them. It is a place of preparation.

Jesus left earth to go to heaven in order to prepare a place for us. But initially he left heaven to come to earth to prepare us for the place. His Spirit who lives in us will continue to sanctify us so that people can see us as Kodak moments of the future state of eternity. People can look at us and see heaven in us. Just by the way our lives are lived, others can get just a sample of what heaven will be like because we are living in a heavenly way by the power of the Spirit.

Gilgal Is a Place of Remembrance

Have you been to Gilgal? Gilgal is also a place of remembrance. The Bible says in Joshua 4:21-24 that children in the future would ask their parents, "What is the meaning of these stones?" Children are by nature inquisitive and curious. Consider a son walking with his father like Isaac did when going up Mount Moriah with Abraham saying, "Daddy, I see the fire, the instruments for making the fire, and the elements for making the fire. I see the wood, but where is the lamb for the sacrifice?" And then picture a little boy going through the Gilgal National Park, and he sees these strange monumental stones. They are not chiseled; God forbade that. There is no mortar; they are just piled together.

Some of the boulders are larger than the others, like Judah and Ephraim are more numerous than Issachar and Asher. However, it makes no difference in terms of the monument's unity. When it comes to the church, by extension, it makes no difference what gift we have received. We are not better or lesser because of our gifts. The foot cannot say to the hand, "I don't need you" (1 Cor 12:21). No. We each put whatever we have into the monument called the church to glorify God. We may not be able to sing like angels, and we may not be able to preach like Paul, but each of us can tell of the love of Jesus, that he died to save us all. Do not despise or look down on smaller things that do not get the kind of prominence other gifts receive. We must use what we have to glorify God and edify others.

When children asked in future times, "What is the meaning of these stones?" parents were to tell them, "God dried up the Jordan River, and we crossed over on dry ground," in order that they might see the hand of God as mighty and fear the Lord. That is what these stones meant.

Everyone ought to have a memorial. I have been gifted some beautiful diplomas, plaques, and jewelry. All of them are valuable; some are not monetarily valuable, but all of them are significant to me. My hospital wrist bands are particularly meaningful to me. One is from January 1996. God brought me through cancer. The related wristband is a memorial. I have another one from 2005. Cancer. There is another one from 2010. Cancer. I keep these to remind myself, "Son, you do not have time to waste. God has been good to you. God has spared you. God has done what no one could do. Had it not been for God, you would not be here. You are not here just to do time in the pulpit. You are here to give glory to him and to carry out the ministry he has given you—not with mediocrity but with excellence because you want to please your Father."

We all need memorials: things that keep bringing us back to the center. When we get sidetracked by other attractions that seem to loom large, do we have memorials to bring us back to where God called us? Gilgal is a place of remembrance, and God brings us back to the place where we remember our call and what he has called us to do. Jesus uses the word *anamnesis* in Luke 22:19, "Do this in remembrance of me." Paul says in 2 Timothy 2:8 to remember Jesus Christ because we have the proclivity, the propensity, and the tendency to forget the Lord. We all need a place of remembrance.

Gilgal Is a Place of Removal

Children of Israel

Have you been to Gilgal in this next sense? Gilgal is a place of removal. The name *Gilgal* is associated with this truth: the reproach of shame has been rolled away. That is what it means.

There is a difference between shame and guilt. Guilt relates to what we have done. We need the conviction of guilt in terms of being conscious of our sin so we turn to God for grace. But shame relates to who we are. For Israel, the shame of Egypt got rolled away at Gilgal. The shame of backlashes, the shame of genocidal attempts, the shame of embarrassment—that shame has been rolled away. The Lord removed it.

Rahab could tell you her guilt had been forgiven and her shame was rolled away, too. She would testify, "I was the prostitute. I was the madam of the best little house of disrepute in Jericho. That's what I was. I also was a pagan, but God washed the shame of it away because, in Hebrews 11:31, I am in the hall of faith and not the hall of infamy." The text says Rahab welcomed the spies and did not perish with the disobedient. She was justified by faith. James 2:25 says Rahab is justified by works because she gave lodging to the spies and sent them another way.

Christians

Justification by faith precedes justification by works. Justification by works is working *from* salvation. God justifies us and declares us righteous. God sees the end from the beginning, and because he knows the end from the beginning, he can declare us as he sees us in glory though we are still living on earth and being sanctified and progressively becoming more and more like his Son.

Psalm 103:10-12 says God forgives our sins and casts them as far as the east is from the west. The east and west never meet. In other words, our sins are forgotten. Corrie ten Boom paraphrases these verses to say that God puts a "no fishing allowed" sign on the shore so no one is allowed to purchase the license to fish up our sins. In fact, we cannot even fish up our own sins. Our forgiven sins are gone. Therefore, there is now no condemnation for those who are in Christ Jesus.

Saint of God, stop walking in condemnation. We have a new identity. We are his children. We can never have that relationship nullified. It can never be abrogated. That relationship must be intact from now even unto eternity. In trusting Jesus, we've been to the place of removal.

Christ

Shame removal is what Jesus does. Installment payments were made for sin all the way throughout the Old Testament. Every sacrifice made for sin was an installment on a debt we could never pay. That obligation was against us, keeping us from God. But Jesus went to the cross, and he took the certificate of debt away. He erased it by nailing it to the cross (Col 2:14). Jesus paid it all, and on the third day, the stone from Joseph's tomb was rolled away and Jesus rose from the dead.

Gilgal Is a Place of Rest

Have you been to Gilgal in this sense? Gilgal is a place of rest. These people were tired. They had been walking around in the wilderness for forty years. They have been mourning the death of Moses for thirty days. A million plus people have crossed the Jordan River. Old women, pregnant women, middle-aged men—all of them crossing over tired. Then the men were circumcised, since no one had been circumcised during the forty-year wilderness journey. After circumcision, they stayed in the camp until they were healed (5:8-9). They needed the rest.

Some of us are really tired. We are tired of infertility; we are tired of going to Mother's Day services and seeing mothers holding babies and we do not have the one we want. We are tired of being turned down by the adoption agencies. We are tired. We are tired of being unemployed or employed in the wrong jobs. We are tired of making the hospital our second homes or the doctor's office our second residences. We are tired, like Fannie Lou Hamer of Mississippi would say—sick and tired of being sick and tired. There seems to always be another surgery that is needed. We ask, "Why can't I be well, live a normal life, and enjoy what everyone else has enjoyed?" We are tired of relationships that have soured. We are tired of the distance in marriages where the dissonance between us and our spouses is deafening. We are tired of the distance between us and our mothers or us and our fathers, sisters, and brothers. Of those relationships in which we have not enjoyed peace since daddy died. We are tired. Some are so tired that we wish at night not to wake up in the morning.

Gilgal is a place of rest, and Jesus epitomizes and personifies that rest. Do you hear him saying, "Come to me, all of you who are weary and burdened, and I will give you rest" (Matt 11:28)? According to Hebrews 4:8-9, the Old Testament Joshua did not give the people of God rest. If he had, then God would not have spoken of another day when the people of God will have their Sabbath. Augustine said in his *Confessions,* "Our souls are restless until they find their rest in thee" (*Confessions,* 1). God has made a God-sized hole in us, and nothing will fill that hole except God. Thus, only he gives us real rest.

Just as the reproach of shame was rolled away at Gilgal, so the reproach of sin is rolled away at Golgotha through the death of Christ raised by the Spirit of God that we may worship him anew in heaven. Jesus is like the ark. In him there is manna-bread and provision. In fact, Jesus is the Bread of Life. In the ark of the covenant, there is Aaron's rod that budded. Aaron's rod represents the power of God, and Jesus is the power of God personified. In that ark are two tablets of stone, which represent the law of God, and Jesus is the Word of God. He is the living Word, and what did he do? The Bible says in John 1:14, "The Word became flesh and dwelt among us. We observed his glory, the glory as the one and only Son from the Father, full of grace and truth." He dwelt—tabernacled—among us. In the words of Eugene Peterson, Jesus "moved into the neighborhood" (John 1:14; *Message*). He tabernacled on earth. John said in Revelation 21:3-4,

Then I heard a loud voice from the throne: Look, God's dwelling is
with humanity, and he will live with them. They will be his peoples,
and God himself will be with them and will be their God. He will wipe
away every tear from their eyes.

Even in eternity he will be our ark. He will be our tabernacle. He will
dwell in the midst of his people. We are bound for glory land. The question remains for you to answer on your way, "Have you been to Gilgal?"

Reflections

The Christological Highway to Jesus

Gilgal is a place of preparation, remembrance, removal, and rest.
Preparation, removal, and remembrance are integral parts of believers'
lives until they come to find their rest in Christ. In fact, preparation,
removal, and remembrance are repeated activities believers experience
that point them to the Savior, just as sin is a reminder pointing to the
need for the Messiah.

Behavioral Response

Jesus dwelt with us and paid the cost to give us the ultimate personal
Gilgal. We must grasp the significance of what Jesus did so that we keep
right focus and will be motivated to tell others how they can join him in
the eternal kingdom.

Reflect and Discuss

1. How has God used a Gilgal of remembrance to bring you to a place
   of surrender to him?
2. What relationship does Gilgal have with Golgotha? In other words,
   what implication(s) does Gilgal have for Golgotha in relation to
   salvation history?
3. What was Gilgal's ultimate purpose for Israel and the surrounding
   nations?
4. Differentiate between guilt and shame. Why is knowing the difference important for true Christian identity?
5. Interpret Hebrews 12:2 in light of the meaning of Gilgal.
6. How has your Gilgal been a place of preparation for you?

7. How has your Gilgal been a place of remembrance for you?
8. How has your Gilgal been a place of removal for you?
9. How has your Gilgal been a place of rest for you?
10. How does *glory* fulfill and fill full the significance of Gilgal and Golgotha?

The Sufficiency of God

JOSHUA 5

Main Idea: God in Christ, the God abandoned, who is our Passover Lamb and manna, empowers believers through the Spirit to proclaim the sufficiency of God.

I.   **Living between the Times**
   A. Joshua: Remember to remember God.
   B. Between crossing the Jordan and the battle of Jericho
   C. Between preparation and execution
     1. Jeremiah
     2. Paul
     3. Jesus
     4. The people of Jericho
II. **Living the Personal Testimony**
   A. Of the obedient flesh—circumcision
   B. Of the disobedient flesh—circumscription
III. **Living Redeemed**
   A. Circumcision—Jesus was cut off.
   B. Passover—Jesus gave himself as the sacrifice for our sin.
   C. Coronation—Jesus is the King of kings.

The Big Ten

Text: Joshua 5
Title: The Sufficiency of God
New Testament Companion: 2 Corinthians 3:4-6
Fallen Condition Focus: Because of the failure of believers to be faithful to the Word, the Lord has to take us back to his commands (circumcision and Passover observed again) before he can move us forward in victorious service at Jericho.
The Whole Counsel of God: Jesus is the commander in chief of God's army, to whom we are brought to worship as Lord through the illuminating power of the Holy Spirit.

The Christological Highway to Jesus: Christ, who is our Passover Lamb, submitted himself to the cross so that the judgment for our sins might be laid on him. As our Bread of Life, Christ's body is broken to provide spiritual sustenance for us as we commune with him.

Intratrinitarian Presence: The Father who commanded the circumcision of the heart and provided manna in the wilderness also provides his own Son as the true, sustaining Bread of Life. The Holy Spirit draws us to this sustaining bread and empowers us to proclaim the sufficiency of God and to worship the God of our sufficiency.

Proposition: God in Christ, the God abandoned, who is our Passover Lamb and manna, empowers believers through the Spirit to proclaim the sufficiency of God.

Behavioral Response: Christians are to live in full confidence that God is sufficient for all our needs. Yahweh-yireh (Jehovah-jireh) will provide, perhaps not in the ways or timing we desire, but God is faithful to keep his promises.

Future Condition Focus (Sermonic Eschatonics): For the Old Testament Jews, circumcision was the physical sign that indicated they were members of the community of Israel, the people of God. No uncircumcised Israelite male could live in the community of Israel. In the eschaton, those who are spiritually circumcised will live in eternal fellowship with God in their midst (Rev 21:3). In the eternal state, the saints who overcame by the blood of the Passover Lamb (Rev 7:14) and have eternal fellowship with God through the Holy Spirit will feed figuratively on Christ the Bread of Life throughout ceaseless ages.

Living between the Times

In Charles Dickens's classic novel *A Tale of Two Cities*, he describes the times in which he lived with these unforgettable words:

> It was the best of times, it was the worst of times; it was the age of wisdom, it was the age of foolishness; it was the epoch of belief, it was the epoch of incredulity; it was the season of light, it was the season of darkness; it was the spring of hope, it was the

winter of despair. We had everything; we were all going direct to
heaven; we were all going direct to the other way. (p. 1)

The Latin phrase *carpe diem* means "seize the day." The Germans call
it *zeitgeist*, which means "the spirit of the times." Victor Hugo has said,
"There is nothing more powerful than an idea whose time has come."[4]
The apostle Paul charges us in Romans 13:11 that our conduct should
reflect this reality—it is high time we wake out of sleep. We are living
between the times—yesterday has passed and tomorrow may never come.

Joshua: Remember to Remember God

Joshua 5 was written for a time between the times. The book of
Deuteronomy, which precedes the book of Joshua, was written to cau-
tion Israel not to forget the law. The book of Judges, which follows the
book of Joshua, was written to remind us to remember the importance
of retaining the truths of the law and not forgetting God. The book of
Joshua was written in order that the people of God would remember to
remember God. Joshua 1:8 declares, "This book of instruction must not
depart from your mouth; you are to meditate on it day and night."

Between Crossing the Jordan and the Battle of Jericho

In chapter 2 spies are sent to Jericho and return with a report that
the people of Jericho are saturated with fear and have heard about
the exploits Yahweh has accomplished in the wilderness and in the
destruction of Og and Sihon and their kingdoms. In chapters 3 and
4 the Israelites have planned and successfully executed their objec-
tive in crossing the Jordan River by the mighty hand of God who held
back the waters until they had completely crossed over. In this chapter, the Israelites are going to reenact the rite of circumcision, renew
the celebration of Passover, and have their leader, Joshua, prepared to
lead them in their first military confrontation: against the fortress city
of Jericho. Therefore, chapter 4 serves in an in-between position for
Joshua and Israel. They are in between crossing over the Jordan and
their battle against Jericho.

---

[4] Victor Hugo, *The Future of Man* (as paraphrased by the artist Robert Vickrey on
a painting in the series Great Ideas of Western Man, 1964; Smithsonian American Art
Museum).

Between Preparation and Execution

The Old Testament reflects the significance of living in between two inescapable realities—preparation and execution. Jeremiah experienced this in Jeremiah 20:9 when, on the one hand, he said he was determined not to mention God again "or speak any longer in his name." On the other hand, he exclaimed that he could not hold back from preaching in his name because, being in the middle, "his message [became] a fire burning in [his] heart, shut up in [his] bones," and he couldn't resist the compulsion to speak it. The apostle **Paul** lived in this in-between ambivalence in Philippians 1:23-24, where he says, "I am torn between the two. I long to depart and be with Christ—which is far better—but to remain in the flesh is more necessary for your sake." **Jesus** also wrestled with this in-between reality in the garden of Gethsemane where he prayed for a release from drinking the cup ahead until he finally concluded his prayer with, "Yet not as I will, but as you will" (Matt 26:39). All of us struggle with this in-between tension. I maintain that God in Christ, the God abandoned, who is our Passover Lamb and manna, empowers believers through the Spirit to proclaim the sufficiency of God anyway.

In the opening verse of Joshua chapter 5, the scene is set for anticipatory living between the times. The author describes the disposition and attitude or mindset of **the people of Jericho**. These enemies' hearts melted and their spirits were dried up. They had no courage in them. This sounds similar to what Rahab said in her confession to the two spies sent from Joshua: "When we heard this, we lost heart, and everyone's courage failed because of you, for the LORD your God is God in heaven above and on earth below" (2:11). Therefore, 5:1 is an update. Rahab's report is a reflection of what she had heard God had done to the two kings in the wilderness. Now this report is what the people of Jericho saw God do in holding back the waters of the Jordan River until approximately a million of his people successfully crossed over. One can only imagine how long it must have taken for over a million people to cross through this body of water with young, old, pregnant women, small children, and animals!

Living the Personal Testimony

Chapter 5 has brought the Israelites to a place of gaining experience. As believers we must know God for ourselves and not simply by secondhand reports. Israelite forefather Jacob's name means "deceiver," "trickster," or "supplanter." He was Isaac's son. When he had the dream in

Genesis 28 of angels ascending and descending, God spoke to him and said he was the God of Abraham and Isaac. He never said he was the God of Jacob. It is only in Genesis 48:15 where Jacob says God had been "*my* shepherd*.*" His own. This personal witness speaks to the importance of an individual experience with God that cannot be borrowed. It is one's own story, and God in Christ, the God abandoned, who is our Passover Lamb and manna, empowers believers through the Spirit to proclaim the sufficiency of God. First, though, we need to trust it personally.

I remember when I was a small boy, my sisters, brother, and I played church at home. I would put on one of my daddy's ties and big coats and shoes and preach to my sisters, who would be dressed in some of mama's oversized attire, and to my brother, who was also in some of daddy's clothes and shoes. That was playing church. But when I had an experience with God years later, playing church became real church. It is important for us to experience the real God in order to experience real worship. Believers must be able to truthfully say, "This is *my* story, this is *my* song" (Fanny Crosby, "Blessed Assurance"; emphasis added).

Of the Obedient Flesh—Circumcision

I believe sometimes God initially concerns himself with bringing his children to a place of weakness so they recognize that their strength is in him and in him alone. This could be why God tells Joshua to bring all of the uncircumcised males to the table in order to undergo the rite of circumcision. What a strange order because circumcision immobilizes a male, yet Israel is getting ready to face the enemy in the fortress city of Jericho. This will be her first battle in the promised land, and the first order of business is not confrontation but rather circumcision? It is like seeing Coach Nick Saban ordering all his University of Alabama players to undergo plastic surgery a few days before the College Football Association Championship Game. That would be ludicrous, for they should be practicing in preparation for the game rather than recovering at the hospital or at home. Israel would need strength, not weakness. But God's ways are not our ways. In fact, in 2 Corinthians 12:10 Paul says, "When I am weak, then I am strong."

All Israel would've recognized that the circumcision order was a call not to rely on their own might; their fitness for battle was being taken away. In Genesis 34 a man by the name of Shechem saw Dinah, the daughter of Jacob, out in the field and desired her. He eventually raped her. The report got back to Jacob and his eleven sons (Benjamin wasn't born yet). They were furious. Levi and Simeon wanted revenge. Hamor the father of Shechem offered Jacob and his family land on which to live. They would share space, and Jacob's sons could marry the pagan daughters. Hamor was informed that Hebrew women would not marry uncircumcised men, so the Shechemites would need to be circumcised. This was really just a ruse to weaken the Shechemite men so Simeon and Levi could take their revenge for the rape of their sister, Dinah. As expected, the Shechemites remained in pain for several days. While they were recovering, Simeon and Levi killed all of them.

In Genesis 17 God commands Abraham and his more than three hundred servants to be circumcised. Abraham is ninety-nine and Ishmael is thirteen. In Exodus 4:24-26 God was about to kill Moses because he had not yet circumcised his son. Circumcision is a requirement for God's people, though the Israelites were not the first to practice circumcision.

Of the Disobedient Flesh—Circumscription

The Egyptians practiced circumcision three centuries before Abraham. Actually, they practiced *circumscription* of the foreskin of the male genitalia and not circumcision. Circumscription was a matter of circumscribing or cutting *around*, whereas circumcision was the cutting *off* of the foreskin. By extension, one might say circumscription represents a partial carrying out of God's direction, whereas circumcision signals complete adherence to God's direction.

Partial obedience to God's instructions happened with Saul in 1 Samuel 15 when he spared Agag and the best of the livestock. God had instructed Saul to kill all the Amalekites and their livestock. In effect, Saul agreed to carry out circumscription and not circumcision. Sometimes in our desire to honor our own wishes, we choose to live lives of circumscription and not circumcision or circumspection. God wanted both physical circumcision for Jewish men and spiritual circumcision for all believers. In Deuteronomy 10:16 the Lord declares he wants the Israelites' hearts to be circumcised, too. In Romans 2:29 Paul says God desires circumcision of the heart by the Holy Spirit. We are to give ourselves and yield our will to God. As the nineteenth-century Scottish pastor and preacher Alexander Whyte often prayed, "Lord, I give myself to thee, and whatever I cannot give I invite you to take." We must give all we know of ourselves to all we know of God. Nothing must be held back. The inspired writer admonishes us in Hebrews 12:1, "Let us lay aside every hindrance and the sin that so easily ensnares us." What is that sin? Regardless, it must be circumcised, removed completely, and not merely circumscribed.

During the nearly forty years of wilderness wandering, no one was circumcised (v. 7). Therefore, individuals who hadn't been born yet or who were younger than eight days of age when the children of Israel made their exodus from Egypt were not as God wanted. That's forty years. The men who were twenty years old and older at the time of Israel's balking at Kadesh-barnea would have since died in the wilderness because of God's judgment against them (Num 14:28-29). So the only older males who would have survived the nearly forty years of wilderness wanderings were Caleb and Joshua, for they returned as spies from Canaan with a faithful report: "If the LORD is pleased with us, he will bring us into this land . . . and give it to us" (Num 14:8).

After the Israelites were circumcised, they stayed in their camp until they were healed (Josh 5:8). Then Joshua was informed by the Lord that the place of Gilgal would have significance for them historically because at Gilgal the disgrace of Egypt was rolled away. That meant the embarrassment of the four-hundred-year Egyptian bondage was no longer on them. The times in which genocide was attempted, the oppressors ordered them to make brick without straw, the sound of the whip on the bare backs of the Israelites—all had been rolled away. The damaging emotional memories and dreams had been addressed.

Living Redeemed

Circumcision—Jesus Was Cut Off

There is a difference between shame and guilt. One of my great sorrows as I preach in churches throughout the world is the recognition that people do not feel they are sinners any longer. I can no longer find any sinners or sin in the church. Of course, it is there, but people refuse to see it. The fact is people don't feel bad about what they have done any longer, for they do not acknowledge what they've done as wrong. We need good guilt. We need to say as David said, "For I am conscious of my rebellion, and my sin is always before me" (Ps 51:3). However, true Christians do not need shame because shame is feeling bad about who you are. We are no longer who we were. We have been declared righteous, faultless, and guiltless. Too many Christians walk around in shame, never able to forgive themselves or to live beyond their pasts. Yes, our sins have consequences. However, we are able to recover by the power and forgiveness of God. If God has forgiven us, we have no right not to forgive ourselves. We must press on from Gilgal to Golgotha to share in the glory of the cross because God in Christ, the God abandoned, cut off, who is our Passover Lamb and manna, wants to empower believers through the Spirit to proclaim the sufficiency of God.

Passover—Jesus Gave Himself as the Sacrifice for Our Sin

In verses 10-12 there is a renewal of the Passover. In Exodus 12 the children of Israel were finally released from their four-hundred-year incarceration in Egypt. The Passover points to Jesus, the ultimate Passover Lamb. Unleavened bread, bread baked without yeast, commemorates the hasty exit Israel made from Egypt in Exodus 12. Their bread did not have time to rise. Unleavened bread also points to our call to be holy as God is holy. The fast from leavened bread reminds us to discipline ourselves and choose obedience. Our firstfruits offering points to our acceptance by God since the offering of Christ, the firstfruits of the resurrection, was accepted (1 Cor 15:23).

Our God brought the Israelites out of Egypt by leading them the challenging way (Exod 13:17). In Joshua 3:15 God commanded Joshua to lead Israel across the Jordan River while the river was at flood stage. This seems to make no sense. Why not wait until the Jordan River is at low tide? This question would be appropriate to ask of a human leader but not of the I AM who reminds Israel that he fights with every mention of their name and does so his way. This might require a supernatural crossing. It would require providential timing.

Once they get into the promised land, there are crops ready for the harvest, just as God had promised in Deuteronomy 6:10-11. Collard greens, carrots, black-eyed peas, lima beans, grain, and the rest are readily available for over a million people in order to celebrate the Festivals of Passover and Unleavened Bread.

God had the Israelites cross the Jordan River when its banks were overflowing with water—a stark reminder their God controls the new land's water. The very people group who complained about the lack of water in Exodus 17:3 should realize their Rock has given them a land, as he promised, with plenty of water for their needs.

Though God commanded the Israelites to observe Passover at its appointed time, it had not been observed during the forty years of the wilderness wandering. This is instructive for believers today. When we choose to wander, we are choosing to disobey God. We must take care not to choose wilderness wanderings with our grumbling, our thoughts, our actions, or our words. We must trust God. The Passover and crossing over prove once again that God's clock keeps perfect time.

Coronation—Jesus Is the King of Kings

In verses 13-15 God prepares Joshua, their leader, to lead them into battle at Jericho. Joshua leaves the camp at Gilgal and begins to survey the land. He had probably seen Jericho forty years earlier when he and Caleb spied out the area. While he is there several miles from the fortress, he is approached by one with a drawn sword. Joshua boldly asks, "Are you for us or for our enemies?" The response was, "Neither. I have now come as commander of the LORD's army." He was on his own side. He was there to take over. Joshua hears this divine presence say, "Remove the sandals from your feet, for the place where you are standing is holy." This is the same order Moses heard well over forty years earlier at the back side of the desert (Exod 3:5).

Joshua begins to worship this divine presence. This is not an angelic being. Here we encounter a theophany, the visible manifestation of God to humans, or a Christophany, the visible manifestation of Christ the Son of God to humans before his birth in Bethlehem. In Revelation 19:10 John the apostle falls at the feet of an angelic being, and the angelic being says to him, "Don't do that! I am a fellow servant with you. . . . Worship God." However, in Revelation 1:17-18, John submits himself to the one who said, "I was dead, but look—I am alive forever and ever." This is Jesus, our Lord, who does not prohibit John from assuming a posture of worship.

In these three actions—circumcision, renewal of Passover, and orientation of Joshua, their leader—we see three foreshadows of the divine. Circumcision represents when Jesus was cut off from the Father at Calvary because he was the sin bearer. There he was abandoned and cried out, "My God, my God, why have you abandoned me?" (Mark 15:34). In the Passover, Jesus is our Passover Lamb. John the Baptist declared, "Look, the Lamb of God, who takes away the sin of the world!" (John 1:29). He does not come to *bring* an offering; he *is* the offering. Finally, the divine presence of Christ as the captain of the Lord's heavenly armies means Christ has come to be King of kings and Lord of lords. He comes to take over. No wonder John said of history's finale, "The kingdom of the world has become the kingdom of our Lord and of his Christ" (Rev 11:15).

Reflections

The Christological Highway to Jesus

Compare Gilgal and Golgotha. At Gilgal, the reproach and shame of the Israelite past in Egypt was rolled away, and at Golgotha Jesus "endured the cross, despising the shame" (Heb 12:2). The cross is a picture of Jesus's physical circumcision, which took place when he was eight days old. His spiritual circumcision took place at the cross when he was thirty-three years old. He was cut off or abandoned by his Father (Mark 15:34) in order that we might be accepted by the Father. In this passage, Jesus, who is our circumcision, is also our manna, our Passover, our firstfruits, and our commander in chief of the Lord's armies.

Behavioral Response

Joshua asked the revealed Lord, "Are you for us or for our enemies?" (Josh 5:13) and also, "What does my lord want to say to his servant?" (v. 14). This anticipates Paul's two questions to the revealed Lord on the road to Damascus: "Who art thou, Lord?" and "Lord, what wilt thou have me to do?" (Acts 9:5-6 KJV). The first question sought information, while the second question focused on action. God expects believers to act on the knowledge they receive from him.

Intratrinitarian Presence

The flint knife used in the circumcision of the Israelite males in this passage is emblematic of the sword of the Spirit, which is the Word of God. The image also brings to mind Jesus, the Great Physician.

Reflect and Discuss

1. Reflect on some of the powerful personal testimonies you have heard. How have they impacted your walk with Christ?
2. How was the circumcision of the new generation in Joshua 5 an act of faith?

3. When has God allowed you to be weak so you would allow him to be your strength?
4. What does "circumcision of the heart" (Rom 2:29) mean? How does it look for contemporary believers?
5. How does Jesus fulfill the Old Testament practices of circumcision, Passover, and the Festival of Unleavened Bread?
6. Reflect on the statement, "The greater the love, the greater the pain." Where have you found this to be true? When have you found it to be false?
7. Have there been layover seasons in your life? How did you feel while experiencing them? How did God refine you during them?
8. How might one learn to live faithfully in seasons of adjustment?
9. God is on his own side. How do believers reconcile this truth with their need to have God on their side?
10. According to Paul in Colossians 3, what should Christians take off? What should Christians put on? How do Christians execute these actions?

Divine Demolition

Main Idea: Through the power of the Holy Spirit, Christ has torn down the dividing wall of hostility that separated us from God and one another by submitting himself to the cross, thus enabling believers to proclaim a gospel of reconciliation to God and one another.

I. **Israel versus Jericho**
   A. Natural position
   B. Divine position
II. **Mercy versus Misery**
   A. Rahab
   B. Believers
   C. Theodicy
III. **Faith versus Unbelief**
   A. Follow God's order.
   B. Obey God's commands.
IV. **Victory versus Defeat**
   A. Rahab and her family
   B. The people of Jericho
V. **Spared versus Destroyed**
   A. Rahab
   B. Barabbas
   C. Zacchaeus
   D. Joshua

The Big Ten

Text: Joshua 6
Title: Divine Demolition
New Testament Companion: Ephesians 2:14-18
Fallen Condition Focus: Because of the sinfulness of humanity, a wall of hostility separates God from humans and humans from one another, which can only be demolished by divinity.

The Whole Counsel of God: Rahab the prostitute was spared from destruction in Jericho. This anticipates God's not sparing his own Son but giving him up for us, only to raise him from the dead three days later (Rom 8:11,32).

The Christological Highway to Jesus: Christ has torn down the dividing wall that separated humanity from fellowship with the Father by submitting himself to God—and to abandonment (Mark 15:34)—in order that believers might be embraced by the Father.

Intratrinitarian Presence: God in Christ removes the barriers between us and him and sends the Holy Spirit to dwell within us.

Proposition: Through the power of the Holy Spirit, Christ has torn down the dividing wall of hostility that separated us from God and one another by submitting himself to the cross, thus enabling believers to proclaim a gospel of reconciliation to God and one another.

Behavioral Response: Believers are not to try to rebuild the wall of hostility Christ has torn down. In Christ we are all one: Jew, Gentile, male, female, slave, free (Gal 3:28).

Future Condition Focus (Sermonic Eschatonics): The reconciled people of God will never again experience the curse of separation because Jesus became accursed in order that believers might have fellowship with God through the power of the Holy Spirit and might worship the triune God with their shouts of praise throughout eternity.

Israel versus Jericho

I wish you could hear the sound of jubilation and expectation I am experiencing in my spiritual ears as I recall a gospel choir singing the Negro spiritual "Joshua Fought the Battle of Jericho." The bass singers provide a deep richness that perfectly accompanies the other voices as hearers like me rejoice in not just the lyrics but the moving reenactment of Joshua 6 in song.

> Joshua fought the battle of Jericho! Jericho! Jericho!
> Joshua fought the battle of Jericho, and the walls came
>   a-tumbling down!

These words have been an encouragement in the African American struggle for freedom and deliverance against their oppressors through the years and are still celebrated as a reminder of deliverance. Believers share similar hope because, through the power of the Holy Spirit, Christ has torn down the dividing wall of hostility that separated us from God and one another by submitting himself to the cross, thus enabling all believers to proclaim a gospel of reconciliation to God and one another.

Natural Position

Jericho was a major city in Canaan. It was surrounded by an outer wall forty feet high and an inner wall twenty feet high, each one being about six feet thick. Israel versus Jericho—this is the typical underdog and powerful warlord story. It is comparable to David versus Goliath.

Divine Position

The only way Israel could defeat Jericho would be by the mighty hand of God, and this is the way they did it.

Mercy versus Misery

The battle of Jericho provides the contrasting theme of mercy versus misery.

Rahab

Essential in chapter 6 is that Rahab and the members of her family who hide in her house during the catastrophic collapse of the walls of Jericho receive the mercy of God and are spared, while the entire city of Jericho receives misery and is destroyed. Rahab and her family receive grace, while the other citizens of Jericho receive judgment.

The people of Jericho were Amorites—pagan worshipers listed among the seven nations Israel was to drive out of the promised land. God, however, had given the Amorites four hundred years to repent of their sins and turn to the true and only God (Gen 15:16). They had not been destroyed up until now because of God's long-suffering toward them. But by the conquest the sin cup of the Amorites was full, and the judgment of God was about to fall. The only exception to God's judgment falling on Jericho was Rahab and those who took refuge in her home. The two spies had made an oath in the name of God that assured Rahab and her family divine protective custody. The scarlet cord hung out of her window as a symbol of sovereign security. God had spared the city previously in part to eventually spare Rahab at this time.

Believers

Second Peter 3:9 says, "The Lord does not delay his promise, as some understand delay, but is patient with you, not wanting any to perish but all to come to repentance." God is a God of justice and grace. All of us have sinned and are worthy of the ultimate judgment of God: hell—eternal separation from him. But God was long-suffering toward us. He spared us even in our sin so he could save us from our sin. Jericho is an instance of sovereignty (the omnipotence of God) and judgment (condemnation by God). God is both all-powerful and all-compassionate. He is full of grace and is long-suffering, but he is also full of justice.

Theodicy

The matter of theodicy, which revolves around the why-ness of God (Why do the righteous suffer and the wicked prosper?), has caused many to think God cannot be both all-compassionate and omnipotent simultaneously. The circumstances in our world where there is the manifold suffering of the innocent and the massive prosperity of the wicked has caused some to believe that while God is all-powerful and could change things and prevent evil, change is not made because God is not compassionate or sensitive to human plight. On the other hand, there are those who believe God is all-compassionate but not all-powerful, that God is sensitive to human plight but does not have the power to effect change.

God is both, though there is mystery in theodicy. The cross is the ultimate example of the omnipotent God married to his perfect compassion. Jesus Christ became as weak as he could by falling underneath the weight of the cross and needing human assistance by way of Simon of Cyrene to carry the cross to the execution site of Calvary. God abandoned Jesus not because he was insensitive to his Son. He loved his Son, but he refused to rescue him through his omnipotent hand in order to rescue us from the depths of eternal perdition. He abandoned Jesus in order to embrace you and me. He would not save Jesus in order that he might save us.

Faith versus Unbelief

In Joshua 6:1, the city of Jericho is completely shut up so that there is no entry and no exit for human travel. There is only one threat: God. John the apostle writes in Revelation 3:7 that God is the one "who opens and no one [can] close." He is the only one who can enter right past any "Do Not Disturb" sign on a door. He is the only one who can pass through what is impassible. When authorities put restrictions on God's children—whether they are health restrictions, relational restrictions, financial restrictions, or even emotional restrictions—even when professionals say there is nothing they can do, there is always something our God can do! Praise God! When doors are shut, he is able to open them.

In Joshua 6:2, the Lord says to Joshua, "I have handed Jericho, its king, and its best soldiers over to you." Once again the chain of command is consistent. God will speak to Joshua, the leader, who will in turn speak to the leaders under him, both military and religious. They will then speak to the congregation.

Notice God's language: "I have handed Jericho . . . over to you." From a divine perspective, Jericho is defeated before the battle is initiated because God sees the end before the beginning begins (Isa 46:10). The entire city, with its citizenry, has already been handed over. All that is needed is the participation of Joshua and the people. They need to participate in what God has already consummated. This is known as divine-human instrumentality. They are to do what they are told to do—march around the walls of Jericho, blow trumpets, and shout. God will bring the walls down.

Follow God's Order

The instructions are given in a clear and systematic fashion in verse 3. The marching sequence is announced. The military is to lead in an advance guard fashion, followed by priests who will carry their trumpets and blow them. They will be followed by the priests who will carry the ark of the covenant, and the procession will conclude with more military who will serve as the rearguard. That is the order, and they are to follow it without any deviation.

Obey God's Commands

God orders them to march around the Jericho walls one time each day. No one is to make a sound. The only noise to be heard is the sound of feet. They are not to talk, chuckle, or make any noise. Such silence had to be challenging for a people known for their murmuring. Their silence must have been deafening to the people of Jericho who stood on top of the walls and looked down. The residents of Jericho were already experiencing the melting of their hearts like water and the total loss of courage. Undoubtedly, they had participated in warfare many times. However, they had never fought the people whose name, Israel, can be translated "God fights." Moreover, they had never seen a battle formation like this one. It was mysterious to them. It came with no indication as to when they were going to be attacked.

They had heard how God fought for Israel in the wilderness. He defeated the two Amorite kings, Sihon and Og. They had watched the children of Israel cross over the Jordan River just a few days prior because God had opened up the river to provide a highway without needing to build a bridge over the water. Strange things were happening, and this silent march added to the great suspense. God instructs Joshua to have *all* the armed men march around the city on six days.

God's instructions continue in 6:4. Seven priests with trumpets are to go before the priests carrying the ark of the covenant. There were to be military personnel before the trumpet-bearing priests and behind the ark-bearing priests. This parade formation suggests that God wants us to worship before he does the work. Trumpets were blowing and people were shouting even before the walls fell. That is a subtle reflection of Abraham, who took Isaac and two of his servants to the bottom of Mount Moriah in Genesis 22. Abraham said to the servants, "Stay here with the donkey. The boy and I will go over there to worship; then we'll come back to you" (Gen 22:5). Abraham knew he was to go to Mount Moriah to sacrifice his son Isaac. Instead, he said he and the boy were going up there to worship and then they would be returning. Somehow, looking through the mist of mystery, he anticipated God's doing the work on top of Mount Moriah so that he could bring Isaac back down to the bottom of Mount Moriah. He knew the promise of God and the God of the promise. He decided to focus on worship and anticipate God's doing the work. Too often we expect God to do the work first and want to worship in response. We react to what God does instead of worshiping before God does it. We must change the order.

On the seventh day this parade was to make seven revolutions around the walls of Jericho. Once the seventh revolution was completed, the priests bearing the trumpets were to blow with an extended blast (vv. 5-9). It is the victory sound. It is interesting that they were not told to blow the trumpets after the victory was gained. Instead, they were to blow the trumpets before victory was realized. They were to blow the trumpets before the walls fell. In African American churches, choirs often sing, "Don't wait 'til the battle is over; shout now!" The blowing of the trumpets and the ensuing shouting of the people would be notes of anticipation even before there was the sign of victory, namely, the collapse of the walls. Surely it must have produced great ridicule on the part of the people of Jericho when they heard the blowing of the trumpets as the priests marched around the walls on that seventh day. Nothing victorious had yet occurred.

This is a picture of faith. Hebrews 11:1 (KJV) says, "Faith is the substance of things hoped for, the evidence of things not seen." Believers must exercise faith—not passively but actively. They must shout in anticipation of deliverance. They must shout in expectation of recovery. They must shout in celebration of overcoming one day. Anyone can shout after the walls fall, but can we shout before they fall, knowing that they will fall because God said they would?

God instructs this group of people to march around the walls one time each day for six days, and seven times on the seventh day. That's thirteen revolutions, thirteen circuits, thirteen rounds. Why all of this marching? Could not God have brought the walls down after one time around on the first day? Yes! Could it be that God wanted this military regime and these priests to become so acquainted with the massive walls that they would recognize the building components were not shifting with each successive revolution? The stones in the wall were not at all weakened. The stones were just as intact upon completion of their thirteenth round as they were when they made their first circuit. Could it be he wanted them to see that they were helpless in gaining entrance to Jericho without him? Could it be that God wanted them to realize, without his telling them, that if the walls were to fall, he would have to bring them down himself?

This is a lesson believers need to learn today. The power to defeat our Jerichos will not come through our methods, skills, reputations, titles, or any of the things we take pride in doing in order to be victorious. God will have to do it! There must be things in our lives that we can look back on and say, "I never would have made it without God." God must be the only explanation for deliverance—not education, money, good looks, strong families, or any other props. The only answer we must be able to provide sometimes is, "God did it."

The question that remains is, How many times must we march around Jericho before we realize our dependence on the King? Israel walked thirteen revolutions. How many will we need? Will we need thirty or three hundred? When will we finally realize that it is "'Not by strength or by might, but by my Spirit,' says the LORD of Armies" (Zech 4:6)?

Verse 5 begins with the word *when*: "When there is a prolonged blast of the horn . . ." What follows the *when* is the *then*: "Then the city wall will collapse." When and then. When we do what God has told us to do (obedience), then we can expect that God will do what he said he would do. We have no reason to expect the *then* of God until we have carried out the *when* of our responsibility.

When the walls collapsed, the rest of the congregation, led by the military regime, would go into Jericho and destroy all human and animal life, take the valuable articles of gold, silver, bronze, and other items, and bring them to Joshua so that he could put them into the treasury of the Lord in anticipation of their being used in the building of the future tabernacle at Shiloh.

Joshua gives the exact instructions he had received from the Lord to the priests and the military leaders. They instruct the people about their responsibilities in this warfare enterprise. Everyone was to be involved. Everyone had a part to play.

Joshua makes crystal clear that no one was to make a sound as they marched around the wall (v. 10). They were not to raise their voices until the seventh day when it was time for them to shout.

The participants in the parade around the wall of Jericho would retire for the night and rest after they had made each single circuit around the wall (v. 11). This was not like a parade down the street of Times Square in New York City. Rather, this was a parade in an arid atmosphere on uneven soil and ground. Nevertheless, he told them to march around it one time each day for the first six days. This gave every person ample chance to share his thoughts with his family and friends. They could tell their family members and friends what the faces of the people of Jericho looked like as they leaned over the walls and watched this mysterious march. If there were jeers and ridicule from the people standing on the walls, they could report this also to their family and friends. Most of all, they could share with them what they sensed God was up to as they marched around the walls in total silence. This was suspense of the greatest magnitude.

Joshua got up early the second morning (v. 12) and had the march continue for the second day. Verse 13 recounts the priests resuming their position and carrying their trumpets as they marched around the walls. They blew the trumpets. The advance guard and rearguard assumed their positions as well, along with the priests carrying the ark of the covenant.

This march went on for six consecutive days. On the seventh day they marched around the walls seven times (v. 14). Now they were to do more on the seventh day than they had done cumulatively for the first six days. After the seventh time around the walls on the seventh day, Joshua commanded the people to shout (v. 16). He announced that the Lord had given them the city. The movement is from silence to sound.

God is in both silence and sound. Too often in our churches we discern the presence of God only in sound or noise. We are too uncomfortable with silence. For many believers, when there is the absence of sound and the presence of silence, they simply say that the worship is dead. Yet there must be time in the worship service for silent meditation, contemplation, and cogitation. Celebration is important, but so is cogitation. In fact, the more we cogitate and percolate about the goodness of the Lord and what he has done for us, the more we tend to celebrate. The more experience we have in solitude and quietude, the stronger we will be when it is time to make a joyful sound. Habakkuk 2:20 says, "The LORD is in his holy temple; let the whole earth be silent in his presence." I love Psalm 150:6: "Let everything that breathes praise the LORD. Hallelujah!" Like David, we Christians love to praise the Lord with stringed instruments and flutes, with resounding cymbals and clashing cymbals. However, God is also in silence: "The LORD your God is among you, a warrior who saves. He will rejoice over you with gladness. He will be *quiet* in his love. He will delight in you with singing" (Zeph 3:17; emphasis added).

Mary, the mother of Jesus, simultaneously and inextricably held silence and sound together. On the one hand, there was great silence after the angel Gabriel informed her she would be the mother of the Son of God. She pondered those things in her heart. This is silence. She meditated and contemplated what the angel said to her. But on the other hand, she expressed sound in the Magnificat saying, "My soul magnifies the Lord, and my spirit rejoices in God my Savior" (Luke 1:46-47). Silence and sound are not antithetical; they are commensurate, and they are both absolutely necessary. Silence and sound: what God has joined together let no one put asunder.

Joshua tells the people what God has told him. The entire city with all of its possessions is devoted to the Lord (v. 17). The city is to be destroyed and the valuable articles are to be devoted to the treasury of the Lord to be used in the building of the future tabernacle. The only persons who are to be spared from destruction are Rahab and all the family members gathered in the house where the scarlet cord could be seen hanging out of her window. God would spare her because she spared the spies.

In verse 18 the concepts of devotion and destruction converge and collide. God says the people are to keep away from the devoted things (those valuable metals and other articles that are to be saved for the building of the tabernacle) so that they will not be destroyed and bring trouble into the nation of Israel. God is saying the only way for the Israelites to avoid destruction is to avoid taking those things that were devoted for tabernacle usage. Silver, gold, bronze, and iron are specified (v. 19). They are sacred and must go into the treasury.

The wall fell down flat when the trumpets sounded and the people shouted (v. 20). The sound precedes the collapse. God moves after Israel has obeyed. This must have been a loud shout (which is what God commanded). They had waited seven days to shout. They had waited thirteen circuits around the wall to shout. Now that it was time to shout, they shouted.

How long can you wait to shout? How long can you delay? How long can you put off shouting? There is a theology of the shout. Perhaps we have become too formal, sophisticated, and dignified to shout. The shout must be based on substance and not merely on emotion and style. The shout must be based on who God is, what God has done, and what God will do. The shout must be based on expectation because of God's promise to carry out his purpose.

The text says that the wall fell down flat. That suggests that not one stone was on top of the other. Flat means flat! This massive wall, this prodigious wall, this double wall fell down flat. This suggests a catastrophic act that had a cataclysmic impact. It is like watching a thirty-floor building that is structurally sound being imploded; dynamite instantly reduces thirty floors to a low pile of rubble. This act of God was miraculous. There was no implosion due to dynamite or a bulldozer. No earthquake was necessary. It was the hand of God that knocked the walls down flat.

Victory versus Defeat

Rahab and Her Family

One question still lingers: How did Rahab and those residing in her house survive with the walls falling flat? These were huge stones. Joshua 2:15 says, "She lived in a house that was built into the wall of the city." So, if Rahab's house was built within the actual infrastructure of the wall, when the wall fell down flat, how did she and her family survive? Once again this may be attributed to selective demolition. Perhaps God kept that section of the wall intact and standing while the rest of the wall totally collapsed. Perhaps her house was built against one of the huge stones and it fell flat intact. In the name of God, the spies had assured Rahab she and her family members who were inside her house would be spared. We may not ever know how God spared her, but we know he did. We also can trust that when everything around us falls and caves in, God is able to spare us from destruction and keep us standing. This is good news for believers.

The People of Jericho

Victory comes in 6:21 after the children of Israel have been obedient. No obedience, no victory. The people destroyed every living thing in Jericho, humans and animals, and saved the valuables to be used in the building of the tabernacle. Thus the Lord destroyed the city.

Joshua sent the two spies, who had made the promise to Rahab, to go and bring Rahab and all of those in her house out of the ruins so they could dwell in safety (v. 22). Apparently, Rahab had been a great evangelist and recruiter for God because her father and mother, brothers, and all she had were spared because of her evangelistic efforts (v. 23). God had given her enough time to knock on doors and tell her family members that if they wanted to be saved, they would need to come into the house.

It is most difficult to evangelize the members of our own families. Evidently, Rahab's family must have seen a tremendous change in her. She was probably not evangelizing them as a person who sold her body and managed a brothel but rather as one who was sold out to God. They apparently saw a wonderful change in her, and even though they were pagans who worshiped a myriad of gods, they believed her testimony

that the Lord is the God of heaven and earth (2:10-11). They were willing to turn to the one true God because Rahab convinced them.

This anticipates the account of the Samaritan woman in John 4. It
involves a woman similar to Rahab. She had been married five times and
was shacking up with a man when she met Jesus at the well. After being
converted to trust in him, she went back to her hometown and began to
evangelize for Jesus. She said to the people, "Come, see a man who told
me everything I ever did. Could this be the Messiah?" (John 4:29). The
people went to hear Jesus, and after listening to him, they made this
confession to her: "We no longer believe because of what you said, since
we have heard for ourselves and know that this really is the Savior of the
world" (John 4:42). Both Rahab and this unnamed woman in John 4
were effective evangelists.

To be spared, Rahab's family had to be in her house when Jericho
was destroyed. They were not required to be the most ethical, the most
spiritual, the most educated persons in the city. They just had to be in
the house of the believer, Rahab the prostitute. This is similar to what
took place at the Passover in Egypt. When the death angel came by the
houses of all the residents in Egypt, the family members of the Hebrew
households had to be not morally perfect but in the houses where the
doorposts were smeared with the blood of unblemished lambs. Our
only security, eternally speaking, is that we have to be in Christ in order
to be spared from eternal damnation.

The whole city of Jericho was burned, and the valuable articles were
brought into the treasury of the Lord's house (v. 24).

Spared versus Destroyed

Rahab

Joshua spared Rahab and her family because she spared the two spies
(v. 25). The wonderful thing is she was not only spared from destruction, but she was spared in order to live within the community of the
Israelites, for the text says, "She still lives in Israel today." What a wonderful explanation of how Rahab was introduced to the Torah—the
teaching of the law and the revelation of the God of Israel. By living
among the Israelites, she was exposed to their worship, their festivals,
and their way of living. No wonder she became the wife of Salmon, the
mother of Boaz, and ultimately one of the ancestors of Jesus Christ.

No wonder she was placed in the hall of faith in Hebrews 11. She was spared to serve.

Spared! What a wonderful word. Romans 8:32 says that God "did not even spare his own Son but gave him up for us all. How will he not also with him grant us everything?" God spared Rahab just as God has spared all of us believers. However, the only way God could spare us was by not sparing his only Son, Jesus Christ.

Barabbas

In the Easter story we are represented by Barabbas, the robber and insurrectionist, who was guilty and should have been crucified. However, he was released while innocent Jesus was crucified in his place. Theologically, this is known as vicarious suffering and substitutionary atonement.

Zacchaeus

Joshua pronounced a curse on the city of Jericho (v. 26). God himself destroyed the city. God pulled down the walls. Joshua cursed the city never to be rebuilt. If it were rebuilt, the builder, or the one who ordered its construction, would lose his firstborn son as well as his youngest son. Centuries later Jericho was rebuilt. No surprise: the person who ordered the reconstruction of the city experienced the loss of his eldest and youngest (1 Kgs 16:34). God has torn down the walls and destroyed the city. What God hath put asunder let not man rejoin together.

Later, Jesus would minister in the city of Jericho even though it was a cursed city. This is good news for sinners. Zacchaeus was a tax collector; he was probably the director of the Internal Revenue Service in Jericho. He was considered a cursed person by the Jews, who despised and hated him. But Jesus went into Zacchaeus's house, changed him, and declared that he was a "son of Abraham" (Luke 19:9). God is able to bring a blessing out of a curse, light out of darkness, and beauty out of ashes.

Joshua

The Lord kept his word. In Joshua 1:5, God assured Joshua, "I will be with you, just as I was with Moses." And in Joshua 1:9, God said to Joshua, "The LORD your God is with you wherever you go." What a word of affirmation and comfort: "And the LORD was with Joshua" (v. 27). What

more do we need than to have the Immanuel, "God with us," with us?
The chapter ends on this note: "His fame spread throughout the land."
The other six nations of Canaan would hear about Joshua.

Joshua's name means "Yahweh is salvation" or "Yahweh saves." God
would save his people by leading Joshua from victory unto victory in his
battle against the other nations in the land. Likewise, believers can go
boldly to confidently share about our Lord and Savior, for through the
power of the Holy Spirit, Christ has torn down the dividing wall of hostility that separated us from God and one another by submitting himself
to the cross, thus enabling believers to proclaim a gospel of reconciliation to God and one another.

Reflections

The Christological Highway to Jesus

Joshua did not fight the battle of Jericho alone. It was Yahweh's battle
to fight. Joshua fought the battle only because God allowed him to participate in the fight that was not Joshua's to win. Jericho was devoted for
destruction because of its sin. God had allowed it, along with the other
Amorite cities, four hundred merciful years of chances to turn from
sin to the sovereign God (Gen 15:16). In doing so, Rahab and those
in her house were spared and received mercy, while Jericho received
the justice it was due: destruction. In an act of substitutionary atonement, Jesus became sin and received death, while we who were sinners
received eternal life (Rom 6:23). In essence, Christ became our *cherem*
(destruction/death), and we received his *chesed* (grace).

The Whole Counsel of God

Both Rahab and the Samaritan woman were saved and subsequently
served in sharing the story of their Lord in spite of their sinful pasts.

Future Condition Focus

The rejection of God by the people of Jericho resulted in the destruction of the city, just like the rejection of the Lord Christ by Jerusalem
would result in its destruction in AD 70 (Matt 23:37; 24:1-2). One day
in the new Jerusalem, however, believers will dwell in a city enclosed by
jasper walls where death and destruction will no longer occur.

Reflect and Discuss

1. How do God's justice and grace relate to one another?
2. Describe a time when you wrestled with God's goodness in the midst of your misery. How did you remind yourself that God is still good?
3. Describe a time when God led you to do something that was completely nonsensical in your eyes. How reluctant or eager were you to obey? Share any obstacles to your immediate obedience.
4. Have you included the practice of the spiritual discipline of silence in your life? Why or why not?
5. Why do you think the ark of the covenant was included in the procession around Jericho?
6. How often do you try to defeat your "Jerichos" with your own skills and methods? How can you better hand your battles over to God?
7. How should Christians respond to the ridicule of those who think obedience to Yahweh is crazy or a sign of low intelligence?
8. What are appropriate times of silence before God? What are appropriate times of sound before God?
9. What is the main challenge you find in accepting the lessons the story of the battle of Jericho teaches?
10. What does the fact that Rahab was spared from destruction and included in the human ancestry of Messiah say about God?

Saved by Wrath

JOSHUA 7

Main Idea: Through the power of the Holy Spirit, believers are enabled to proclaim the God who demonstrated his love for them by pouring out his wrath on his Son, Jesus Christ, to redeem sinful humanity to himself.

I. **Sin Concealed**
   A. Joshua failed to consult God.
   B. Achan failed to obey God.
II. **Sin Revealed**
   A. Joshua
   B. Achan
   C. Israel
   D. Judas
III. **Sin Appealed**
   A. Cherem
   B. Tragedy to triumph
   C. Redemption through Christ

The Big Ten

Text: Joshua 7
Title: Saved by Wrath
New Testament Companion: Romans 5:6-8
Fallen Condition Focus: As Adam's sin brought death and defeat to all humanity, so Achan's sin brought defeat to the Israelites in their battle at Ai. One man's death (Jesus's) is needed to redeem humanity from spiritual defeat and death.
The Whole Counsel of God: Unlike Achan who attempted to hide his sin, we are convicted of our sin by the Holy Spirit of God (John 16:8). This moves us to confess our sin (1 John 1:9) so we can be covered by the blood of Christ (Ps 32:1).
The Christological Highway to Jesus: As Achan, who was from the tribe of Judah, sinned, causing the death of thirty-six men in the

war with Ai, so the death of Christ, who is also from the tribe of
Judah, brought salvation to those who would believe in him.

Intratrinitarian Presence: Human sin is a direct affront to God. The
Father, Son, and Holy Spirit take the initiative in providing an
atoning sacrifice for it. Jesus the Messiah reconciles sinful and
confessing humanity to God.

Proposition: Through the power of the Holy Spirit, believers are
enabled to proclaim the God who demonstrated his love for them
by pouring out his wrath on his Son, Jesus Christ, to redeem sinful humanity to himself.

Behavioral Response: As the Holy Spirit convicts us, we are to confess our sins daily to God so we may receive Christ's forgiveness
and walk in the power of the Holy Spirit as the light of the world
(1 John 1:7-9).

Future Condition Focus (Sermonic Eschatonics): In the eschaton,
death will die and be no more and the saints of God will live eternally in the presence of the glory of the one on whom the wrath
of God was poured out on our behalf.

Sin Concealed

The Israelites are riding the momentum of a great initial victory in the
central campaign of Canaan against Jericho. They had experienced
this after crossing through the parted waters of the Jordan River. God
had delayed their pursuit of victory against Jericho until they under-
went healing from circumcision and celebrated the Festivals of Passover,
Unleavened Bread, and firstfruits. After they successfully conquered
Jericho with Yahweh as the commander in chief, though the Lord puts
the brakes on their attempt at victory over the city of Ai. Chapter 6
ended with these delightful words: "And the LORD was with Joshua, and
his fame spread throughout the land." However, chapter 7 begins with
these disappointing words: "But the children of Israel committed a tres-
pass" (KJV). The story of Achan teaches us to appreciate that through
the power of the Holy Spirit, believers are enabled to proclaim the God
who demonstrated his love for them by pouring out his wrath on his
Son, Jesus Christ, to redeem sinful humanity to himself.

In the KJV, chapter 7 begins with the conjunction *but* (CSB has the
equivalent word *however*). A conjunction is one of the eight parts of

speech and serves to join sentences, clauses, phrases, or words. The conjunction *but* highlights the difference made when *but* is placed within a sentence. The phrase preceding the conjunction is different from the one succeeding the conjunction. When the conjunction *but* is placed before God, the rest of the sentence is seen in a different light. For example, in Genesis Joseph announces to his brothers who betrayed him, "You meant evil against me, *but* God meant it for good" (Gen 50:20 ESV). In the New Testament, Paul highlights God's intention to offer salvation as a gift for those who would believe the gospel: "For the wages of sin is death, *but* the gift of God is eternal life in Christ Jesus our Lord" (Rom 6:23). When the conjunction *but* is placed after God in a sentence, it often signals something negative. This is the case in Joshua 7:1. Joshua 6 ended victoriously with the fame of Joshua spreading throughout the land, for God was with Joshua. However, chapter 7 opens with a conjunction *but* indicating the anger of the Lord is burning against Israel because of Achan's sin. As a result, Israel would lose in their first battle against Ai.

Joshua Failed to Consult God

It appears that, for the first time in the book, the divine protocol has not been followed. Formerly, God communicated his instructions for each event and encounter to Joshua, who conveyed them to the leaders, and the leaders transferred the instructions to the people. God does not tell Joshua to send three thousand fighters to Ai. Joshua does not consult God about the upcoming encounter with Ai. Joshua simply sends some of his militia to spy out the city of Ai like he did prior to confronting Jericho (2:1). The Israelites were successful in capturing Jericho; however, they prove unsuccessful in their battle with Ai. What was the difference? It was not that only three thousand soldiers were sent in this conflict. All forty thousand men (4:13) who had prepared for war at the crossing of the Jordan River could not have prevented the loss at Ai. So, what brought about the loss at Ai? The Lord had given precise and specific instructions concerning what was to be done with the silver, gold, and vessels of bronze and iron of Jericho: they were to be consecrated to the Lord and deposited in his treasury for erecting the tabernacle. Any violation of these instructions would lead to Israel's falling under a curse and experiencing trouble. In the case of Ai, disobedience would lead to defeat.

The spies returned to Joshua beaming with excitement. They recommended Joshua not tax the army by sending a large military unit, since Ai was a small city and only had twelve thousand citizens. Joshua followed this human reasoning and sent three thousand men to Ai. After all, there must have been a sense of confidence among the military after having participated in the devastation of a much more formidable foe at Jericho.

But if God had been consulted *before* Joshua sent the three thousand soldiers to Ai, God could have warned, "I know we did a clean sweep in Jericho, but do not send the military to Ai. Do not send one, and do not send three or three thousand because I am not going to be with you. You will lose if you go." After all, at Kadesh-barnea, God had said, "Go and take the land, and I will be with you." The Israelites said, "No!", and paid the price. Here, forty years later, the Israelites say, "We will go and take the city of Ai," but God will say, "No. I will not be with you because Israel has sinned."

We must learn to lean on God and not on our own understanding. We go when he says go. Conversely, if the Divine does not go with us, we should be just as adamant about not going anywhere. We must not go on our own because all believers are united in Christ. Our individual actions matter to the whole body.

Today's American believers seem to live in isolation. We live in neighborhoods and do not know the names of our next-door neighbors. We go to school and do not know the names of our classmates. We go to church and do not speak to the people on the same row. We go to a store after church and do not speak to someone who just heard the same sermon and worshiped with us in the same building. We live in selfish isolation, but this should not be. Are we our brothers' and sisters' keeper? God says we are. We must correct our failure and begin to love and witness like our lives depend on it. We are saved to work together because, through the power of the Holy Spirit, believers are enabled to proclaim the God who demonstrated his love for them by pouring out his wrath on his Son, Jesus Christ, to redeem sinful humanity to himself.

Achan Failed to Obey God

Achan from the tribe of Judah had stolen consecrated elements during Israel's victorious battle at Jericho and had deposited them under the ground in his tent. This angered the Lord and prevented him from giving Israel the victory against Ai. They not only lost the battle but also lost thirty-six men in the battle. If these soldiers were married, this would have left thirty-six wives as widows and undoubtedly numerous children fatherless. The people of Jericho had endured melting hearts and courage-less spirits, knowing that the God of the Israelites was fighting against them (2:11; 5:1). After the loss at Ai, the Israelites felt this same heart-melting fear.

Sin Revealed

Joshua

When the loss of the battle and the thirty-six soldiers was reported to Joshua, he expressed great dejection, disappointment, and sadness. He asked God the age-old question, "Why, Lord?" He could not comprehend why God would bring them to Canaan to evict the Amorites from the land only to let Amorites evict them.

Joshua did not show disrespect for God when he asked questions. God is not fragile; he is omniscient. We must be aware that God knows what we will think before we think it. He is strong enough to handle our honest questions and our deepest pain. He is not temperamental. He knows the end before the beginning begins. Joshua could ask God what was on his heart. His honesty demonstrates his trust in the Master. Joshua seems to insinuate that the two and a half tribes of Reuben, Gad, and the half-tribe of eastern Manasseh made the better choice of settling on the east side of the Jordan. However, his greatest concern seemed to be about the high and holy name of God being erased from the earth.

Had Joshua asked God prior to going to war with Ai, God would have informed him that the devoted things had been stolen and advised him to call a halt to the battle against Ai until the offender was confronted.

Bereft, Joshua tore his clothes and fell facedown to the ground before the ark of the covenant, the symbol of God's presence (v. 6). But how could God be in their presence when they had lost the battle at Ai and suffered thirty-six casualties? Joshua was so confused and devastated by this that he remained on his face before God until the evening. The elders and leaders assumed the same posture and sprinkled dust on their heads—a sign of great sorrow and great regret. This is similar to Job's experience. After hearing Yahweh answer him out of a storm about divine sovereignty and majesty, Job referred to himself as dust and ashes as a sign of repentance (Job 2:12).

Achan

Joshua did not have the opportunity for a long, lamenting conversation with God about his sorrow like Job did. God brought Joshua's inquiry about this matter to an end by saying, "Stand up!" (v. 10). God told Joshua about Achan's sin. Perhaps Joshua should have had an idea one of the Israelites had sinned against God because God had promised Joshua that no one in the land would be able to stand before him. When something seems to contradict the word God has given us, we should stop to consider the human part of the divine-human instrumentality. Any failure is human; it is never divine.

Israel

Achan's sin was so pervasive that God saw it in the light of a congregational offense: "Israel has sinned" (v. 11). When Achan sinned, there was a collateral and collective effect on Israel. His sin was not his alone. It belonged to the entire nation.

Paul teaches that Christ's body, the church, is an organism that can be affected by the experience of one member. He teaches us in 1 Corinthians 12:26, "So if one member suffers, all the members suffer with it." This is why we witness and share the love of God with one another. We are blessed through the blood of Christ together because, through the power of the Holy Spirit, believers are enabled to proclaim the God who demonstrated his love for them by pouring out his wrath on his Son, Jesus Christ, to redeem sinful humanity to himself.

The greatest loss in the battle of Ai was the loss of God's presence. The Israelites had the *symbol* of God's presence in the ark of the covenant (which they apparently did not take to the battle at Ai as they did at Jericho), but they lost the *real* presence that the ark of the covenant pointed to—God's! God would not be with them in the upcoming battles in Canaan until they removed the offender, Achan. Just as they had sanctified themselves before the crossing of the Jordan River (Josh 3:5), they must sanctify themselves again as they prepared to expose and exterminate the offender. The people must be holy and ready to enact a holy command in order to once again enjoy the presence of their holy God.

It is selection day. The offender is selected by tribe, family, and household. Upon being exposed, the offender, his family, the items he stole (a beautiful Babylonian garment, two hundred shekels of silver, and a bar of gold) are burned along with his livestock in the Valley of Achor, which can be translated "Trouble."

What we as individual Christians do affects others. The effect of our actions reaches well beyond our immediate spheres of influence. The devastation we invite visits those who are innocent. What an effective tool Achan's story is to warn humans about our self-centeredness. Can you imagine how Achan must have felt when he realized his sons and daughters, his wife, and his animals would die because of his greed?

We can be tempted just as Achan was tempted. However, we do not have a nation waiting to stone us to restore unity with God. The church does not have to kill us for our sin, but we must crucify our own flesh for the good of the body of Christ and the sake of the cross. We do not want to trample the blood of Christ underfoot by disregarding the high price he paid to be our Kinsman Redeemer. He allowed them to crucify him. That's love! But that wasn't the end of the story; he rose again on the third day. The conjunction *but* changes the entire redemption story. Praise God, death could not keep him in the grave!

Judas

This chapter is an exposé of God's perspective on sin. Sin offends God and separates us from fellowship with him—though believers' salvific relationship can never be annulled. Achan resembled Judas on selection day. Both knew they were guilty. Both refused to willingly and openly confess their offense initially. Both had to be exposed. Joshua exposed Achan. Jesus, the greater Joshua, exposed Judas. Achan and his family were stoned, and they, the devoted elements, and his livestock were burned in the Valley of Achor. A stone was placed over their bodies, the stolen elements, and their possessions as a memorial to infamy and sin. Judas hanged himself, and a field was named as a memorial to the same.

Sin Appealed

What disaster unfolded in Achor Valley! Yet Hosea writes, "There I will give her vineyards back to her and make the Valley of Achor into a gateway of hope" (Hos 2:15), and Isaiah comments, "Sharon will be a pasture for flocks, and the Valley of Achor a place for cattle to lie down" (Isa 65:10). Following the execution and cremation, the Lord turns from his anger.

How do we defend God's goodness to an unbeliever or even to a believer? How do we justify his letting one person bring death to a nation and his own family? We explain by telling his-story. Through the sin of one man, Adam, sin entered the world. From our first breaths, we all are headed toward an eternity separated from our Father. *But* God! *But* God took that text of terror written by human decision and gave us grace and redemption through his Son. So, we embrace his-story! Through the power of the Holy Spirit, believers are enabled to proclaim the God who demonstrated his love for them by pouring out his wrath on his Son, Jesus Christ, to redeem sinful humanity to himself.

Cherem

Why should soldiers die and children be cremated for the misdeeds of just one man? We may not be able to untie the theological knots or to escape the deep pain behind the question. But offering the greater story gives hope for the future.

Tragedy to Triumph

God ultimately dealt with sin through another man from the tribe of Judah: Jesus. The place was not a valley; it was a hill called Calvary. Christ took on the sin of humanity by becoming our *cherem*—devoted to destruction for us though he is without sin. He died—the guiltless for the guilty. He was raised from the dead three days later by the power of the Spirit (Rom 8:11). Calvary, the apparent symbol of tragedy, became the place of triumph for all who believe in him. "For God loved the world in this way: He gave his one and only Son, so that everyone who believes in him will not perish but have eternal life" (John 3:16).

Redemption through Christ

We share this great news, for through the power of the Holy Spirit, believers are enabled to proclaim the God who demonstrated his love for them by pouring out his wrath on his Son, Jesus Christ, to redeem sinful humanity to himself. In the eschaton, death will die and be no more, and the saints of God will live eternally in the presence of the glory of the one on whom the wrath of God was poured out on our behalf.

Reflections

The Christological Highway to Jesus

Achan from the tribe of Judah was guilty of taking the "devoted things" that should have been put into the treasury for the future building of the temple. To be guilty of this offense was to be committed to *cherem* or destruction. His sin was not considered to be a sin of individualism, for God said, "Israel has sinned" (v. 11). Achan is akin to Adam. The *first* Adam's sin brought death to all mankind. As for this *intermediate* Adam, Achan from the tribe of Judah, his sin brought defeat and death on the nation of Israel. The *second and last* Adam, Jesus, was also from the tribe of Judah. He took the sin of the entire world upon himself and became sin, assuming the plight of *cherem* so that we might escape the plight of eternal separation from God (1 Cor 15:21-22,45-47). He became the *curse* so that we who were *accursed* might be blessed.

Behavioral Response

We must learn this invaluable lesson: Our victory does not rest on the presence of our organizations and ecclesiastical machinery. Rather, we succeed in kingdom work by the presence and power of God as we obey his Word and walk together as one.

Reflect and Discuss

1. Do you find the story of Achan's sin difficult to read? Why or why not?
2. What are some examples of how one person's sin can negatively affect those around them?
3. Can you think of any sin that only affects the sinner?
4. How did Joshua fail in the Ai campaign? How was his failure costly to the nation of Israel?
5. When is it proper to ask God about something we do not understand?
6. How can we explain justice and judgment to those who believe a good God would not allow tragedy?
7. What is the difference between remorse and repentance?
8. How is confessing sin a way to praise God?
9. It is often said sin starts in the heart. How is this true?
10. How do our actions as believers impact the body of Christ? How are our actions indicative of our attitudes toward the blood of Christ?

The Second Time Around

JOSHUA 8

Main Idea: Because God is faithful and he redeemed sinful humanity by sparing not his own Son, God's people must choose to obey and tell the story of their second chance in the power of the Holy Spirit.

I.   **Second Chance to Review**
  A. Joshua and Israel
  B. Us—Have you been to Ai?
II. **Second Chance to Obey**
  A. A trick at God's command
  B. Destruction at God's word
  C. Redemption from defeat at God's plan
III. **Choose Blessings or Curses.**

The Big Ten

Text: Joshua 8
Title: The Second Time Around
New Testament Companion: James 1:22-25
Fallen Condition Focus: Because believers do not consistently worship God and commit themselves to his Word even after he has given them victory in their Ai battles, God has to call them to the altar of recommitment at Shechem.
The Whole Counsel of God: Redemption means to "buy back." It signals a second-chance transaction. Just as God gave Joshua and Israel a second chance to defeat Ai, God sent Jesus, the greater Joshua, to redeem humanity lost as a result of Adam's sin. Redemption was not purchased by silver and gold but by the precious blood of the Lamb of God who died and was raised for our justification by the Spirit of God (Rom 4:25; 8:11).
The Christological Highway to Jesus: Christ, the living Word, took the curse of Mount Ebal in order that believers might enjoy the spiritual blessings of the salvation of Mount Gerizim.

119

Intratrinitarian Presence: God gives his Word through Jesus, the Word made flesh, and sends the Holy Spirit to help us keep his Word.

Proposition: Because God is faithful and he redeemed sinful humanity by sparing not his own Son, God's people must choose to obey and tell the story of their second chance in the power of the Holy Spirit.

Behavioral Response: True worship is exhibited when doctrine and practice are held together in an inextricable relationship. "Be doers of the word and not hearers only, deceiving yourselves" (Jas 1:22).

Future Condition Focus (Sermonic Eschatonics): In the eschaton, the spiritual curse of evil will be eliminated, and the saints will join in an eternal spiritual chorus of praise, for there will no longer be a curse (Rev 22:3). The saints of God will eternally experience the spiritual blessings of Mount Gerizim because of Christ, who gave them a second chance through the second birth. He will come again at the second coming.

Second Chance to Review

How do the people of God recover from a loss? How do the people of God regain lost ground? Undoubtedly this is the question Joshua, the leaders, and the congregation of Israel ponder as they lick their wounds from their recent defeat at the hands of Ai. They are still mourning the death of thirty-six soldiers. They had trusted that the Israelite army outsized the army of Ai, and their whole congregation of over a million outnumbered Ai with its population of only twelve thousand. Yet Israel sits defeated by the underdog, Ai. When God was on Israel's side, Jericho with its thick walls and secure fortress fell at a commanded shout, but when God was not with Israel, neither a shout nor a sword could help her win.

Joshua and Israel

God is a God of the second chance. It is a second time around for Joshua and Israel. Jonah was given a second chance after initially refusing to go to Nineveh and preach to the adversarial nation. Scripture records, "Then the word of the LORD came to Jonah a *second* time. 'Get up! Go to the great city of Nineveh and preach the message that I tell you'" (Jonah 3:1-2; emphasis added).

Israel is not ready to wage war against another opponent. Israel must face Ai a second time. Some places and experiences cannot be evaded or avoided; they must be faced again. Jacob had to go back to Bethel, and the prodigal son had to go home to the father. In Revelation 2 the Lord tells the Ephesian church they must return, remember, and repent because they had left their first love. In Hosea 3:1 the Lord commands Hosea to go back and buy his wife back and take her into his home. Joshua and Israel must go back and face Ai a second time.

Us—Have You Been to Ai?

It is difficult to go back to places where we have suffered defeat, hurt, and embarrassment. We would rather move on and not revisit the past. We all are products of the past; however, we must not be prisoners of the past. The past is oftentimes a necessary place to visit, but it is a terrible place to live. We must remember God's graciousness to us. Because God is faithful and he redeemed sinful humanity by sparing not his own Son, God's people must choose to obey and tell the story in the power of the Holy Spirit.

The Israelites lost at Ai, and now God is telling them to go back and fight a second time. In professional sports it is standard for teams to go back and review game film so they can see their errors, correct them, and play the next game with a new game plan designed to give them victory. I have heard Dr. Gardner C. Taylor say, "It is better to fail with a plan than to succeed without a plan."[5] He means if a person succeeds without a plan, the individual will not know how to succeed the next time he faces or participates in a similar situation. However, if a person had a plan and failed, the individual can go back and rethink the plan, tweak the plan, and adjust the plan in an effort to come up with a plan that will bring success during the next encounter. Sometimes God calls us to review the film of our lives so we can see where we have failed and come short of his intended purpose for us. There is no need to adjust the plan he has for our lives; it is written in the Bible. Our responsibility is to adjust our lives to the unadjustable Word of God so that we can live victorious lives. Because God is faithful and he redeemed sinful human-

---

[5] I heard Dr. Taylor make this statement in various settings.

ity by sparing not his own Son, God's people must choose to obey and tell the story in the power of the Holy Spirit.

Have you been to Ai? This is a metaphor for returning to past reality. At times, Ai cannot be avoided. It is difficult to revisit those places of defeat and pain. Ai is a place we go to help us return to the original blueprint of God's plan for our lives. Christ came to address what happened in the ultimate Ai of human history, where our father Adam failed the first time. When Christ came to the planet Earth, he came as our Savior. The next time he comes, he will come as the Judge. He came the first time because humanity had been defeated here. He came to rescue us from sin. The next time he comes, he will come to receive us unto himself—a people made victorious in living through the power of the Holy Spirit.

Second Chance to Obey

Between the loss at Ai and the return to face Ai again, the Lord gives Joshua the same instructions he gave him before they crossed the Jordan River, before the battle of Jericho, and before this second war with Ai: "Do not be afraid or discouraged" (Josh 1:9; 8:1). In fact, the Lord gave Joshua essentially the same assurance against Ai that he had given in the battle against Jericho: "Look, I have handed over to you the king of Ai, his people, city, and land" (v. 1). God had said to Joshua prior to the conflict with Jericho, "Look, I have handed Jericho, its king, and its best soldiers over to you" (6:2).

Today, God is not saying anything new to his people. There is no new revelation being added to Scripture. There is no extrabiblical book of the Bible. Psalm 119:89 says, "LORD, your word is forever; it is firmly fixed in heaven." God's people need to appropriate the word that God is speaking to them from his Word, the Bible. We cannot say to others with confidence and bold assurance, "*Thus* saith the Lord," until we first know *what* saith the Lord.

Like Jericho, the city of Ai is to be burned and its king exterminated. Unlike Jericho, Ai's spoil and plunder could be kept for the use of the Israelites (v. 2). Achan could have prevented the premature deaths of his family and the destruction of his properties had he obeyed God and been patient. Jesus reminds us, "But seek first the kingdom of God and his righteousness, and all these things will be provided for you" (Matt 6:33). Believers are admonished to do God's will every time.

A Trick at God's Command

Strange are the ways of our God. He orders the priests to carry the ark of the covenant to the edge of the Jordan River and touch the waters at the shoreline with the soles of their feet. They do this and the water parts. The Lord orders a parade to process around Jericho's walls once a day for six consecutive days and seven times on the seventh day. They do this, and after the shout the walls fall down. Now God orders Joshua to carry out a ruse, a subterfuge, a trick during their second-time-around battle against Ai. What? A ruse? A trick? The God of truth employing a military trick? How can this be? The Lord operates in many different ways, his wonders to perform. Whatever God permits and allows, he has a purpose to promote.

In chapter 9 the Gibeonites will use a trick or ruse to prevent defeat and destruction by Joshua and the army of Israel. They are successful because Joshua did not inquire of the Lord (9:14). Had he inquired of the Lord, he would have known the Gibeonites were not foreigners who lived far away from Canaan, but they were actually neighbors who lived in Canaan. Joshua knew it was forbidden to make a covenant with idolatrous neighbors who would be a threat and entice the Israelites into idolatry. The Lord would not have favored the Gibeonites' attempt to gain residence within the Israelite community by a ruse. Yet this is just the kind of thing God commanded Joshua to instruct Israel to do in their second battle against Ai. He used a ruse as the strategy.

In Genesis 22, the Lord orders Abraham to sacrifice his son, Isaac, on an altar on Mount Moriah. Only idolatrous nations practiced human sacrifice! God generally opposed it and stopped Abraham before allowing him to plunge the knife into Isaac. Strange are the ways of our God. God cannot be put in a proverbial box. As Paul says, "How unsearchable his judgments and untraceable his ways!" (Rom 11:33). God stopped Abraham, but for you and me, he allowed his own Son, sinless and perfect, to be sacrificed in our stead. Believers must remember that regardless of the mystery of God's plan, whatever God permits he has a purpose to promote. We must remember, because God is faithful and he redeemed sinful humanity by sparing not his own Son. We must choose to obey God and tell the story in the power of the Holy Spirit.

In the battle against Ai, God employs a redemptive ruse to bring about the defeat of that city. Joshua is to orchestrate a military ambush (v. 2). A military unit is to take their position behind the city of Ai

(v. 4). A larger military unit would draw the Ai army out of the city with a frontal approach. Once the Ai army came out of the city to do battle, the military unit lying in wait behind the city would enter the unguarded city, kill all its residents, and set it on fire. It happened just as planned (vv. 14-19). When the advancing army of Ai saw the smoke of their unguarded city ascend, they turned to return and defend their city, but it was too late. When they began to go back to the burning city, the Israelite army that had set the city on fire met them. Then the larger retreating Israelite army turned and began to make an advance on the army of Ai (vv. 20-22). Ai's army is therefore sandwiched. They are caught in the middle. There would be no escaping the will of God exercised through the hands of his obedient people. Ai was not able to stand before Joshua and God's people.

Destruction at God's Word

Every person in Ai was killed—all twelve thousand. There were no survivors. The king was captured and brought to Joshua, who executed him and hanged his body on a tree until the evening, at which time his corpse was taken down, placed at the entrance of the city gate, and covered with a pile of stones (v. 29). According to Deuteronomy 21:23, to prevent the profaning and polluting of the land, a dead body hanging from a tree must not remain after the sun has gone down. This injunction finds its ultimate fulfillment in Christ hanging and dying on a tree (a wooden cross) and being taken down from the cross and put into a grave of stone before the sun went down. The people of Ai and their king would die because of their sin, while Jesus the King of kings would die and rise from the dead by the power of the Spirit for sinners like you and me.

Redemption from Defeat at God's Plan

The defense at Ai ended with stones raised over the dead body of its king. The final section of Joshua 8 captures the erecting of a stone memorial compiled to renew the covenant between God and Israel. The ceremony is held in Shechem, a place of significant history in the lives of Abraham and his posterity. In fact, Shechem was the first place Abraham set foot in Canaan after his exit from Ur of the Chaldeans. Joshua built an altar on Mount Ebal, and burnt offerings and fellowship offerings were offered on it to the Lord. Burnt offerings and fellowship offerings are sacrificed as a sign of the people's gratitude to God for their victory at Ai. A burnt offering is wholly given to God—nothing is left. This is a symbol of their giving their whole selves to God. The fellowship offering signifies that the children of Israel are in covenant relationship with God.

Choose Blessings or Curses

According to Moses's command in Deuteronomy 27, Joshua had the Israelites stand on either side of these twin towers—Mount Ebal, the mount of cursings, and Mount Gerizim, the mount of blessings (v. 33; see Deut 11:29). This area at Shechem provided a natural amphitheater for this gathering. Joshua read from the book of the law (v. 34). Those who obeyed God's law would receive the blessings of Mount Gerizim. Those who disobeyed would undergo the cursing of Mount Ebal. Joshua wrote a copy of the law of Moses (v. 32). He did not add or take away a single word from the law of God. It was a copy of the law of Moses already recorded on stones. It was not a revision or redaction of the law. Joshua read and wrote all the blessings and cursings of the law as the entire nation stood and listened (v. 35).

Training in God's law was not reserved for adult males (v. 35). All God's people listened to the reading of the law because all God's people are responsible for obeying the law. This act reminded God's people of their covenant promise, covenant relationship, and covenant lives. The Lord would successfully lead them in their campaign against the Canaanites in the promised land as he said, and they would obey as he commanded. Any deviation from the law of Moses would detract from their success.

Believers are people of the Word. We are to adhere to God's Word written in the canon of Scripture. Being led by philosophical reasoning, political personalities, social correctness, or emotional leanings is sin. If we want God's blessings, we must live God's way as revealed in the Book. We must be true worshipers who live in obedience because the day will come when sin will be no more. There will be judgment, and those who live according to God's Word will have no more tears, no more pain, no more sorrow, and no curse. We will worship God eternally because through the crucified, risen, and living Christ we have been given a second chance so we can go with him at his second coming. Because God is faithful and he redeemed sinful humanity by sparing not his own Son, we people must choose to obey him and tell the story of our second chance given through the blood of Jesus in the power of the Holy Spirit.

Reflections

The Christological Highway to Jesus

The king of Ai getting hanged on a tree until the evening and covered by a pile of stones did not bring redemption. That was a picture of utter ignominy and condemnation. Jesus, the King of kings, was also hanged on a tree, the cross of Calvary, and put in a rocky grave only to emerge three days later, on Sunday morning. The king of Ai would die because of his own sin, while the King of kings would die sinless on behalf of sinners. God informed Joshua that he had already given the king of Ai, his people, his city, and his land into Joshua's hand. Victory was assured *before* the battle even took place. Similarly, salvation was assured before the fall. According to the predetermined counsel of God, the sovereign God had already orchestrated the death of Christ and his resurrection in preexistent eternity (Acts 2:23-24; Rev 13:8) and choreographed it in historical time.

Behavioral Response

The children of Israel were allowed to keep the articles of value following the battle of Ai. They were prohibited from taking such valuables in connection with the battle at Jericho. The principle this emphasizes is that we are to give God the "first," and the other things will be given to us, his people. Jesus stated this principle in Matthew 6:33: "But seek first the kingdom of God and his righteousness, and all these things will be provided for you." We must apply the principle of divine firstness to our lives and ministries and trust God to bless our obedience and our willingness to prioritize his work and will.

Reflect and Discuss

1. Who are some biblical characters who received undeserved second chances from God?
2. What was different about Israel's second battle with Ai compared to the first?

3. What is the difference between being a "product of the past" and a "prisoner of the past"?
4. God allows the Israelites to keep the spoils of war this time. What does that say about God? What does it mean for his people?
5. In Joshua 8, how does God show that he is with Joshua as he was with Moses?
6. Read about who the assembly attending the reading of the law was composed of. Why does the composition of the assembly matter?
7. According to God's law, what leads to blessings? What leads to curses?
8. How can we be sure we hear God's voice, since we cannot put God in a proverbial box? His ways are not our ways. How can we learn to trust his voice when we do not know the specifics of his plan?
9. Describe benefits of hearing God's Word read aloud. Why is this an important practice?
10. How did Jesus become a "curse" for us?

From Gibeon to Golgotha

JOSHUA 9

Main Idea: The Son of God, who carried his cross of wood to Calvary for the glory of God, enables believers through the Spirit of God to take up their crosses and follow him in the service of God.

I.   **The Gibeonites Deceive the Senses.**
   A.   What the Gibeonites knew
   B.   What the Israelites saw
   C.   How the Israelites failed
   D.   How we fail
II. **The Israelites Conceive the Senseless.**
   A.   A covenant with liars
   B.   A covenant with truth
III. **The Gibeonites Receive the Sentence.**
   A.   The ruse
   B.   The restriction
   C.   The result
IV. **The Savior Receives the Service.**

The Big Ten

Text: Joshua 9
Title: From Gibeon to Golgotha
New Testament Companion: 2 Peter 3:9
Fallen Condition Focus: Like the Israelite leaders who did not consult the Lord (Josh 9:14), believers have a tendency to trust in their own wisdom rather than in the God of wisdom or the wisdom of God, which is found in his Word.
The Whole Counsel of God: Joshua failed to consult with God through the Urim and Thummim of the high priest, which resulted in the Israelite leaders succumbing to the deception of the Gibeonites. Jesus the greater Joshua, being the wisdom of God, is anointed by the Spirit of God (Luke 4:18) and sends the Holy Spirit to lead his followers to all truth (John 16:13).

The Christological Highway to Jesus: All human beings are spiritual Gibeonites because they are guilty of sin. Yet Christ, who was laid in a wooden manger as a babe and died on a wooden cross as a man, was raised from the dead by the Spirit in order that believers might take up their own crosses, follow him daily, and worship him both now and forever.

Intratrinitarian Presence: On the cross, the Father abandons the Son and the Son gives up his spirit. In an act of immeasurable grace, the Holy Spirit is given to deceitful sinners who repent and place their faith in Christ.

Proposition: The Son of God, who carried his cross of wood to Calvary for the glory of God, enables believers through the Spirit of God to take up their crosses and follow him in the service of God.

Behavioral Response: Preach the gospel to the deceiver, knowing that you, too, were once deceived.

Future Condition Focus (Sermonic Eschatonics): In eternity, believers who have been given the right to eternal life will enter the gates of the celestial city to worship God (Rev 22:14). This is made possible because of the one who died on the tree at Calvary.

The Gibeonites Deceive the Senses

When I was a little boy, I went to school with my older sister. At school one day, a boy took my lunch money. He obviously did not know I was my sister's brother. He knew to avoid any conflict with her; he just did not know bullying me put him directly into her line of fire. What happened to him helps me remember believers must do due diligence before we act. We are instructed not to rely on our own understanding (Prov 3:5-6). If we acknowledge Yahweh in all our ways, he will direct our paths. That is exactly what Joshua and the men of Israel did not do in their dealings with the Gibeonites.

What the Gibeonites Knew

If you can't beat 'em, join 'em! This seems to be the Gibeonite mentality. They live in Canaan, not far from Gilgal, the location of the Israelite camp. The Gibeonites had a mighty army. However, they knew Israel's God had been fighting for Israel and Gibeon did not stand a chance. They knew Israel's distant history: how God worked wonders in Egypt to

---

deliver Israel from a four-hundred-year period of slavery. They knew at the end of that national incarceration, God delivered Israel by dividing the Red Sea so Israel could cross over to their freedom. They heard how God fought for Israel in the defeat of the two Amorite kings, Og and Sihon, and their people during Israel's forty-year trek in the wilderness. They also knew Israel's recent history: how God had opened up the Jordan River so Israel could pass over to Canaan on dry ground. They were fully aware Israel's God had demolished the seemingly impregnable walls of Jericho and had redeemed Israel from their initial loss at Ai by giving them victory over Ai at their second military encounter.

What really brought pressure and produced anxiety on the part of the Gibeonites was that Israel had come to their vicinity to do battle with them. They were certain Israel's God would fight for Israel and win. Fearing this reality, they resorted to a ruse. After learning of Israel's distant and recent history, the Gibeonites decided to withdraw from the six-nation confederacy formed to attack Joshua and Israel. The Gibeonites knew six or even sixty nations against the God of Joshua and Israel would suffer defeat, for Israel's God is the awesome God.

Somehow the word had spread through the land that Israel's God is the God of all the earth. He is not limited by territories or borders. Rahab the prostitute knew and feared, and the Gibeonites knew and feared. Somehow they heard, their hearts melted, and they devised a plan to ingratiate themselves to God's people.

What the Israelites Saw

The Gibeonites, who were Hivites, pulled off an Oscar-worthy performance in their theatrical debut. They took old sacks and loaded them on their donkeys. They carried tattered and torn wineskins, wore old and patched sandals, and dressed in old garments. To make the Gibeonite ambassadors more convincing to Joshua and the Israelite elders, they brought dry and moldy bread, contending that it was hot and fresh the day they left their homes in a far and distant land. They pleaded for a covenant with Joshua and Israel in order to avoid a fight they knew they could not win.

The Gibeonites were wise enough to divulge some of their knowledge of Israel's distant history. They talked about what God had done in delivering Israel from Egypt and making Israel victorious over the two Amorite kings on the west side of the Jordan. They knew if they revealed to Joshua and the elders their knowledge of Israel's recent history in Canaan, they would blow their cover, and Joshua and the elders would know they were neighbors and not foreigners. Consequently, death would be imminent.

How the Israelites Failed

Joshua 9:14 records the great mistake the Israelite leadership made: "Then the men of Israel took some of their provisions, but did not seek the LORD's decision." They trusted their senses instead of consulting with the sovereign One. They had made a mistake the first time at Ai in trusting their senses—they trusted what they could see. They saw Ai, a much smaller city than Jericho with fewer citizens and a smaller military force. This led them to ignore inquiring of God and to recommend to Joshua the taking of two to three thousand soldiers to fight against Ai instead of employing the entire military regime and presumably wasting unnecessary manpower. They lost that battle because they relied on what they could see and did not inquire of the Lord whom they could not see, even though they had indeed seen God's provisions and his love for them demonstrated over and over. Had they sought God's directions this time, God could have revealed the deception to them.

George Santayana, the great philosopher, said, "Those who cannot remember the past are condemned to repeat it" (*Life of Reason*, 5). Israel failed in the first battle against Ai because they neglected to inquire of the Lord beforehand, and here they were neglecting to do so again. The nation of Israel would suffer because leaders would choose to rely on their own senses. They forgot their distant and recent past. They sampled the provisions. That is, with carnal eyes they looked at the moldy and dry bread; they smelled its staleness; they saw how cracked the sacks and wineskins were; they looked at the worn-out clothes and the sandals; they may have felt the dryness of the sacks and noticed the wineskins were empty and no longer supple; they may have even tasted the dry and stale bread. But they did not inquire of the Lord.

How We Fail

Oftentimes we fail in our Christian living because we are driven by our senses rather than inquiring of the Lord and discerning by his Spirit. Eve got into serious trouble because she *saw* that the fruit was good for food. She proceeded to eat it and then gave it to her husband who also ate it. We must inquire of the Lord in spite of what we can discern with our sensory system. Feelings can deceive; sight can mislead. We must seek God, who looks not on the outward appearance but rather on the heart (1 Sam 16:17). God looks beyond the visible and sees the invisible.

Joshua 9 urges believers to search their own hearts: Do I seek God's guidance in the things that seem inconsequential? Do I seek his guidance in big decisions? Do I stop to pursue him in emotional decisions? Do I seek his hand, and not just his plan, when I lay out my five-year plan?

The Israelites Conceive the Senseless

A Covenant with Liars

The Israelite leaders entertained the possibility that the travelers just might share their zip code (Josh 9:7). The leaders knew that God had forbidden their making an alliance with any neighboring nation to avoid idolatrous infestation. However, there was no prohibition about forming a covenant with nations from a distant country (Deut 20:10-15). On the basis of their senses and sympathy, Joshua made a covenant with the Gibeonites to let them live. The leaders of Israel affirmed and confirmed the covenant. This covenant, like the one the two spies had made with Rahab, was apparently made in the name of the Lord. It was therefore irrevocable because it would negatively reflect on the reputation and character of God if broken. The covenant was ratified.

Satan attacks believers by coming to them in disguise as an angel of light. We must beware of Satan by being aware of his devices and schemes (2 Cor 2:11).

A Covenant with Truth

It is interesting how believers feel bound by a covenant made with other humans, yet they ignore the solemnity of the covenant ratified with the blood of God's only begotten Son, Jesus the Christ. The Son of God, who carried his cross of wood to Calvary for the glory of God, enables believers through the Spirit of God to take up their crosses and follow him in the service of God. Believers must take this covenant seriously or risk trampling the blood of Christ underfoot with their words and actions (Heb 10:29).

The Gibeonites Receive the Sentence

The Ruse

Three days after the covenant was made, Joshua and the congregation heard that the Gibeonites were their neighbors! An Israelite embassy was sent to the Gibeonite cities. Joshua asked their leaders for their reason for using deceptive measures. Once again they cited their knowledge of Israel's God. They admitted hearing Israel's God intended to make the Israelites permanent residents of Canaan by destroying the present occupants. They believed there was no other option available to them if they wanted to survive extermination. So they resorted to disguise and deception. In the face of the truth and what must have felt like impending doom, the Gibeonites pleaded for mercy from Joshua and from the leaders of Israel.

The Restriction

Joshua and the leaders knew if they annulled the recent covenant made between the Israelites and the Gibeonites, God's name and reputation would be dishonored among the rest of the Canaanites. The wrath of God would subsequently fall on the Israelites. Joshua and the leaders chose to honor the covenant and let the Gibeonites live. However, they relegated the Gibeonites to being cutters of wood and carriers of water for the sacrifices of the tabernacle and, ultimately, the temple. Instead of being sacrificed, Gibeon participates in providing wood for the temple's sacrificial offerings. History will show that this line of the Gibeonites will even survive the seventy-year Babylonian captivity and return to Jerusalem (Neh 7:25), apparently continuing in the temple service.

The Result

Undoubtedly, by staying so close to the temple, the Gibeonites heard the Torah consistently read, prayers regularly offered, and psalms continuously sung. Many of them were likely converted to the God of the Hebrews. This gives great hope for unbelievers we know. If they can be kept near the church or brought to the church, even if it's only occasionally, there is hope that they will become devoted believers after hearing the gospel preached and the songs of praise sung in the midst of the worship of God by the people of God.

The Savior Receives the Service

How great is the grace of our God! The juxtaposition of lying sinners being saved while a sinless Son who is the truth dies in our stead is the greater story. This is a greater truth than what took place in the midst of the Gibeonites. The greater truth emerges from the one who would go to Golgotha. The Gibeonites lied, and God looked beyond their fault and saw their need. It is not that God blessed the lie; rather, God blessed his own name. Jesus, who is one with the Father, is the truth. The Gibeonites lied and were blessed in spite of their lie. Jesus, who is the truth, told the truth and was crucified at the hands of sinners who could not recognize truth. He said, "I and my Father are one" (John 10:30 KJV). Referring to his death and resurrection he said, "Destroy this temple, and I will raise it up in three days" (John 2:19). He said he would be crucified and would be resurrected on the third day. He said he was the Son of God. He told the truth, and most liars could not stand to hear it.

This is the reason we must live worshipful lives in compliance with the costly covenant. The Son of God, who carried his cross of wood to Calvary for the glory of God, enables believers through the Spirit of God to take up their crosses and follow him in the service of God. Truth was crucified on Friday, but he rose on Sunday morning. In his famous "We Shall Overcome" speech, Martin Luther King Jr. quoted the longtime editor of the *New York Evening Post*, William Cullen Bryant, by saying, "Truth crushed to earth will rise again."

The Gibeonite ruse resulted in redemptive implications. God is so gracious! All believers were once Gibeonites—sinners with a determined destiny that would lead to destruction and hell. We had no merit. We had no understanding. We had no truth of our own to share. Even our approach to the greater Joshua, Jesus, was faulty and flawed. We pled to him for mercy and not justice. Now, we live by the grace of him who died as a ransom for our sins. His precious, sinless blood paid the price we could never pay so we liars, backbiters, whoremongers, adulterers, thieves, manipulators, the unrepentant—yes, all sinners—could have the chance to come to the table and eat. Jesus, the Son of God, who carried his cross of wood to Calvary for the glory of God, enables believers through the Spirit of God to take up their crosses and follow him in the service of God. Because of this we move from identifying with Gibeon to with Golgotha.

Reflections

The Christological Highway to Jesus

Jesus is the opposite of deception, for he is the truth (John 14:6). His resurrection body was not a phantom. Therefore, he invited Thomas to touch the hole in his side so Thomas could be assured he was who he said he was—Christ, the Son of the living God. Upon examination of it, Thomas exclaimed, "My lord and my God!" (John 20:28). Similar to the Gibeonites becoming woodcutters and water carriers, veritable slaves, Jesus the Master became a slave and was obedient to death, even death on the cross (Phil 2:7-8). He carried his own wood, and water flowed from his pierced side. Now he is exalted and is seated on the throne. We submit to him in covenant allegiance as our Lord, for we are his servants.

Behavioral Response

God keeps his promises to us. As a reflection of God, we as his children must keep our promises to one another as the Israelites kept theirs to the Gibeonites. When we become promise breakers and not truth sayers and promise keepers, we taint our testimony and bring disrepute on the church of God instead of bringing glory and honor to the name of God.

Intratrinitarian Presence

Joshua and the leaders were deceived by the Gibeonites because they did not seek the counsel of the Lord. Today we are to seek the Lord's counsel, for he is the Wonderful Counselor (Isa 9:6). Jesus promised the disciples he would send the Holy Spirit who would be our Counselor (John 14:16; 14:26; 15:26), and the Spirit would lead and guide us into all truth. We must not trust appearances or our own senses. We must be guided into truth by the Spirit of truth (John 16:13).

Fallen Condition Focus

We are innately and intrinsically compelled to rely on what we can see and sense rather than to be led by the one, the Holy Spirit, whom we cannot see.

Future Condition Focus

During this earthly pilgrimage, we must walk by faith and not by sight. However, one day we will walk by sight and not by faith, for in the eschaton we will no longer need faith or hope, for faith and hope will have reached their expiration point.

The Gibeonites, who were foreigners, became a part of the Israelite congregation throughout the Old Testament period. They even survived the seventy-year Babylonian captivity. This serves as a foretaste of the eschaton in which there will be people from every nation, tribe, people, and language standing before the throne of God (Rev 7:9).

Reflect and Discuss

1. What connection do the Gibeonites share with Rahab?
2. Why would God forbid his people to make treaties with foreign nations?
3. Do you think the Gibeonites had genuine faith in Yahweh? How can we know?
4. Do you inquire of the Lord before you make important decisions? Why or why not? What size decision do you take to him, and what size do you feel comfortable making on your own?
5. How are we driven by our senses in our decision making? Give some examples.
6. How may we become more discerning in our interactions with those who may wish to manipulate us?
7. How were the Gibeonites blessed in spite of their deception?
8. Why is it good for unbelievers to be near the church of believers even though they don't believe?
9. Does Joshua's reaction to the Gibeonite deception surprise you? Why or why not?
10. Why does God allow sinful pagans into the Israelite family?

Prayer That Promotes Divine Purpose

JOSHUA 10

Main Idea: As Christ our great high priest intercedes for us, believers must pray in the power of the Holy Spirit for changes that promote the purpose of God.

I. **Our Sovereign God Can Direct What Is Heard for His Purposes.**
   A. Rahab and the people of Jericho
   B. The Amorite kings from the west
   C. The Gibeonites
   D. The confederacy
   E. Joshua
II. **Our Sovereign God Directs Divine-Human Instrumentality.**
   A. Joshua and Israel
   B. Israel and five kings in a cave
   C. Sinners redeemed by the blood of the Lamb

The Big Ten

Text: Joshua 10
Title: Prayer That Promotes Divine Purpose
New Testament Companion: Romans 8:26-28
Fallen Condition Focus: Unlike Joshua who prayed for extended daylight in order to pursue his enemies and accomplish the purpose of God, believers have a propensity to pray selfishly, which does not promote the purpose and will of God.
Whole Counsel of God: As Joshua interceded for his advancing army in his prayer to God, our high priest, who is the greater Joshua, and the Holy Spirit make intercession for the saints of God (Rom 8:26; Heb 7:25).
The Christological Highway to Jesus: Unlike the five allied kings whose bodies lay dead in a cave covered by large stones, Christ our high priest upon his resurrection, ascension, and enthronement intercedes for the saints (Heb 7:25) in order to give us victory in matters that promote the purpose and glory of God.

Intratrinitarian Presence: King Jesus reigns forever at the Father's right hand, and the Holy Spirit intercedes before him on our behalf.

Proposition: As Christ our great high priest intercedes for us, believers must pray in the power of the Holy Spirit for changes that promote the purpose of God.

Behavioral Response: Believers are to pray bold prayers of great faith that align with the Scriptures.

Future Condition Focus (Sermonic Eschatonics): The last prayer in the Bible focuses on the return of Christ (Rev 22:20). As God gave Joshua victory over opposing nations, so the returning Christ will gain victory over opposing nations (Rev 11:15).

Introduction

Anyone who has had the pleasure of teaching a young child to pray might remember the feeling of leaning in to hear what the child says to God. The astounding thing about this rich narrative in chapter 10 is not that the sun stood still but rather that the sovereign God listened to his servant Joshua's request. God, the Father, listened to his child, Joshua, pray, and he listens when we pray. That seems so commonplace, but it is actually an amazing blessing for fallen humankind. God attends the prayers of his children. Moreover, our Messiah intercedes for us (Heb 4:14-16)! As Christ our great high priest intercedes for us, believers must pray in the power of the Holy Spirit for changes that promote the purpose of God.

Joshua is not changing God in any way with his prayer because prayer is not overcoming God's reluctance; it is laying hold of God's willingness. In response to his child's prayer, God suspends the laws of nature because Joshua's prayer lined up with God's will. When our will aligns with God's will, and when we delight ourselves in the Lord, he gives us the desires of our hearts because his desire becomes our desire and his will becomes our will (Ps 37:4). The greatest visual of this truth is when Jesus asked his Father to let the cup pass from him. This "cup" is symbolic of the separation that would occur between the Son of God and the God of the Son when Jesus would die on the cross as the sin bearer. The third time he prayed to his Father, he said, "Not my will, but yours, be done" (Luke 22:42) and acquiesced to the Father's will without praying further for the cup to pass.

Our Sovereign God Can Direct What Is Heard for His Purposes

Rahab and the People of Jericho

So far the dominant sense prevailing in the book of Joshua is the sense of hearing. Rahab the prostitute of Jericho confessed to the spies sent from Joshua,

> For we [the people of Jericho] have heard *how the* LORD *dried up the waters of the Red Sea before you when you came out of Egypt, and what you did to Sihon and Og, the two Amorite kings you completely destroyed across the Jordan.* (Josh 2:10; emphasis added)

Rahab goes on:

> When we heard *this, we lost heart, and everyone's courage failed because of you, for the* LORD *your God is God in heaven above and on earth below.* (2:11; emphasis added)

The Amorite Kings from the West

The author of the book includes the Canaanite kings' response to what they heard about Israel's God:

> When all the Amorite kings across the Jordan to the west and all the Canaanite kings near the sea heard *how the* LORD *had dried up the waters of the Jordan before the Israelites until they had crossed over, they lost heart and their courage failed because of the Israelites.* (5:1; emphasis added)

In chapter 9, the author of Joshua once again apprises the reader of the significance of hearing with these words:

> When all the kings heard *about Jericho and Ai . . . they formed a unified alliance to fight against Joshua and Israel.* (9:1-2; emphasis added)

The Gibeonites

Even the Gibeonites prefaced the rationale for coming to make a covenant with Joshua on the basis of what they had heard about Israel's God:

> Your servants have come from a faraway land because of the reputation of the LORD *your God. For we have* heard *of his fame, and*

> *all that he did in Egypt, and all that he did to the two Amorite kings*
> *beyond the Jordan—King Sihon of Heshbon and King Og of Bashan,*
> *who was in Ashtaroth.* (9:9-10; emphasis added)

Furthermore, three days later, after making a covenant with the Gibeonites, Joshua was informed they were not distant travelers but residents of Canaan. Joshua approached their leaders and asked for an explanation for their deception. They answered him:

> *It was clearly communicated to your servants that the LORD your God*
> *had commanded his servant Moses to give you all the land and to*
> *destroy all the inhabitants of the land before you. We greatly feared for*
> *our lives because of you, and that is why we did this.* (9:24)

Centuries later, the apostle Paul says that faith comes from what is *heard* (Rom 10:17).

The Confederacy

In the previous examples the Lord directed what Rahab and the people of Jericho, the Amorite kings of the west, and the Gibeonites *heard* to serve his purpose—to deliver or to destroy. Rahab and those residing in her house were delivered *from* destruction, while the opposing cities and their kings were delivered *for* destruction. Joshua 10 opens with these words:

> *Now King Adoni-zedek of Jerusalem heard that Joshua had captured*
> *Ai and completely destroyed it, treating Ai and its king as he had*
> *Jericho and its king, and that the inhabitants of Gibeon had made*
> *peace with Israel and were living among them.* (10:1)

The Lord subtracted one of the cities of what had been planned as a six-city confederacy against Israel and added victory to Israel. The Gibeonites made a treaty, or a covenant, with Israel.

Joshua

God assured Joshua they would be victorious over the remaining confederacy, saying, "Do not be afraid of them, for I have handed them over to you. Not one of them will be able to stand against you" (10:8). Aren't these the same words God repeatedly uses when he speaks to Joshua? God is not saying anything different; rather, he is saying the same thing. Fear is natural when one faces cities gathered to fight against him, but he tells Joshua not to be afraid. Joshua needs to hear once again that God had already delivered these next cities into his hand. He needed to receive the words that not one of the cities would be able to stand against him. These are the same words from the same God as Joshua faces a different situation.

Oftentimes, God speaks the same words to us, not because God doesn't have anything new to say but because we either get amnesia or we are hard of hearing. If God is doing anything new, then the newness is based on the oldness of his established Word. He never says anything that contradicts what he has already said. Psalm 37:23 teaches us the Lord orders the steps of a good person. God not only orders our steps; he also orders our stops. We oftentimes cause ourselves a great deal of trouble if we step when he says stop, and we stop when he says step. And as Christ our great high priest intercedes for us, believers must pray in the power of the Holy Spirit for changes that promote the purpose of God.

Our Sovereign God Directs Divine-Human Instrumentality

Joshua had *heard* these words at the beginning of his leadership ministry: "No one will be able to stand against you as long as you live. I will be with you, just as I was with Moses. I will not leave you or abandon you" (1:5). But now there are multiple cities aligned against Joshua! Regardless, the Lord used what these five kings had heard about Joshua and his God for his purposes. He permitted these five kings to unite so that Joshua could kill five birds with one stone; that is, so Joshua could defeat all five kings and their cities in one battle instead of five separate battles. Fighting solo wars would have required more time, manpower, and effort. God's ways are inscrutable (Rom 11:33), and "we know that all things work together for the good of those who love God, who are called according to his purpose" (Rom 8:28).

Adoni-zedek urged the kings of four other Amorite cites to join him in attacking the Gibeonites for making a treaty with the archenemy, Israel, who was threatening the existence of the entire population of Canaan. Interestingly, it is the king of Jerusalem who initiates the alliance. Today we know what would become of Jerusalem—King David's capital city, the site of the temple, and the location of Christ's crucifixion and resurrection. There are several ascribed meanings to this king's name. For our purposes, because of the time, place, leadership personality, and pagan beliefs of this king, his name Adoni-zedek means "[the god] Zedek is lord." When the five-nation union formed, these kings and their armies marched to Gibeon and took their positions, prepared to attack.

The Gibeonites sent an urgent message to Joshua at the camp at Gilgal: "Don't give up on your servants. Come quickly and save us! Help us, for all the Amorite kings living in the hill country have joined forces against us" (v. 6). Joshua is drawn into the battle with the National Alliance of Canaanite Territories (NACT) because of his allegiance to the Gibeonites. He is not only committed not to destroy them, thus honoring the dictates of the covenant made in God's name, but he is also committed to moving beyond covenantal commitment and defending the Gibeonites against any people who would try to destroy them. The Gibeonites receive grace from Joshua, and the situation offers an opportunity for Joshua to exterminate five neighboring peoples at one time.

Joshua and Israel

Joshua and Israel participate in the dynamic of divine-human instrumentality. Joshua takes the entire army (which he did not do at Ai; 7:3), and they march all night from their camp at Gilgal and surprise the NACT. The confederacy is at the doorstep of the Gibeonite people, likely waiting to attack and destroy them as soon as the darkness was replaced by the light of the day. The Israelites were doing their part from a human standpoint, but the divine would do what they could not do. The Lord infiltrated the ranks of the NACT with a spirit of confusion. This confederacy lost its composure, knew it would be soundly defeated by Joshua and the Israelites at Gibeon, and began to retreat.

Daylight was nearly gone as the Israelites continued to chase their enemies. The Israelites must have felt the time crunch because enemies could escape in the darkness of the night. Joshua, who had not consulted the Lord in the matter of the Gibeonite deception, sought God in prayer regarding this matter. Joshua knew they needed continued daylight if Israel was to pursue and defeat their enemies. He knew that God put the sun in the sky, and he put it there to shine until further notice. Therefore, Joshua appealed to the Creator in this prayer: "Sun, stand still over Gibeon, and moon over the Valley of Aijalon" (v. 12). In response, God literally established a daylight saving time in order to provide enough light for Joshua to overtake Israel's enemies. The astounding thing about this rich narrative is not merely the standing still of the sun. The astounding thing is the love God demonstrates by inclining his ear to hear his child pray and by impacting the forces of nature in answer to his child's prayer. As Christ our great high priest intercedes for us, believers must pray in the power of the Holy Spirit for changes that promote the purpose of God.

God, the Father, listened to his child, Joshua, pray, and he listens when we pray. Believers should be confident in the power of our omnipotent God who bends his ear to listen to his children praying. We may lay hands on one another in order to help one another, but God lays ears on us because he wants to hear the cries of our hearts.

In granting Joshua's petition, God allowed the Israelites to pursue and kill some of their enemies. However, the Lord did not release his role as Israel's strong protector. As the divine marksman who never misses a target, God hurled large hailstones, killing more NACT soldiers than the Israelites killed with their swords.

We cannot overlook the standing still of the sun. Great attention has been given to this cosmological shift. John Jasper, a former slave who would pastor the Sixth Mount Zion Baptist Church in Richmond, Virginia, preached a sermon from this passage: "The Sun Do Move." He was uneducated yet was a powerful and eloquent preacher. He not only preached to crowds of African Americans, but throngs of white people came to hear him preach. He was conservative regarding Scripture. He was a literalist. He believed the sun actually paused.

Before the Copernican revolution, science purported the earth as the center of the solar system. Since that revolution, we know that the sun is the center of the solar system and does not move, but the Earth revolves around the sun and rotates on its axis. At issue in the biblical text is not whether the sun moves. The Bible is not a scientific book. Joshua is just reporting the cosmology and the perspective of the people who lived in the fifteenth century BC. There need not be a major debate on whether this was a figurative or a literal pause of the sun. Had the night ensued, then Joshua and his men would not have been able to overtake the enemy, for they would not have been able to see them. So God held back the night and extended the day in order for Joshua and his men to completely overthrow this five-nation confederacy. If God could hold back the waters of the Red Sea and the Jordan River, it would not have been a struggle for God to hold back the night. This event in Joshua 10 is also recorded in the Book of Jashar, a book of poetry that was extant at this time but has since disappeared.

The crucial matter does not concern cosmology but the power of God, the greater one who extended the day and delayed the night so

Joshua and his troops could defeat their enemies. This is divine-human instrumentality. As Christ our great high priest intercedes for us, believers must pray in the power of the Holy Spirit for changes that promote the purpose of God. Joshua did not presume on God but did what he and his troops could do and watched God do what only God could do in bringing about victory.

The author of the book says, "There has been no day like it before or since" (v. 14). This cosmological shift of the night being withheld and the sunlight being prolonged, however, anticipated a time fourteen hundred years later when God would advance the day and bring on the night prematurely—it happened at the cross. "It was now about noon, and darkness came over the whole land until three, because the sun's light failed" (Luke 22:44-45). God set both the sun and the moon in the sky and can adjust their work schedule in order to accomplish his purpose whenever he desires. That day Christ, the sun of righteousness (Mal 4:2), was abandoned by God the Father, who did not verbally answer his question, "My God, my God, why have you abandoned me?" (Mark 15:34). That day on Calvary's hill, the death of the Son of God, the greater Joshua, transcended the day the sun stood still. In Joshua 10, God provided Joshua and his army with extended daylight, enabling them to overtake or overcome their pursuing enemies. However, the day will come when both the sun and the moon will be unemployed— there will be no more *night*. We will not need the light of the lamp or the sun, for the Lord God will be our light (Rev 22:5).

Israel and Five Kings in a Cave

Joshua was informed that the five kings of the confederacy were hiding in a cave. Joshua gave orders for the cave to be temporarily sealed by large stones until the enemy's retreating armies were captured. Joshua said to his officers what he had heard God say to him: "Do not be afraid or discouraged. Be strong and courageous" (v. 25). This is God's intention in our communication. We are to say what we have heard God say. This is what hermeneutics (the science of interpreting the biblical text) is all about. We are to say what God says (exegesis) and not twist the text so it says what we want it to say (eisegesis). Joshua proceeds to tell his officers, "Your foot being on the necks of these enemy kings is what the Lord intends for you to do to all the enemies you are going to fight." God intended for them to go from victory to victory. This is also a picture of what God intends for contemporary believers. Figuratively speaking,

God desires for us to put our feet on the necks of Satan and his agents. We are to be in a position of victory and not defeat, of strength and not weakness, of valor and not fear. The Israelite victors resting their feet on the necks of their defeated foes foreshadows what God has promised to do to all evil since as early as Genesis 3:15. Righteousness will trounce evil, and God's will *will* prevail.

Sinners Redeemed by the Blood of the Lamb

Ultimately, Joshua and the Israelites soundly defeat and destroy the retreating soldiers and their cities. The victors executed the five kings who had hidden in the cave and buried them in the cave that had been their hiding place. God gave the southern cities into Israel's hands, and once again Joshua is a mighty conqueror respected in the eyes of Israel (vv. 30,32).

If Joshua, not having the benefits of the historical incarnation, crucifixion, resurrection, and ascension of Christ the greater Joshua, could pray and see God work a miracle for him to accomplish his purpose, certainly we can cast our cares on him. What problems can we have that God cannot handle? Is there anything too hard for God? As Christ our great high priest intercedes for us, believers must pray in the power of the Holy Spirit for changes that promote the purpose of God. Saint Augustine famously put it this way: "Pray as though everything depends on God, and work as though everything depends on you."

Reflections

The Christological Highway to Jesus

This confederacy of five kings against Joshua was a personal attack against God and a threat against the fulfillment of the promise of God to Abraham (Gen 12:1-3). If this coalition had defeated Joshua and Israel, it would have wiped out the tribe of Judah. Therefore, the corridor or channel through which Jesus was to be born would have been forever closed. God had to ensure Joshua's victory by routing the enemies before Israel, killing them, chasing them, striking them, and casting down large hailstones until they all died (Josh 10:10-11).

One day Jesus, the greater Joshua, would be born in Bethlehem of Judea and later, on Calvary, would win the greatest battle against Satan and the coalition of hell through his death and resurrection. The author of the book of Joshua says, "There has been no day like it before or since" (v. 14). We must look fourteen hundred years later to see the sun stand still again (Luke 23:44-45), yielding its will to the moon-veiled day, paving the way for the Son of righteousness to rise three days later with healing in his wings (Mal 4:2).

Behavioral Response

If the Old Testament Joshua could pray with such faith and power that God listened to him and responded to him by putting the sun on daylight saving time and providing Joshua with sufficient daylight to pursue and defeat his enemies, then Christians who live on the other side of the incarnation and Pentecost can pray with power that accomplishes the purpose of God for the church and for their own lives.

Reflect and Discuss

1. Adoni-zedek can mean "the Lord is righteousness" or "Zedek is lord." How is this ironic?
2. When have you seen opposition on all sides, yet God still fought for you?
3. What are possible consequences if you step when God says stop?
4. Do you find it easier to step, i.e., push forward with reckless abandon, or stop, i.e., wait without anxiety and worry?
5. How do we remind ourselves and one another to yield to God who fights our battles?
6. Do you hesitate to pray for seemingly impossible things? If so, why? If not, how did you learn to pray boldly?
7. How might you teach your children to pray with faith to believe God has all power?
8. "The Bible is not a scientific book." What kind of book is it?
9. Of the supernatural miracles God has performed in the book of Joshua thus far, which one(s) speaks to a situation in your life?
10. Reflect on and react to this statement: "Pray as though everything depends on God, and work as though everything depends on you."

Ain't Gon' Study War No More

JOSHUA 11

Main Idea: The God who fights for us in Christ Jesus will bring us to a land of eternal rest by his Spirit.

I.   **No Need to Study War**
   A.   Flee from sin.
   B.   Flee from enemies of God.
   C.   Flee from complacency.
II. **The Futility of Fighting Our Merciful, Holy, and Righteous God**
   A.   Jabin
   B.   The Anakim
III. **God Fights for His Own.**

The Big Ten

Text: Joshua 11

Title: Ain't Gon' Study War No More

New Testament Companion: Revelation 19:11-16

Fallen Condition Focus: As Joshua and the Israelites were successful in exterminating their external enemies, believers must always be cognizant of the enemies who lurk within their own congregations—and indeed within themselves—who are capable of bringing them to utter defeat (Josh 22).

The Christological Highway to Jesus: While Joshua brought Israel rest from war by God's hand, he was unable to bring complete *shalom* to the world. Jesus, the new and better Joshua of the New Testament, inaugurated complete salvation and total peace through his death and resurrection.

The Whole Counsel of God: Just as Joshua left nothing undone of that which God commissioned him to do (Josh 11:15), Yeshua, sent by the Father and anointed by the Spirit, declared, "I have glorified you on the earth by completing the work you gave me to do" (John 17:4).

> **Intratrinitarian Presence:** God is faithful to keep his promises. As he
> fulfilled his promise to Israel and gave them their inheritance, so
> he fulfills his promise to give saved humanity their inheritance by
> dwelling in believers through the Holy Spirit and bringing them
> to their ultimate destination—heaven.
> **Proposition:** The God who fights for us in Christ Jesus will bring us to
> a land of eternal rest by his Spirit.
> **Behavioral Response:** We must live in expectant hope of the day
> when all wars will cease and death will be no more. Our God
> fights for us, and he has already won the final battle.
> **Future Condition Focus (Sermonic Eschatonics):** We live in the
> already-not yet—Jesus has already conquered sin and death,
> but we have not yet reached the true shalom that will permeate
> the new creation: "He will wipe away every tear from [our] eyes.
> Death will be no more; grief, crying, and pain will be no more,
> because the previous things have passed away" (Rev 21:4).

No Need to Study War

No survivors! "The LORD handed them over to Israel, and they struck them down. . . . They struck them down, leaving no survivors" (v. 8). No survivors! "They struck down everyone in it with the sword, completely destroying them; he left no one alive" (v. 11). No survivors! "But they struck down every person with the sword until they had annihilated them, leaving no one alive" (v. 14). No survivors! This is God's intention for Israel. Israel is to be more than a conqueror. No one is to be able to stand against Israel all the days of Joshua's leadership (1:5). The Lord knew that the presence of Canaanite survivors elevated the potential and inevitability of these idolatrous worshipers leading Israel into idolatry.

Flee from Sin

Believers often play with fire and leave parts of themselves unsurrendered to God, opening themselves to the onslaughts of the devil. Satan knows Joshua 8 and 9 and uses that strategy on the people of God. Satan draws the saints out of their stronghold only to ambush them once they leave their stronghold unguarded. Believers cannot flirt with sin or, like Achan, hide sin in their tents. We must obey the admonition of

Hebrews 12:1: "Let us lay aside *every* hindrance and the sin that so easily ensnares us" (emphasis added).

Flee from Enemies of God

In the economy of the kingdom of God, partial obedience is disobedience. God's intention and command was for the Israelites to completely defeat and destroy the Canaanite residents because they threatened Israel's devotion to God. As part of this danger, they imposed a threat to the preservation of the tribe of Judah, the channel and corridor through which the Messiah, Jesus, would come. The God who fights for us in Christ Jesus will bring us to a land of eternal rest by his Spirit.

If all Scripture is profitable for teaching and reproof (1 Tim 3:16), how are long lists of kings and place-names, like in verses 1-5 of Joshua 11, profitable to us? Why are they detailed? Dale Ralph Davis ponders the effect of omitting these details:

> [T]he text would lose its punch. You see, it is precisely in reading this extended, detailed, particularizing description of Israel's opposition that you begin to feel how overwhelming the enemy is, to sense in line-upon-line fashion the almost hopeless situation Israel faces. (*Joshua*, 92)

Flee from Complacency

There are no human reservations about God's proclamation in this chapter. There are no interrogations about God's directions in this chapter. There are no interruptions in military action against Israel's enemies in this chapter. Like dominoes, their adversaries fall one after another without the Israelites having a break or chance to savor the previous victory. This way, the Israelites avoid complacency. The Lord knows they are prone to take their eyes off him, the source of their strength, and rely on their own military might.

The Futility of Fighting Our Merciful, Holy, and Righteous God

Jabin

Jabin, the king of Hazor, solicits the help of other kings in the northern part of Canaan to assist him in preventing Israel from completely conquering Canaan. God orders Joshua to instruct the Israelite army to hamstring the enemy horses and burn their chariots with fire (vv. 6,9). This act would remove the temptation for Israel to use the horses and chariots in upcoming battles and attribute victory to the newly acquired military equipment instead of to God alone.

The combined size of their rivals' armies is described in the following way: "They went out with all their armies—a multitude as numerous as the sand on the seashore—along with a vast number of horses and chariots" (v. 4). Israel had a history of not needing horses and chariots in their quest to possess their inheritance in Canaan. They defeated Jericho without horses and chariots, and the walls came tumbling down. They destroyed Ai during the second battle and burned the city. They eliminated the southern five-king confederacy and turned the kings' hiding place into their mausoleum. Now, they decimate the kings and their kingdoms during the northern conquest.

We may feel tempted to bypass the book of Joshua because of these reports of violence. But God is a merciful, holy, and righteous God, and the Canaanite cities were overrun with sin and devoid of the desire to accept God's grace or acknowledge his patience. The locals were like thieves practicing their crimes in the presence of police officers. For a long while, the officers could see but were lenient, hoping the criminals would change their behavior. But after patiently waiting for change, the officers finally incarcerated the criminals. Should there be an outcry against delayed justice? Most would look at this situation and understand the punishment came long after the crimes were committed originally. In Canaan, the nations had been sinning in the presence of the God of all the Earth for centuries, and they did not repent or renounce their ways.

The Anakim

Even the formidable Anakim were removed from the land (vv. 21-22) as noted in the commendable and celebrative summary of this chapter: "So Joshua took the entire land, in keeping with all that the LORD had told Moses" (v. 23). These were the Canaanite "giants" who had struck fear in the Israelite spies decades before (Deut 1:28 MSG).

God Fights for His Own

All these battles were won without horses and chariots. How? Because the Lord was fighting for Israel. The God who fights for us in Christ

Jesus will bring us to a land of eternal rest by his Spirit. The Lord told Joshua, "Do not be afraid of them, for at this time tomorrow I will cause all of them to be killed before Israel" (v. 6). In fact, the Lord influenced these Canaanite kingdoms to fight against Israel by affecting their desire. God knew the desire of their hearts was to oppose Israel at war. As a result, God provided the opportunity for their will to be carried out. Yet when they fought against Israel, they signed their own death certificates, for in fighting against Israel, they really were fighting against God. Joshua 11:20 recalls what God had done similarly to Pharaoh and his officials in relation to the Hebrews in Egypt over four hundred years prior: "For it was the LORD's intention to [totally] harden their hearts" since they had long hardened themselves against him (see Exod 10:1,20).

The Israelite army did not need horses and chariots. They had all they needed in God. God is always enough. His grace is always sufficient. As Paul rhetorically asked, "If God is for us, who is against us?" (Rom 8:31). The implication is, if God is for us, no one can be against us and win! The Israelites were thoroughly victorious because they were consistently obedient to their military commander, who was obedient to the Word of God and the God of the Word: "Just as the LORD had commanded his servant Moses, Moses commanded Joshua. That is what Joshua did, leaving nothing undone of all that the LORD had commanded Moses" (Josh 11:15). God calls his children to trust and obey him. That is the formula for being successful in the work of the kingdom:

> Above all, be strong and very courageous to observe carefully the whole instruction my servant Moses commanded you. Do not turn from it to the right or the left, so that you will have success wherever you go. This book of instruction must not depart from your mouth; you are to meditate on it day and night so that you may carefully observe everything written in it. For then you will prosper and succeed in whatever you do. (1:7-8)

"Trust and obey, for there's no other way!" (John Henry Sammis, "Trust and Obey"). Joshua will take the entire land, just as the Lord had directed Moses, and be prepared to parcel out a territorial inheritance to each of the tribes according to their tribal divisions. The God who fights for us in Christ Jesus will bring us to a land of eternal rest by his Spirit. This chapter in Joshua ends with a *shalom* note: the land had rest from war.

Reflections

The Christological Highway to Jesus

The Old Testament Joshua left nothing unfinished of all that the Lord commanded Moses (v. 15). But the law had come by Moses and could at best only serve as a tutor, a schoolmaster, to lead us to Christ. The law had its limits. John said, "The law was given through Moses; grace and truth came through Jesus Christ" (John 1:17). Therefore, Joshua could only lead the people to the extent of the law. He could not convert or save them. However, the greater Joshua went beyond Moses and the Old Testament Joshua in that he converted and saved us by his grace through the truth of the gospel.

Behavioral Response

Hamstringing horses was the Lord's way of reminding his people to completely rely on him for victory rather than on earthly schemes and instruments. God's grace is sufficient (2 Cor 12:9).

Reflect and Discuss

1. How is partial obedience the same as disobedience?
2. What does God's "fighting" for us look like in the church today?
3. How might Joshua's experiences fighting in the central and southern regions have informed his approach to the north?
4. God promised to hand Israel's enemies over to them, but he also gave them instructions to ensure that victory happened. Do you see a tension there? Why or why not?
5. How important is human personal responsibility to God?
6. Why do believers often keep "pet sins" when the Lord has demanded "no survivors" of sin in our lives?
7. In the face of all this violence, is God still loving? Is God still good? How do we know?
8. What does the mention of Moses in this chapter do for the Joshua narrative?
9. What does it mean that God "hardened the hearts" of Israel's enemies?
10. How does Jesus bring rest from war?

Count Your Blessings

JOSHUA 12

Main Idea: God lavishes blessings on his people, who must remember and count them, beginning with his greatest blessing—salvation offered by Christ through the Spirit.

I. God Keeps His Promises.
II. God's Record Produces Confidence in His Word.
III. God's Success Rate Is Perfect.
IV. God's Blessings Must Be Counted and Remembered.
V. Salvation through Christ Is God's Most Important Blessing.

The Big Ten

Text: Joshua 12
Title: Count Your Blessings
New Testament Companion: Ephesians 3:20-21
Fallen Condition Focus: Joshua 12 lists thirty-one kings and kingdoms that fell in defeat to Joshua and the Israelites. Thirty-one seems to be a trivial number. However, because believers have a propensity to underemphasize the amazing and astounding power of God working wonders on their behalf, thirty-one is inserted in Holy Writ.
The Whole Counsel of God: With the exception of the loss at Ai, Joshua had an impressive military record—thirty-one victories over thirty-one kings and kingdoms (v. 24). Our heavenly Joshua, empowered by the Holy Spirit of God, won his greatest victory at Calvary and is worthy to receive this attribution: "The kingdom of the world has become the kingdom of our Lord and of his Christ, and he will reign forever and ever" (Rev 11:15).
The Christological Highway to Jesus: As God secured the Israelite victory over the Canaanites, so does Jesus secure our victory over sin, death, and the devil. Because of his sacrifice and resurrection,

Christians await the arrival of our grand inheritance. We owe him eternal gratitude.

Intratrinitarian Presence: God is a merciful God who gives his people gifts they do not deserve. This is best evidenced by the fact that God gives himself in Jesus Christ and does not leave saved humanity as orphans but sends us the Holy Spirit to empower us.

Proposition: God lavishes blessings on his people, who must remember and count them, beginning with his greatest blessing—salvation offered by Christ through the Spirit.

Behavioral Response: Believers are to give thanks in all circumstances, remembering the many ways God in Christ has blessed us.

Future Condition Focus (Sermonic Eschatonics): The Israelite inheritance of the promised land was an amazing blessing, but that land pales in comparison to the new heaven and new earth. In the eschaton, the land God's people will inherit will be without curse and without night (Rev 22:1-5).

Introduction

I enjoy watching a good action movie. There is movement and excitement. I am on the edge of my seat waiting to see what happens next. That is not the case with this chapter. Some texts are more tantalizing, other texts are more doctrinally dramatic, and some texts cause the readers seeking spiritual information and edification in Scripture to wonder about their benefit. Joshua 12 appears to be that last kind of text. It calls into question whether Paul had it in mind when he wrote 2 Timothy 3:16: "*All* Scripture is inspired by God and is profitable for teaching, for rebuking, for correcting, for training in righteousness" (emphasis added). But indeed he was urging readers to remember its value. God lavishes blessings on his people, who must remember and count them, beginning with his greatest blessing—salvation offered by Christ through the Spirit. It is doubtful Joshua 12 would be the pick of most readers seeking spiritual growth. On the surface, it is a military report of Israel's victories over their enemies—both on the east side of the Jordan River (wilderness) and the west side of the Jordan (Canaan). This chapter concludes with the names of the kings and number of the victories Israel had over these kings and kingdoms: thirty-one in all.

God Keeps His Promises

That's it. Where is worship in chapter 12? Where are the actual dramatic events in the book of Joshua—parting waters, falling walls, burning cities, extension of light and delay of night, and hailstones hurled by the divine? Where are the dramatic cries from the kings and the people? They are absent from Joshua 12. However, Joshua 12 has a lot to say to us by what it does not directly say to us.

First, this chapter communicates that God makes good on his promises. The Lord promised if the two tribes of Reuben and Gad and the half tribe of Manasseh would share in the conflict with their brothers, the nine and a half tribes on the west side, then God would give them the land promised to them on the wilderness side of the Jordan. The two and a half tribes were faithful to their promise, and God was faithful in his provision.

God lavishes blessings on his people, who must remember and count them, beginning with his greatest blessing—salvation offered by Christ through the Spirit. Some promises and covenants are unconditional like the Noahic covenant, in which God promised the whole world would never again be destroyed by flood (Gen 9:11). However, this covenant with the two and a half tribes is a conditional covenant, contingent on the tribes doing their part in fighting alongside their fellow tribes until Canaan had rest from war. Then and only then was the land promised to them on the east side of Jordan definitely theirs.

If we as believers abide in God and live out his Word, he will bless us with the fruit of his promises found in his Word. This is not prosperity preaching; it is standing on the promises of God in obedience and reaping the benefits God has promised. We reap them according to obedience to his Word, not according to our wishes.

God's Record Produces Confidence in His Word

Second, this chapter articulates the significance of past experience with God producing present confidence in God. Whenever Israel faced any present challenge or encounter, they could always look back and see how God had delivered them in the past. This assured Israel that God could surely deliver them in the present.

This was the basis of David's confidence when he faced Goliath the giant, champion of the Philistines. Goliath was shocked that King

Saul, a great warrior, would send a youth with no military experience to fight him. But David came with the experience of serving God, who allowed him to kill a lion and a bear that had threatened his father Jesse's sheep. David reasoned that if God could help him succeed in the past, God would empower him in the present against Goliath, the uncircumcised giant.

When believers face what appear to be unconquerable challenges in the present, they must rehearse and review their pasts. They must dust for divine fingerprints in their biographies in order to remember that God was with them in the past and will be with them now. This should give believers great confidence in God.

God's Success Rate Is Perfect

Third, this chapter clearly and powerfully makes the undeniable statement that there is no failure in God. God inspires the writer to list the kings of the territories Joshua and the Israelites conquered on the west side of the Jordan. The names run like credits at the end of a movie. They seem to be unnecessary. Why doesn't the author just settle for the fact he has already reported the whole territory of Canaan had rest from war and the entire land was taken under the leadership of Joshua (Josh 11:23)? The author takes the extra step of naming the territories these kings ruled. In fact, in verse 24 they are counted and numbered. Thirty-one kings in all were defeated. Some of the territories are readily known even though the name of the king is omitted: Jericho, Ai, Jerusalem, and Bethel. Other names are unfamiliar: Eglon, Debir, Geder, Hormah, Tappuah, and Jokneam. Yet God inspires the writer to list these names in chronological order based on when they fell to the swords of Joshua and the Israelites.

God's Blessings Must Be Counted and Remembered

Our God is an omniscient God! He is an accountant. He keeps track of numbers. God's people should be accountants, too. After all, God lavishes blessings on his people, who must remember and count them, beginning with his greatest blessing—salvation offered by Christ through the Spirit. As we consider what is before us, we must remember what is behind us. We each have a testimony if we would but stop to tell it. Therefore, we each have the responsibility to join the Believer's Accounting Firm and count our blessings.

God puts our tears in bottles so that he knows the weight of the many tears we have shed (Ps 56:8). For God, tears are liquid love and a language he understands. How many tears have flowed down your cheeks? Tears over relational rifts? Over tragic and premature deaths? Tears over devastating habits? God keeps track. As if to emphasize this, Jesus said, "But even the hairs of your head have all been counted" (Matt 10:30). God keeps track of souls that are added to the kingdom, too. Luke writes, "So those who accepted his message were baptized, and that day about three thousand people were added to them" (Acts 2:41). The Lord put your name in the Lamb's Book of Life as one of the innumerable host of saints approaching the heavenly throne. They have "washed their robes and made them white in the blood of the Lamb" (Rev 7:14). Surely since God is that meticulous about keeping up with details seemingly so mundane, then he is even more meticulous in keeping up with our heartaches and our pain.

Salvation through Christ Is God's Most Important Blessing

The listing of thirty-one kings demonstrates Joshua and the Israelites' total victory. Jesus Christ came to bring about total victory, too. When he said in John 19:30, "It is finished," he meant he had done everything his Father sent him to do. Every enemy was defeated, and the last enemy, death, was given notice of utter defeat. Jesus took the sting out of death, and his resurrection by the Spirit robbed the grave of its victory. Like Joshua, he left nothing undone. As the Old Testament Joshua completed his work and addressed all he was to do (Josh 11:15), so the New Testament Joshua will complete his work and will leave nothing undone (John 19:30). Presently, Jesus is interceding for his spiritual siblings as the great high priest. The ministry of salvation and redemption is complete; however, the ministry of intercession is ongoing. Hebrews 7:25 says that Jesus is a high priest who always lives to make intercession for us. We, as God's children, survive because he is interceding and praying for us. We are to follow his example and leave nothing undone.

Joshua 12 is a resounding announcement to Christians as they face foe after foe: God is our mighty fortress. This list is an example of our need to recount, as is Matthew 1:1-17. In that list, which believers might skip to get to the meat of the book, is the story of all of us. Regardless of our origins, our pasts, our sins, or our failures, we are important to God, who lavishes blessings on his people. We must remember and count them, beginning with his greatest blessing—salvation offered by Christ through the Spirit.

Reflections

The Christological Highway to Jesus

Our Lord God is our accountant. The thirty-one names recorded in Joshua 12 are significant and are not just a superficial listing. Sometimes small details become matters of enormous importance for the one whose ways are not our ways and whose thoughts are not our thoughts (Isa 55:8). Like Abraham, we have no innate righteousness in our accounts, but faith was accounted to Abraham and to us as righteousness (Gen 15:6; Rom 4:9). Christ became our sin, and we became his righteousness, not by our works but by faith.

Reflect and Discuss

1. How do you approach texts like Joshua 12 that many deem boring?
2. How is Joshua 12 profitable for teaching?
3. How is Joshua 12 profitable for correction?
4. How is Joshua 12 profitable for training in righteousness?
5. How does knowing God is an accountant, a God of the meticulous details, impact your daily life? How should it impact your daily life?
6. Where else do we see meticulous detail in Scripture?
7. What value do verses 1-6 of Joshua 12 contribute to the chapter and to the book of Joshua?
8. How might an Israelite in Joshua's day have responded to this record?
9. Have you ever itemized the Lord's blessings in your life? How can this practice affect you and those around you?
10. In this chapter, God attributes the victories to the Israelites even though he was the one who really won their battles. Why does God choose to partner with us in accomplishing his purposes?

Finishing Well

JOSHUA 13

Main Idea: Because of the victory won by God in Christ, Christians can walk by faith in the Spirit even when they cannot see the assurance of the victory.

I. **Claim God's Promises.**
   A. Joshua
   B. Caleb
   C. Believers
II. **Remember God's Promises and Recount Them.**
III. **Keep Promises to God.**
   A. The two and a half tribes
   B. Joshua and the Israelites
IV. **Possess the Promised Land.**

The Big Ten

Text: Joshua 13

Title: Finishing Well

New Testament Companion: Philippians 1:6

Fallen Condition Focus: Joshua and the Israelites had much land to possess even after their central, southern, and northern military campaigns were complete. Believers must avoid the spirit of complacency and adopt the spirit of Paul, who resolved to keep reaching forward to what was ahead (Phil 3:13).

The Whole Counsel of God: Joshua would finish well yet recognize in his old age there was still much land to be possessed. Jesus, the greater Joshua, declared from the cross, "It is finished" (John 19:30), committed his ongoing work to his followers, and told them they would do "even greater works than these, because [he was] going to the Father "(John 14:12). These works are carried out in the book of Acts by the apostles and today by Christians through the power of the Holy Spirit.

The Christological Highway to Jesus: The life, death, and resurrection of Jesus Christ have proved God is faithful to keep his promises.

Intratrinitarian Presence: "All things work together for the good for those who love God and are called by Christ to fulfill his purposes" (Rom 8:28; author's paraphrase). We live with Spirit-empowered confidence to take faithful actions without fear of failure.

Proposition: Because of the victory won by God in Christ, Christians can walk by faith in the Spirit even when they cannot see the assurance of the victory.

Behavioral Response: Believers are to have an expectant faith that God will fulfill all his promises regardless of how hopeless a situation may look. As we hold in tension God's sovereignty and our personal responsibility to do what he has called us to do, we can live with expectant faith.

Future Condition Focus (Sermonic Eschatonics): As we live in the "already of the here and now" and look forward to the "not yet of the hereafter," we can live in tiptoe anticipation of the blessed hope as we await our Savior (Phil 3:20).

Claim God's Promises

I have a friend who has been married to her husband for over a half century. She revealed to me she received a letter from a company concerning monetary funds. She put the letter aside, thinking it irrelevant or a hoax. After a long period of time had passed, she noticed the envelope containing the letter was from a rather obscure place. She opened the envelope and began to read it. Then she asked herself the question, "What do I have to lose if I follow up on the directions in this letter?" The letter requested her to contact the Department of Unclaimed Funds. Several weeks later, she and her husband received a check for multiple thousands of dollars! Though she didn't even know it existed, the money had been there waiting for her the whole time. Because of the victory won by God in Christ, Christians can walk by faith in the Spirit even when they cannot see the assurance of the victory.

Joshua

Joshua was now an old man. He would live to be 110 years old (Josh 24:29). He accomplished a great deal. He had lived a life of faithfulness to God.

In fact, Joshua 11:15 offers a commendable summary of his service: "That is what Joshua did, leaving nothing undone of all that the LORD had commanded Moses." Although Joshua was advanced in age, the Lord reminded him, "A great deal of the land remains to be possessed" (Josh 13:1). God had promised Israel the entire land of Canaan, "from the wilderness and Lebanon to the great river, the Euphrates River—all the land of the Hittites—and west to the Mediterranean Sea" (Josh 1:4). There were still some unclaimed packages of land that needed to be possessed. And what faith Joshua had in God's promises!

Caleb

Believers may retire from jobs but not from ministry. The Lord said to the church at Smyrna, "Be faithful to the point of death, and I will give you the crown of life" (Rev 2:10). In the next chapter (14), Caleb, the octogenarian, will pursue his greatest challenge: the conquering of the Anakim in order to possess Hebron, the territory the Lord had promised forty-five years before (Josh 14:10-12).

It is important for believers not only to begin ministry well but also to finish ministry well. Saul, the first king of Israel, began his kingship well but ended it tragically on the wrong side of his sword (1 Sam 31:4). By contrast, Saul, the great apostle of the New Testament, preceded his ministry with persecution of the church but ended his ministry victoriously (2 Tim 4:6-8).

Believers

Christians must strive to be consistently faithful so they do not leave behind an unfinished past. Because of the victory won by God in Christ, Christians can walk by faith in the Spirit even when they cannot see the assurance of the victory. Joshua was reminded by the Lord of unpossessed and unclaimed territories. What areas and possibilities remain unclaimed and unpossessed in your life, work, and ministry? What doors have you failed to enter, and what mountains do you refuse to tunnel through? What talents and gifts remain undeveloped?

Remember God's Promises and Recount Them

Joshua 13 notes there would be promised land territories the Israelites would allow the Canaanites to continue to inhabit. The Israelites did not drive them out. The list is an indictment of Israel's failure to possess unclaimed packages of territory: "But the descendants of Judah could not drive out the Jebusites who lived in Jerusalem. So the Jebusites still live in Jerusalem among the descendants of Judah today" (Josh 15:63). "However, they did not drive out the Canaanites who lived in Gezer. So the Canaanites still live in Ephraim today, but they are forced laborers" (16:10). "But the Israelites did not drive out the Geshurites and Maacathites. So Geshur and Maacath still live in Israel today" (13:13). This was land on the west side of the Jordan. The trend continued in the east: "The descendants of Manasseh could not possess these cities, because the Canaanites were determined to stay in this land" (17:12). The failure to completely follow God's commands but leave some Canaanite peoples in the land would bring about much crisis down the road. God's ways are not our ways, and his thoughts are not our thoughts. It is in our best interest as believers to completely obey him because only God knows the beginning before the beginning begins!

In addition to these territories still in the hands of the original dwellers (13:3-6), there were other unpossessed territories occupied by the Canaanite enemies of Israel. Only the two and a half tribes who chose to set up residence in the land on the east side of the Jordan had received their territorial inheritance. The nine and a half tribes of Israel who would live on the west side of the Jordan were still waiting to receive their land allotments, and Joshua was to be the Secretary of Housing. He was to direct the apportioning of the tribal lots to the nine and a half tribes. No, it was not time for his retirement but for a renewed engagement and investment in his expanded role.

The Lord had given Moses, the senior statesman, what he needed to complete his mission. It was said of Moses, "Moses was one hundred twenty years old when he died; his eyes were not weak, and his vitality had not left him" (Deut 34:7). Caleb said at the age of eighty-five, "I am still as strong today as I was the day Moses sent me out" (14:11). And now that Joshua is advanced in years, he is ready to write yet another chapter in his autobiography. He is not simply a senior citizen; he is a man of God who possesses *xyz*'s—extra years of zest.

Keep Promises to God

The Two and a Half Tribes

In Numbers 32, Reuben, Gad, and the half-tribe of eastern Manasseh applied to Moses for an early settlement on the east side of the Jordan,

the wilderness side. God had promised Abraham the entire land of
Canaan for all twelve tribes of Israel to dwell in, not just the nine and
a half tribes. The two and a half tribes liked the Gilead territory on the
east side because of its lush and rich pastureland for the livestock. But
Moses reminded them that the children of Israel had been in a thirty-
eight-year wilderness wandering holding pattern before they crossed
over the Jordan River. Ten of twelve spies sent to the land of Canaan
returned to the congregation of Israel with a doubtful and discouraging report. The people adopted the report and subsequently declined
to engage the Canaanites for the promised land. Moses was thinking
that the two and half tribes' intention was to abandon their brothers as
they fought to evict their enemies from the promised land. In Moses's
mind, the two and a half tribes would forego the fighting to enjoy a
conflict-free and carefree life on the east side. That would communicate another doubtful and discouraging message to the other nine and
a half tribes. But when the two and a half tribes assured Moses they
would leave their families and livestock on the east side and join their
brothers in battle on the west side, Moses approved of their early settlement on the east.

This is a conditional covenant. If the two and a half tribes would
live up to their promise, then they could definitely inherit the land on
the east side. However, if they reneged and went back on their promise,
then they would have sinned greatly against the Lord: "But if you don't
do this," Moses said, "you will certainly sin against the LORD; be sure
your sin will catch up with you" (Num 32:23). Based on this covenant,
Moses distributed the land inheritance on the east side to the two full
tribes of Gad and Reuben and half the tribe of Manasseh.

Joshua and the Israelites

Joshua, Moses's assistant and now successor after his death, was to dis-
tribute the land inheritance on the west side to the nine full tribes of
Judah, Ephraim, Benjamin, Simeon, Zebulun, Issachar, Asher, Naphtali,
and Dan as well as to the half tribe of western Manasseh. But wait: isn't
Levi a tribe? What happened to Levi? Had they been left out of the
inheritance? Levi was a son of Jacob, too.

God is Levi's inheritance! For the Levitical tribe the Lord would
provide furnished pasturelands and dwelling places through the forty-
eight Levitical cities scattered across Israel (Josh 24:41). The reality of
Levi's inheritance is made clear throughout the book of Joshua: "He

did not, however, give any inheritance to the tribe of Levi. This was their inheritance, just as he had promised: the food offerings made to the LORD, the God of Israel" (13:14). Also, "But Moses did not give a portion to the tribe of Levi. The LORD, the God of Israel, was their inheritance, just as he had promised them" (13:33). And again, "No portion of the land was given to the Levites except cities to live in" (14:4).

Possess the Promised Land

The land of Canaan is of supreme importance in salvation history because God promised Abraham that he would give his posterity a great land. Canaan is this land. In this land the Messiah, Jesus Christ, would be born in Bethlehem of Judea (Mic 5:2). What a blessing, then, that the land of Canaan goes beyond a physical reality for Israel to a spiritual reality for all who believe in Christ and accept him as Savior! Because the Father and the Son sent the Spirit, God lives within people! The Holy Spirit has been given as an inheritance to every believer in Christ. Paul wrote to the Ephesians concerning Christ, through whom we receive the inheritance of the Holy Spirit:

> *In him we have also received an inheritance. . . . In him you also were sealed with the promised Holy Spirit when you heard the word of truth, the gospel of your salvation, and when you believed. The Holy Spirit is the down payment of our inheritance, until the redemption of the possession, to the praise of his glory.* (Eph 1:11,13-14)

All Christians are a part of a royal priesthood (in contrast with Israel's priests, who came from the tribe of Levi), and therefore all believers have the Holy Spirit as their inheritance. Because of the victory won by God in Christ, Christians can walk by faith in the Spirit even when they cannot see the assurance of the victory. We can be sure of our salvation.

Reflections

The Christological Highway to Jesus

We are heirs of God and coheirs with Christ who has purchased us. He is our inheritance. Joshua's author notes, "A great deal of the land remains to be possessed" (Josh 13:1). The two and a half tribes of Reuben, Gad, and eastern Manasseh had possessed their land on the east side of the Jordan River, yet they needed to fight in solidarity with the nine and a half tribes on the west side until they had received the land of their inheritance. This is a picture of believers growing in Christ as they are being transformed from glory to glory (2 Cor 3:18). It is also a picture of life in the fellowship of Christ's church body, where believers who are the body of Christ participate with one another in victorious Christian warfare (1 Cor 12).

Intratrinitarian Presence

The Spirit of God is continually transforming and conforming us into the image of God until we reach the place of glorification when we see him as he is (1 John 3:2).

Reflect and Discuss

1. Knowing God's Word is perfect, how can believers reconcile the list of unconquered lands in 13:1-6 with the pronouncement in 11:16-23 that the entire land was taken?
2. How might we reconcile other seeming contradictions?
3. Why do you think God mentioned Joshua's age?
4. How does faithfulness unto death (Rev 2:10) look?
5. What are your thoughts on God's command to divide the land before it has even been completely conquered?
6. Has God ever prompted you to act before you felt ready? When and how did you react?
7. Where else in Scripture have these "leaps of faith" been commanded?
8. What will be the consequences of Israel's failure to drive out some of the Canaanite peoples?
9. What might Christians today learn from failing to completely obey God's commands?
10. What does it mean to have God as your inheritance?

The Blessedness of Secondness

JOSHUA 16

Main Idea: Christ, the ruler who came to serve God and others, calls believers to render service to others through the fruit of the Spirit of humility rather than through competition.

I. **Caleb's Reward for Patient Loyalty**
   A. Caleb spied with Joshua.
   B. Caleb served behind Joshua.
   C. Caleb is the first individual to receive a land inheritance.
II. **God Rewards Loyalty.**
   A. Caleb
   B. Simeon
   C. Paul
   D. Dietrich Bonhoeffer, Martin Luther King, Jr., and Gardner Calvin Taylor
   E. Caleb conquered what God promised.
   F. Jesus conquered death as God promised.
III. **Believers Must Be Loyal to God in All Things.**

The Big Ten

Text: Joshua 14
Title: The Blessedness of Secondness
New Testament Companion: Romans 12:3
Fallen Condition Focus: Christian leaders too often compete with one another for preeminence instead of supporting each other in a complementary relationship like Joshua and Caleb did. Leaders should support one another for the purpose of fostering healthy congregational life to the glory of God who is preeminent.
The Whole Counsel of God: Caleb of Judah led the victory over the Anakites in the hill country of Hebron and gave that territory as an inheritance to his descendants. Jesus, also from Judah, through his death on a hill, conquered Satan, the archenemy of God. Jesus was resurrected from the dead by the Spirit three days

later. He brought salvation and guaranteed eternal inheritance for the believer (Eph 1:14).

The Christological Highway to Jesus: Christ, who alone is preeminent, stooped to wash his disciples' feet as a visual example of servanthood that believers are to embrace.

Intratrinitarian Presence: The holy God lowered himself to take the form of a servant in Christ Jesus, who, with God, sent the Holy Spirit to transform sinners into servants.

Proposition: Christ, the ruler who came to serve God and others, calls believers to render service to others through the fruit of the Spirit of humility rather than through competition.

Behavioral Response: Older believers draw on Christ's strength to finish the race well. Younger believers are to honor the older believers in the congregation and seek their wisdom.

Future Condition Focus (Sermonic Eschatonics): One day every individual's knee will bend in acknowledgment of the one who stooped and washed the disciples' feet. Believers will confess that only Christ is worthy to receive glory as an acknowledgment of their secondness to his preeminence.

Caleb's Reward for Patient Loyalty

Caleb Spied with Joshua

Wait for the LORD; be strong, and let your heart be courageous. Wait for the LORD" (Ps 27:14). Those words could exude from the pores of Caleb's body. He had been waiting for forty-five years to receive his land inheritance. As one of the two faithful spies (Joshua being the other), Caleb undoubtedly saw the land of Hebron about forty-five years prior to the time of the text. He spied out the land of Canaan. Already Hebron was rich with Hebraic history. The bones of many of Israel's ancestors were there. As a faithful spy, Caleb had consoled the Israelite congregation who had become discouraged and despondent by the report of the ten spies. The ten did not believe the Israelite army had the ability to take the land because of the Canaanite nations' mighty soldiers, the seemingly impregnable fortresses, and the presence of the Anakim—giants. However, Caleb told the people, "Let's go up now and take possession of the land because we can certainly conquer it!"

(Num 13:30). The ten spies had their eyes on the inhabitants of the land, while Joshua and Caleb had their eyes on the God of the promise. Believers must keep their eyes on God.

The Lord promised that Caleb and his descendants would inherit the land, namely Hebron: "But since my servant Caleb has a different spirit and has remained loyal to me, I will bring him into the land where he has gone, and his descendants will inherit it" (Num 14:24).

Caleb Served behind Joshua

Forty-five years of waiting was over. It was time for Caleb to capture the promised territory of Hebron. Once again, God operates through the process of divine protocol or order. God would give instructions to Joshua, the human commander in chief of the Israelite military forces and congregation. Joshua would convey those directives to the leaders under his command: Eleazar the high priest and the tribal heads. They would then communicate those orders to the congregation. In this instance, the matter being addressed is the distribution of land inheritance to the nine and a half tribes. It was to be done by the casting of lots. (Most likely the Urim and Thummim stones embedded in the breastplate of the high priest were used to determine the will of God concerning which territorial plot went to which tribe.) The two tribes of Reuben and Gad and the half tribe of Manasseh had already received their territorial inheritance forty-five years previously under Moses's administration on the east side of the Jordan River. Of course, the Levites did not receive an inheritance because God was their inheritance, and they were granted forty-eight Levitical cities in which to live and raise their livestock.

God selected Joshua to succeed Moses even though Caleb had been just as faithful as Joshua had been. Both Joshua and Caleb were born in Egypt. Both were slaves in Egypt. Both witnessed the miraculous opening of the waters of the Red Sea. Both received manna from heaven and water from a rock. But when Moses died, the Lord made this announcement: "Moses my servant is dead. Now you [Joshua] and all the people prepare to cross over the Jordan to the land I am giving the Israelites" (1:2). Joshua is chosen to be Israel's leader, and Caleb walks behind him.

Caleb Is the First Individual to Receive a Land Inheritance

But in this chapter, Caleb is the first individual to receive his land inheritance. Joshua will be the last individual to receive his inheritance: "When they had finished distributing the land into its territories, the Israelites gave Joshua son of Nun an inheritance among them" (Josh 19:49). In the economy of God, the first becomes last and the last becomes first (Matt 20:16).

God Rewards Loyalty

Caleb

In this chapter, Caleb and a group from his tribe approach Joshua, the leader of the Israelite congregation. They remind Joshua of some unfinished business that has been on the agenda for forty-five years. Memory can be a blessing. Caleb remembered those times when the nation of Israel was in a difficult position. Other than Joshua and Caleb, all the original adults had died during the thirty-eight years in the wilderness. And now Caleb and Joshua could say by God's grace they were the only ones who survived that wilderness death march. Though others died, God had brought them through. What a blessed memory! They were able to look back and say, "Look where he brought me from." Kadesh-barnea is a place of crisis, a turning point—a place of deliverance and rescue.

Now that the Israelites had seized control of Canaan, it is time to act on the business of securing the territorial inheritance the Lord promised to Caleb forty-five years ago. Joshua remembered hearing Moses give the message from the Lord concerning the faithful servant: "But since my servant Caleb has a different spirit and has remained loyal to me . . ." (Num 14:24). Caleb plays some scenic reruns for Joshua of that unfortunate day when God delayed Israel's entrance into the promised land. They were delayed for nearly forty years because at Kadesh-barnea Israel balked and refused to cross over into Canaan and fight its peoples. Caleb was forty at that time.

Even though the ten spies gave over to unbelief, Caleb followed *completely*. Three times a form of this expression occurs in this chapter: "But I followed the LORD my God completely" (Josh 14:8); "because you have followed the LORD my God completely" (14:9); and "because he followed the LORD, the God of Israel, completely" (14:14). In Hebrew, the name *Caleb* means "dog." Caleb was like a dog who had gone to canine training school and followed the master's directions without deviation—without turning to the right or to the left. Caleb followed the Lord without exception. He believed the Lord's promise to keep him alive until he received what he was promised (14:10). God made the promise to Caleb when Caleb was forty years old, and now, forty-five years later, he is eighty-five. A believer who remains in the will of God is immortal *until* God's purpose for his or her life is fulfilled. How long can we wait on the promise of God to be fulfilled in our lives? Time does not matter. Whether it takes four years, forty years, or forty-five years, we must remember: God is not in time. Time is in God. If God said it, he will do it.

Simeon

In New Testament days, Simeon the priest did not die before God's promise to him was fulfilled. Mary and Joseph entered the temple with the infant Jesus. Luke writes, "It had been revealed to him [Simeon] by the Holy Spirit that he would not see death before he saw the Lord's Messiah" (Luke 2:26). When Simeon saw the baby Jesus, he took him in his arms and said, "Now, Master, you can dismiss your servant in peace, as you promised. For my eyes have seen your salvation" (Luke 2:28-30).

Paul

After Jesus's ascension, Paul was on a ship with 275 other passengers and crew members bound for Rome. After many days of going without food and not seeing the sun or the stars, the passengers and crew panicked and gave up all hope for survival. There was only one person on board who still had hope—Paul. Paul testified to the others aboard the ship that the Lord sent an angel at night and told him, "Don't be afraid, Paul. It is necessary for you to appear before Caesar. And indeed, God has graciously given you all those who are sailing with you" (Acts 27:24).

Dietrich Bonhoeffer, Martin Luther King Jr., and Gardner Calvin Taylor

Sometimes God's purpose for his children is fulfilled at thirty-nine years of age. Dietrich Bonhoeffer and Martin Luther King Jr. are examples of this. Both died at thirty-nine—one by hanging and one by an assassin's bullet. Sometimes God's purpose is not fulfilled until age ninety-six. The inimitable American preacher Gardner Calvin Taylor died then. We cannot explain God's timing. My mother died at ninety-five, but my youngest son died at thirty-four. In the face of death, especially premature death, believers must cling to the hope of the promised resurrection.

The important matter is not counting the number of years one has but making the number of years count.

Caleb Conquered What God Promised

Now, at age eighty-five, Caleb claims to be as strong as he was forty-five years ago. Is this hyperbole? Is this an extreme exaggeration? Is dementia setting in? Or is he simply lying? How can a person be as strong at eighty-five as he was at forty? Caleb even says that he is just as vigorous and dexterous to go into battle as he was forty-five years ago. Most persons you talk to who are advanced in years will outright refute such statements. Because for many it becomes more difficult to lift objects, go upstairs, bend over and tie up shoes, or do many things that were previously done without thinking earlier on, Joshua's claims can seem unrealistic. But what he says is not based on physiology; it is based on theology. This could only be possible by God supplying supernatural strength for Caleb to perform extraordinary service. Isaiah is right: "Those who trust in the LORD will renew their strength; they will soar on wings like eagles; they will run and not become weary, they will walk and not faint" (Isa 40:31). So, may we be vigilant against the sin of ageism.

The word *entitlement* was not in Caleb's vocabulary; rather, the word *inheritance* dominates his thought. Yes, he was from the tribe of Judah, the fourth son of Jacob. The messianic promise emerged from this tribe: "The scepter will not depart from Judah or the staff from between his feet until he whose right it is comes and the obedience of the peoples belongs to him" (Gen 49:10).

Caleb did not want the territory of Hebron without a struggle. No, he said, "Now give me this hill country" (Josh 14:12); that is, give me the opportunity to possess it by defeating the current landlords of it. This is exactly what Caleb did in conquering Hebron: "Caleb drove out from there the three sons of Anak: Sheshai, Ahiman, and Talmai, descendants of Anak" (15:14). Caleb was successful not because of his senior strength but because of the strength of the sovereign One—strength beyond Caleb's strength. He said, "Perhaps the LORD will be with me and I will drive them out as the LORD promised" (14:12). Is "perhaps" a word that indicates faith? Dale Ralph Davis thinks so:

> Taken as a whole Caleb's words in verse 12 simply exude
> expectancy. "Perhaps . . . it may be . . . who knows . . . what

However, some of those children will turn out to be Annie Armstrongs, Martin Luther King Jrs., Rosa Parkses, Wilfredo de Jesuses, and Haik Hovsepian-Mehrs. A sense of unified diversity mirrors the eschatological reality when people from "every tribe and language and people and nation" (Rev 5:9) will say with a loud voice, "Worthy is the Lamb who was slaughtered to receive power and riches and wisdom and strength and honor and glory and blessing!" (Rev 5:12).

Reflections

The Christological Highway to Jesus

Caleb, one of the two faithful spies, was from the tribe of Judah. He is the first to receive a land inheritance on the west side of the Jordan in Canaan. He had undoubtedly seen the territory of Hebron and the hill country in it over forty years prior when he and Joshua were two of the twelve spies sent to spy out the land in Canaan. He waited forty-five years to possess this hill country. Jesus was also from the tribe of Judah, and he saw Mount Calvary prior to his death on the cross. In fact, he saw it from the foundation of the world. And in the mind of God, he was slain there in preexistence before the historical actuality (Rev 13:8). Like Caleb who said, "Now give me this hill country" (Josh 14:12) and proceeded to take it, Jesus "determined to journey to Jerusalem" (Luke 9:51) to purchase our salvation through his death on a hill called Calvary.

Behavioral Response

Caleb had waited forty-five years to see the promise of God fulfilled in the acquisition of Hebron. Finally, God's promise came true. How long can we wait on God's promise made to us through his Word? Can we wait through disappointments, moments of wandering, and the rejection of congregations we are serving? Can we trust God will keep his promise to us as he did to Caleb? The latter said, "As you see, the LORD has kept me alive these forty-five years as he promised" (Josh 14:10).

Intratrinitarian Presence

The Spirit of God rested on Caleb and gave him a different spirit and disposition (Num 14:24). This was evident through his complete devotion to God. He was confident based on what he had seen God do at the Red Sea, in the wilderness, and in the conquest of Canaan. This enabling power of God equipped Caleb to face the giants in the hill country of Hebron. He would be able to defeat the imposing men there and take possession of the territory. The Spirit of the Lord God rested upon Jesus, too, for God anointed him to preach the gospel and carry out his three-year ministry. The victories won in our ministries are to magnify Christ who leads us from victory to victory.

Reflect and Discuss

1. What is God's relationship to time?
2. Place yourself in Caleb's shoes. How would you have reacted when Joshua was selected as Moses's successor?
3. When in life have you played second fiddle? What did God show you through that experience?
4. What does loyalty to the Lord look like for believers today?
5. What does Caleb have in common with Jesus?
6. What saints in your life have maintained a robust service to Christ in the midst of old age?
7. How might we best equip the elderly in our churches to fulfill their callings?
8. What ministries in your church would benefit from elderly volunteers?
9. How was Caleb able to maintain strength after so many years in the wilderness and in battle?
10. Caleb takes the initiative in asking for his promised inheritance. Do you approach God with such boldness? Why or why not?

Water That's Not from the Well

JOSHUA 15

Main Idea: Jesus Christ, the Son of God, will give living water drawn from the well of the Spirit to all who ask and believe in him.

I.   **Courage Is Water That's Not from the Well.**
   A.   God allocates allotments.
   B.   God delivers allotments as allocated.
   C.   God protects allotments he gives.
II. **Courage Yields Freedom to Serve without Jealousy.**
   A.   Caleb and Joshua
   B.   Paul to the churches
III. **Jesus Is the Living Water.**
   A.   He gives courage to cease striving.
   B.   He is our inheritance.

The Big Ten

Text: Joshua 15
New Testament Companion: John 4:13-15; 7:37-39
Title: Water That's Not from the Well
The Christological Highway to Jesus: Achsah courageously asks her father for a blessing—springs of water. Centuries later, a Samaritan woman will ask Jesus for living water. That living water is Christ himself—the only one who can bring us everlasting refreshment.
Intratrinitarian Presence: As the Father and Holy Spirit are present at the baptism of the Son in the Jordan, so is the triune God present in the life of every believer who turns to God for salvation (John 14:26; 15:26).
Proposition: Jesus Christ, the Son of God, will give living water drawn from the well of the Spirit to all who ask and believe in him.

The Whole Counsel of God: In Scripture, water is seen as an emblem of the Holy Spirit. As Caleb from the tribe of Judah gave his daughter Achsah springs of water, Jesus, also from the tribe of Judah, offers a Samaritan woman water springing up for eternal life (John 4:14). In reference to water, Jesus was speaking of the Spirit of God when he stated that the one who believes in him "will have streams of living water flow from deep within him" (John 7:38). In the eschaton, Jesus will shepherd the saints and "guide them to springs of the waters of life" (Rev 7:17).

Fallen Condition Focus: Although Judah is the fourth son of Jacob, Judah is the first tribe of the nine and a half tribes to receive a land inheritance in the promised land. The firstborn tribe, Reuben, had received its land inheritance on the east side of the Jordan earlier. Simeon, the second-born son of Jacob, received its land inheritance after Judah, not before. Believers have a tendency to try to put God in a traditions box and to expect God to transact business according to conventional patterns. Isaiah reminds us that God's ways are not our ways (Isa 55:8).

Behavioral Response: Those who approach God's throne with boldness can share Christ the living water with those with whom they come in contact.

Future Condition Focus (Sermonic Eschatonics): In the presence of Christ, our eternity will be lived free from physical and spiritual thirst, for the Lamb who cried out, "I'm thirsty" (John 19:28), will "guide [us] to springs of the waters of life" (Rev 7:17).

Introduction

God is the God of *creatio ex nihilo*, the God who creates out of nothingness and causes what appears to become something of great importance in the life of the believer and the church. Joshua 15 appears to lack concrete significance. If it had to be put in the book of Joshua, then why is it given more verse space than the other twenty-three chapters have—sixty-three verses? Couldn't this chapter of border limits and geographical directions have been reduced to fewer verses? Joshua 16 contains only ten verses indicating the border limits and geographical directions of Ephraim, a large and great tribe (see also 17:14). Why so many verses in Joshua 15? They are certainly not there to fill up space in an already lengthy historical book. On the surface, this chapter cannot compete with or compare to the dramatic chapter 6, which has the engaging processional marching and the demolishing of the Jericho walls.

Courage Is Water That's Not from the Well

Chapter 15 initially may appear to be insignificant and at best bordering on boring reading about borders and boundary lines. Why is so much attention given to specific details of real estate in this chapter? I contend it's because Jesus Christ, the Son of God, will give more than enough living water drawn from the well of the Spirit to all who ask and believe in him. Consider the wealth of insight here. The extreme southern boundaries of Judah are listed:

- 15:1—"Now the allotment for the tribe of the descendants of Judah by their clans was in the southernmost region"
- 15:2—"Their southern border began"
- 15:3—"and went south of . . . , [and] ascended to . . . passed . . . turned to"
- 15:4—"It proceeded to . . . and so the border ended at"

God Allocates Allotments

Is this interesting reading that will keep you up at midnight—curving land, going up the one place to another, and going down and passing along and reaching other places? Is this what you want to hear when the storm of life is raging and there are financial, relational, and physical struggles? Is this the kind of encouragement you need to get you through a difficult day? Your response, if you're really honest, is, "Absolutely not!" Yet there is a purpose for the territorial boundaries. Land and matter *matter* to God. In the new heavens and new earth, we will dwell on a renewed earth. God does not trash his creation. This is upcycling at its best.

In this chapter, God is trying to show each of these tribes that he has planned ahead for the acquisition. He wants them to know what is for them is for them. There is no need for jealousy and strife. He also does not want them to be confused, for confusion will lead to internal strife and fighting. They have already fought the enemy on the outside; they must not turn in on themselves and fight one another as if they were the enemy. Just as God gives New Testament believers specific gifts to be appreciated but never to create division, so God gives these nine and a half tribes specific territories with boundaries to distinctively separate each territory. If you had a home built, it would be of the utmost importance to know the boundary lines of your property so you did not illegally build anything on someone else's property, nor anyone else unlawfully build anything on yours. Land, boundaries, and possessions matter to God.

God Delivers Allotments as Allocated

Judah is the first western tribe to receive its allotment, and perhaps this is no coincidence. McConville and Williams theorize,

> It has . . . clear theological purposes . . . as the kingdom of Judah
> will endure longer than the remainder of Israel and even form
> the basis of the people who occupy the land again after the
> Babylonian exile. (*Joshua*, 69)

Not only that, but it is the tribe of the Lion of Judah, our Christ. First, Caleb of the tribe of Judah received Hebron as an inheritance for himself and his descendants. This was promised by God because of Caleb's faithfulness (Num 14:24; Josh 14:10,12). The boundary lines are extremely important for him and his progeny.

Nonfamily members do not go to court to listen to the reading of a benefactor's will upon his or her death unless specifically invited as beneficiaries. Participation would not be interesting for nonfamily members or those who can not receive a benefit. But to the recipients of the benefactor, details about the estate, numbers, figures, properties, and valuables would be of the utmost importance at such a legal hearing! The same is true as it relates to Joshua, Eleazar, and the tribal leaders who cast lots and provide territorial boundaries for Judah and the rest of the tribes settling on the west side of the Jordan.

God Protects Allotments He Gives

God is a God of order. Paul admonishes the Corinthian church that "everything is to be done decently and in order" (1 Cor 14:40). The Lord knows how jealous and contentious his children can be over their so-called ministry space. Judah is the first of the nine and a half tribes settling in Canaan to receive an inheritance. It is no accident that the first tribe to receive its inheritance in the promised land is the tribe out of which the Messiah will be born. The name *Judah* means "praise." Out of Judah would come the one most worthy of all praise! Caleb leads the way for his tribe by being the first individual of a tribe to receive a land inheritance.

Courage Yields Freedom to Serve without Jealousy

Caleb and Joshua

Caleb is known for a giving spirit and not a grabbing spirit. Caleb gets Hebron as the inheritance for his family and his descendants. He offers incentive for a man to capture Kiriath-sepher—marriage to Achsah. We do not know if Caleb offered the incentive because he did not want to fight. We know he was still strong. Perhaps he was looking for leaders and offered the incentive to see who would rise to the top. Perhaps he wanted to give others a chance to prove themselves loyal. We do know Othniel took the challenge and met it successfully. So Caleb gave his daughter, Achsah, to marry Othniel, Caleb's nephew, son of his brother Kenaz. Then Caleb gave Othniel and Achsah the upper and lower springs in order to water their new field.

Caleb was a giver and not one who practiced *grabbing*. Caleb was satisfied with the gifts God had given him without being jealous of the gifts God had given Joshua, the leader chosen to replace Moses. Caleb was not like the two Joseph tribes who wanted more territorial space than had been given to them. They asked, "Why did you give us only one tribal allotment as an inheritance?" (Josh 17:14). We work together as one body in Christ without jealousy or counting and resenting the blessings of others. We remain focused on Christ and count our own innumerable and unearned blessings because Jesus Christ, the Son of God, will give living water drawn from the well of the Spirit to all who ask and believe in him.

Paul to the Churches

Paul is instructively helpful in guiding believers to interact with fellow believers in their use of spiritual gifts. Gifts are used to glorify God and dynamically and effectively edify others. He writes in 1 Corinthians,

> *Now there are different gifts, but the same Spirit. There are different ministries, but the same Lord. And there are different activities, but*

the same God works all of them in each person. . . . One and the
same Spirit is active in all these, distributing to each person as he
wills. . . . Now you are the body of Christ, and individual members of
it. (12:4-6,11,27)

Though we have different gifts, we have all received the same living
water from the same well of the same Spirit. There is no room for jealousy in the church of Jesus Christ.

Jesus Is the Living Water

Joshua 15 opens with a positive declaration: "Now the allotment for the
tribe of the descendants of Judah by their clans was in the southernmost
region" (v. 1). It closes with a negative admission: "But the descendants
of Judah could not drive out the Jebusites who lived in Jerusalem" (v. 63).
What happened? Caleb drove out three sons of Anak: "Sheshai, Ahiman,
and Talmai, descendants of Anak" (v. 14). Why did Israel fail to drive out
the Jebusites, the inhabitants of Jerusalem who would be a nemesis to
Judah and a source of great pain for centuries? King David would expel
the Jebusites and make Jerusalem the capital of the united monarchy.

He Gives Reason to Cease Striving

Jesus, who came from the line of Caleb and David, would do something
greater than casting the Jebusites out from Jerusalem. Jesus would die
outside the gates of Jerusalem and give himself over to death on Friday.
Jesus cast out the power of sin and guilt in the lives of believers through
his holy blood. The writer to the Hebrews articulates this in the following manner: "Therefore, Jesus also suffered outside the gate, so that he
might sanctify the people by his own blood" (Heb 13:12). Three days
later, on a Sunday morning, Jesus would be resurrected by the Spirit
(Rom 8:11). He conquered death and sin, our greatest enemies. "Death
has been swallowed up in victory" (1 Cor 15:54). Jesus's defeat of sin
and death provided the water of life for all the members of his body, the
church. Believers must cease striving with one another concerning the
inheritance of gifts and talents.

He Is Our Inheritance

Christ is our inheritance, and the gifts and talents we receive must be
used to glorify God and to build fellow believers up. Jesus Christ, the

Son of God, will give living water drawn from the well of the Spirit to all who ask and believe in him.

Reflections

The Christological Highway to Jesus

Jerusalem was once known as Jebus and was occupied by Jebusites. Early on, only pagan foreigners resided there (Judg 19:12). It would later become the place where God would establish peace between God and humanity by sending Jesus, who is our peace. Jesus would die in Jerusalem so we could have peace with God (Rom 5:1).

Intratrinitarian Presence

The Holy Spirit of God continually enables us to fight against the Jebusites of sin in our spiritual warfare (Eph 6:10-18), just as Christ fought against Satan in the wilderness of temptation (Matt 4:1-11).

Reflect and Discuss

1. Recall the narrative of Joseph in Genesis 37. What kind of brother was Judah?
2. What does Jesus's relation to the tribe of Judah mean?
3. Discuss the importance of Judah receiving his allotment first even though Judah was the fourth born of Jacob.
4. How can land allotment texts like this one bring us confidence, comfort, and hope?
5. How do detailed land allotments set Israel up for success as one united family?
6. Caleb drives out the descendants of Anak (the Anakim). How does this relate to the events of Numbers 13:31-33?
7. Achsah tries to persuade her husband to petition her father, but her father addresses her directly. Have you tried to circumvent talking directly to your heavenly Father?
8. Would you describe Achsah's request as bold? Why or why not?
9. Have you ever prayed, "Give me a blessing"? What happened?
10. Springs are an important image in the Bible. What do they signify?

Unfinished Business

JOSHUA 16–17

Main Idea: God assigned believers to defeat Satan and his demons by pressing on in Christ to higher ground through the power of the Holy Spirit.

I. **Remember**
   A. Zelophehad's daughters remember God's promise to their father.
      1. They had the courage to ask for it.
      2. They trusted God to keep his word.
   B. Believers must remember God's instructions.
      1. We must have the will to have sin eradicated from our lives.
      2. We must trust the blood of Christ to empower us to live holy lives.
      3. We must remember the example of the ancestors and choose God's ways.
II. **Obtainment or Entitlement? The Motive Matters.**
III. **Testimony or Title? The Life Matters.**

The Big Ten

Text: Joshua 16–17
Title: Unfinished Business
New Testament Companion: 2 Timothy 4:6-8
Fallen Condition Focus: Like the two Joseph tribes (Manasseh and Ephraim), believers are mistaken in thinking their blessings and inheritance come from entitlement rather than election and grace.
The Whole Counsel of God: Jesus, the Son of God, went to the wood country of the cross where he died and was resurrected by the Holy Spirit, thus defeating Satan and his kingdom. He ascended into heaven where he has prepared a place of many rooms for believers (John 14:2). One day we will worship our God in a land where there will be no more pain (Rev 21:4).

The Christological Highway to Jesus: Christ Jesus was victorious over the kingdom of Satan when he ascended to the wood country of Calvary and rose from the grave, thus robbing death of its sting and the grave of its victory (1 Cor 15:55-56).

Intratrinitarian Presence: The Holy Spirit strengthens and empowers those blessed by God to press on and claim what is theirs in Christ.

Proposition: God assigned believers to defeat Satan and his demons by pressing on in Christ to higher ground through the power of the Holy Spirit.

Behavioral Response: Believers must not squander the blessings the Lord has lavished on us; we must press on using our talents and resources to fulfill God's calling on our lives.

Future Condition Focus (Sermonic Eschatonics): The resurrected Lord has gone away to prepare a place for believers in the spiritual Mount Zion of heaven and will one day return to receive them to himself that where he is they will be also (John 14:3).

Remember

Zelophehad's Daughters Remember God's Promise to Their Father

The time has come for the tribe of Manasseh, the firstborn son of Joseph, to receive its territorial inheritance and allotment. The female voice has been rarely heard in the patriarchal society of the book of Joshua. But in Joshua 2, Rahab the prostitute vocalized her desire for mercy, that her life and those of her family might be spared from the inevitable destruction of Jericho by Israel's God. In chapter 15 Achsah, the daughter of the conquering Caleb, requested a field with accompanying springs of water from her father. Now, in chapter 17, the daughters of Zelophehad, a descendant of Manasseh, represent their father and request their own tribal inheritance.

About forty-five years previously, during the final and fading moments of Moses's forty-year administration, these same five daughters of Zelophehad (Malah, Noah, Hoglah, Milcah, and Tirzah) approached Moses, Eleazar the high priest, the representative leadership of the tribes, and the congregation of Israel (Num 27:1-11). They presented their unique case of a father who had not participated in the Korah conspiracy but eventually died without fathering a son, though he did have five daughters. This was problematic in the matter of the transference of his inheritance. A son was required for the passing on of the inheritance and keeping a father's name and legacy alive. Such was the issue cited when the daughters of Lot, a man who also had no sons, got Lot intoxicated and had illicit sexual relationships with him after their mother's death. They sought to become pregnant with sons of their own father so that their father's name would continue (Gen 19:30-35). Producing an heir to inherit God's promise to his family had also been the dominating thought in Abraham's mind (Gen 15:2-3; 16:1-2). Zelophehad's daughters were adamant about their father's name remaining extant among his family even though he did not have a son.

They had the courage to ask for it. Their request had been straightforward and simple: "Give us property among our father's brothers" (Num 27:4). Doing that was unprecedented; there was no record in the archives of Israel's history of anything resembling it. Like a good spiritual leader, Moses had taken this case before the Lord. He did not deny the request of the women on the basis of tradition or acquiesce to his community's feelings of patriarchy. He agreed with God. The Lord told Moses Zelophehad's daughters' request was right and proper, and they were to receive the inheritance that had been given to their uncles, their father's brothers (Num 27:7). This Old Testament episode anticipates the New Testament word of nondiscrimination in the church, the body of Christ: "There is no Jew or Greek, slave or free, male and female; since you are all one in Christ Jesus" (Gal 3:28).

They trusted God to keep his word. Moses died in the wilderness and did not enter the promised land to honor the request of these five daughters personally. They had to wait about forty-five years because their request could not be processed and executed until the new national leader was chosen to replace Moses. Under Joshua's administration, though, Zelophehad's name would indeed continue within the tribe of Manasseh, and his daughters received an inheritance among their father's brothers. The story shows God deals with people on an individual level.

What a start to the distribution of land to the families of the tribe of Manasseh! However, there must have been a feeling of detachment within the tribe of Manasseh—a feeling of incompleteness. The half tribe of eastern Manasseh's warriors would soon depart to return to their families, whom they had not seen for the seven years of military engagement. They would be leaving their western brothers and sisters to reunite with their other relatives on the east side. It had to be a bittersweet parting for the half tribes of Manasseh on either side of the Jordan. They may have felt the painful impact experienced by one who has had to say goodbye to a loved one crossing to the other side. Even when the departing one is a believer, the pain is deep and crushing. Those two half tribes of Manasseh would be equal, for they emerged from the loins of Joseph, but they would be separate.

Believers Must Remember God's Instructions

We must have the will to have sin eradicated from our lives. Like their brother Ephraim, who could not drive out the intractable and obstinate Canaanites (Josh 16:10), Manasseh had the same disappointing experience of being unable to completely expel the Canaanites (17:12-13). These verses—Joshua 15:63; 16:10; and 17:12—remind contemporary believers of how important it is to dislodge the enemy from our lives. It is not enough to be victorious in most things; our goal is to be completely victorious. We are not allowed the luxury of retaining evil in any part of our lives. All habits that do not meet the approval of God must go. All propensities, all tendencies, and all proclivities lurking in the innermost recesses of our beings that are in opposition to God's purpose in our lives must go.

We must trust the blood of Christ to empower us to live holy lives. God assigned believers to defeat Satan and his demons by pressing on in Christ to higher ground through the power of the Holy Spirit.

We must remember the example of the ancestors and choose God's ways. If we don't drive out the evil inclinations, they will pop up and drive us out of the will of God. We will be weakened by them, and our vision will be dimmed by them so we cannot confidently discern or hear clearly what God is saying to us.

Inheritance or Entitlement? The Motive Matters

The tribe of Ephraim and the half tribe of western Manasseh had received their territorial land distribution. However, they were not content with the size of the territorial space as it related to their historical greatness and tribal sizes. Listen to their dissatisfaction: "Why did you give us only one tribal allotment as an inheritance? We have many people, because the LORD has been blessing us greatly" (17:14). Is this the sound of inheritance or the sound of entitlement?

Caleb, a leader of honor, must have been greatly disappointed when he learned the person responsible for the first and only defeat in Israel's seven-year campaign and the loss of thirty-six soldiers, Achan, was from Caleb's own tribe of Judah. In the same vein, Joshua must have been uneasy when he heard the representatives of his own tribe, Ephraim, along with Manasseh, express a spirit of *entitlement.*

Joshua challenged Manasseh and Ephraim to prove their greatness by going up to the wood country, cutting down trees, clearing out paths and roads, and driving out enemies, especially the giants, in order to expand their usable territories and create more agricultural and residential space for their communities. Joshua is challenging these two tribes to embrace the extent of what they have rather than complaining about it.

The leaders of these two tribes continued to complain, though, and told Joshua the mountain and wood country were still not enough space for their people. Additionally, they lamented, the Canaanites who lived in that region of the land possessed iron chariots. In the eyes of the half tribe of western Manasseh and the tribe of Ephraim, chariots made the Canaanites superior to Ephraim and Manasseh, whose armies were comprised only of foot soldiers. However, the Lord had delivered the Israelites about forty-five years earlier at the Red Sea when Pharaoh and his army, consisting of soldiers with horses and chariots, were in hot pursuit of the Israelites (Josh 24:6). How soon we forget the abilities of the Lord! These two tribes had anxiety about giants, but Caleb had requested Hebron knowing there were Anakim (giants) on that mountain. Ephraim and the half tribe of western Manasseh had their focus on oversized people while Caleb kept his focus on God. At that time, Caleb had said to Joshua, "Now give me this hill country the Lord promised me" (14:12).

Joshua affirmed Ephraim's and Manasseh's status as the descendants of Joseph: "You have many people and great strength. You will not have just one allotment" (Josh 17:17). Once again he challenged them to be proactive and not presume on God to do the work of clearing the territorial space. They were to go to the mountain, clear it by cutting down trees, extend their territorial borders, and drive out the Canaanite opposition even though the enemy was strong and had iron chariots.

Joshua does not scold them for their ambition, for, after all, Israel was to conquer the whole land. It was not, however, to be a matter of *entitlement* but rather one of *inheritance,* for the Lord said, "I have given you every place where the sole of your foot treads" (Josh 1:3).

Joshua 15 is the longest chapter in the book. It consists of sixty-three verses. The shortest chapter in the book of Joshua is chapter 20; it contains nine verses. Chapter 16 is the next shortest chapter in the book, consisting of ten verses. The representatives of the Israel Real Estate Committee (IREC), consisting of Joshua the nation's leader, Eleazar the high priest, and the heads of each tribe, take their places before the tribes of Ephraim and Manasseh to cast lots for their territorial inheritance. Ephraim will receive its inheritance first.

Manasseh and Ephraim were not the sons of Jacob; rather, they were the older and younger sons of Joseph, the eleventh son of Jacob. Of the twelve sons of Jacob, Joseph was Jacob's favorite. In an act revealing his nepotism, Jacob made Joseph a special garment (Gen 37:3,32). Joseph's brothers resented and envied him and eventually sold him to Ishmaelite traders as a slave. He ultimately became a slave in Egypt. However, the Lord orchestrated Joseph's ascent from a prison there to the palace, and he would ride in the second chariot behind the pharaoh. The former slave became second in power in Egypt.

Manasseh and Ephraim were born in Egypt. By virtue of their father's governmental position, Manasseh and Ephraim were born into royalty and grew in prominence in Egypt. The aged Jacob and his entire family, consisting of his other eleven sons and their families, came to make their new home in Egypt, too, because Joseph, the son of Jacob and prince of Egypt, was there. Altogether, a total of seventy persons from the family of Joseph went to live in Egypt (Gen 46:27).

One day Joseph went to see his ill father, Jacob, before he died. At that time he brought his two sons, Manasseh and Ephraim, with him (Gen 48). Joseph positioned his two sons before the dying Jacob so Jacob could place his right hand on Manasseh, the elder, and his left hand on Ephraim, the younger. However, Jacob crossed his hands so his right hand was placed on Ephraim, the younger, and the left on Manasseh, the elder. The act was contrary to family order and tradition. In this case, order was important because the righthand son was the inheritor of two portions of the father's estate. Traditionally, the younger son would only receive one-third of the estate. In this case, Ephraim, the younger, would get Manasseh's share of the inheritance. Manasseh, the elder, would receive the younger son's share.

Joseph protested and said to his father, "Not that way, my father! This one is the firstborn" (Gen 48:18). The aged and dying Jacob refused to switch his hands back to the traditional order. He simply responded to Joseph by saying, "I know, my son, I know!" (Gen 48:19). Jacob was speaking out of divine revelation, not from human tradition.

God cannot be put in a traditional box. By his design, the messianic blessing did not come from the firstborn Ishmael but through the younger son Isaac, not from the firstborn Esau but through the younger son Jacob, not through the firstborn Reuben but through the fourth-born Judah. This crossing of hands scene is ended with these words:

> So he blessed them that day, putting Ephraim before Manasseh when he said, "The nation Israel will invoke blessings by you, saying, 'May God make you like Ephraim and Manasseh.'" (Gen 48:20)

The borders and boundaries and villages for the tribe of Ephraim are given according to the needs of the people. Joseph would not become a tribe; therefore, there is no tribe of Joseph. Levi as a tribe would receive no territorial inheritance. This would leave two territorial openings to be distributed. They are filled by descendants of Joseph's two sons, Manasseh and Ephraim. The borders of Ephraim are revealed in Joshua 16:5-9. Chapters 14 and 15 had described Judah's and Caleb's inheritance. Chapter 16 continues the narrative with the announcement of Ephraim's land inheritance and boundaries: "This was the territory of the descendants of Ephraim by their clans" (16:5). Chapter 16, like the previous chapter, also closes on a disappointing note: "However, they did not drive out the Canaanites who lived in Gezer. So the Canaanites still live in Ephraim today, but they are forced laborers" (16:10). The descendants of Ephraim, the son who was elevated above his firstborn brother, Manasseh, left behind unfinished business and did not achieve complete Canaanite expulsion.

The Josephite tribes wanted more. We must remember that God allotted the land with its markers and plots. Therefore, the Josephites were both criticizing God and unwilling to do their part in driving out the Canaanites who lived in their territory. They coveted, and covetousness is a sin. Haddon Robinson offered this definition: "Covetousness is wanting more of what you already have enough of."[6]

The Josephite tribes have a James and John spirit in them—a spirit of the Chief Seats Syndrome. These two tribes had a spirit of entitlement:

---

[6] I heard him say this at a conference sermon on Luke 12:16-21.

"We are a great people. We are the sons of Joseph, the savior of both the Egyptians and the Israelites in a day of famine and starvation. Joseph even interpreted the dream of Pharaoh." Regardless of their semi-royal blood, their attitude was wrong.

None of us are entitled. We are sons and daughters of inheritance. Inheritance is a grace gift. These tribes were assigned a duty, yet they had not finished their work. They did not cast out the Canaanites in their territorial plot (Josh 16:10; 17:18). There was territory available for them; however, the enemy forces needed to be driven out.

Testimony or Title? The Life Matters

Like many believers today, these two tribes need to be indicted for grumbling over generosity. They said, "How can you just give us one plot since we are a great people?" The children of Israel had a history of grumbling: at the Red Sea, before a rock when they wanted water, and about manna that was not appetizing. Currently, we are raising a generation of children who are ungrateful and who do not want to put in the sacrificial work to acquire what they want. They grab and grumble. You can never give greedy persons enough to satisfy them. They must learn to depend on the Lord because God assigned believers to defeat Satan and his demons by pressing on in Christ to higher ground through the power of the Holy Spirit.

Past experience ought to have brought present confidence in the God who had taken the wheels off Pharaoh's chariots and who would enable the Josephites to defeat the giants in their territory though they were equipped with chariots. We must trust in the God of the heretofore (yesterday), the here and now (today), and the hereafter (tomorrow; Heb 13:8). But when we struggle to do so, we must remember God, whose *helps* are greater than our *hindrances*, whose *invitations* are greater than our *intrusions*, whose *opportunities* are greater than our *oppositions*, whose *possibilities* are greater than our *problems*.

We must be willing to go to the hill country with confidence in our God. There are some areas in the hill country of our society that we need to explore as it relates to the church, family, and culture: the hill country of industry, enterprise, the neglected AIDS society, and racism.

We also must beware making too much of titles. Titles are not as important as testimonies. The Josephites were proud of their connection to Joseph because of Joseph's reputation. Undoubtedly this was a great stimulus for their spirit of entitlement. Pilate had a title, but John the

Baptist had a testimony, for Jesus called him the greatest. Pharaoh had a title, but Moses had a testimony of being the meekest man in all the earth. Ahab had a title, but Elijah had a testimony for being the prophet of God who could, through the power of God, withhold rain from falling for three and a half years. Herodias had a title, but Mary Magdalene had a testimony for being the first human being to see the resurrected Christ. The Joseph tribe *said* they were a great people. Joshua was at first called Moses's assistant (1:1). However, at the end of his life, he is called the Lord's servant (24:29). Greatness should not be announced but rather demonstrated. You've got to know who you are. We are the sons of God.

We must humbly go to the wood country, for there we find salvation. Helmut Thielicke noted that the wood of a crib and the cross are the same (*Being a Christian*, 101). Jesus went to the wood country/hill country: from the cradle to the cross. He even wore a crown of thorns (wood). He is called the carpenter's son, a craftsman of wood. Yet the carpenter's son rose with healing in his wings. He is our great salvation!

Reflections

The Christological Highway to Jesus

Just as the daughters of Zelophehad received an inheritance regardless of their gender, in Christ there is no distinction between male or female—we are one in Christ.

Fallen Condition Focus

Ephraim and Manasseh were the sons of Joseph, the vice-regent of Egypt. They were royalty. They lived in the best homes and went to the best schools. However, when the land lots were being distributed, they received an inheritance because of their relationship to Joseph. Joseph was not given a tribal allotment; rather, two tribes were named after his sons. They were not entitled to an inheritance, but it came as a gift by the grace of God. It was *chesed*. Believers are not entitled to receive God's blessings. We inherit them through grace because of our relationship to Jesus, the Son of our heavenly Father.

Reflect and Discuss

1. The daughters of Zelophehad remind us that the fulfillment of God's promises is not contingent on a person's gender. In what

other Old Testament passages are women shown dignity and favor in God's eyes?

2. In what New Testament passages do you see Jesus dignify women in a patriarchal culture?

3. What might female believers learn from the daughters of Zelophehad?

4. What might male believers learn from the daughters of Zelophehad?

5. What Christian women in your life have encouraged you to stand up and claim your inheritance?

6. The Israelites do not drive out some of the Canaanites, but they subject them to forced labor (16:10; 17:12-13). How are we similarly tempted to compromise today?

7. How is the request of Ephraim and Manasseh an arrogant one?

8. Is it always arrogant to ask for more? Why or why not?

9. Where in the church today has the "spirit of entitlement" prevailed?

10. How might we guard ourselves from entitled attitudes?

How Long Will You Delay?

JOSHUA 18–19

Main Idea: The Father has sent his Son into the world to save sinners; therefore, we must not delay in taking possession of the salvation he offers in the gift of the Spirit.

I. **The Danger of Delay in Taking Possession of God's Promises**
    A. Delay leads to complacency.
    B. Delay impacts others.
        1. The two and a half tribes were waiting to go home.
        2. The tribes needed to conquer territory so the nation could realize its promise.
    C. Delay leads to sin.
        1. Faith helps us participate in possessing what God has given.
        2. Lack of faith makes us want more or strive for less than what God has promised.
II. **Salvation Is in Christ.**
    A. Possess it.
    B. Live in it.

The Big Ten

Text: Joshua 18–19
Title: How Long Will You Delay?
New Testament Companion: Hebrews 10:37-38
Fallen Condition Focus: Like the remaining seven tribes, believers must resist the urge to be overeager to obtain their possessions that were promised by God (18:3).
The Whole Counsel of God: Joshua leads the nine and a half tribes of the west to possess their possession. This is a picture of progressive sanctification in the life of the New Testament believer. Through the power of the Holy Spirit of God, Jesus transforms the believer from glory to glory (2 Cor 3:18) until the day when each will be glorified and be like him (1 John 3:2).

193

The Christological Highway to Jesus: In the mind of God, Jesus as the Lamb of God was slain in preexistent eternity (Rev 13:8). In human history, Jesus was crucified on a Roman cross and raised from the dead by the Holy Spirit. One day he will come without delay to reign as King of kings in postexistent eternity.

Intratrinitarian Presence: The Father, Son, and Holy Spirit initiate and accomplish human salvation. As the Father sends the Son to purchase our salvation through his redeeming blood, so the Son sends the Holy Spirit as a down payment on our eternal inheritance.

Proposition: The Father has sent his Son into the world to save sinners; therefore, we must not delay in taking possession of the salvation he offers in the gift of the Spirit.

Behavioral Response: If you have not received the salvation that comes from faith in Christ, place your faith in him today. If you have received his blessed salvation, make evangelism a priority. Do not delay! Since life is temporary and like a vapor, we as witnesses must be urgent in delivering the gospel.

Future Condition Focus (Sermonic Eschatonics): When time will be no more and the terrestrial is exchanged for the celestial, the Lord will no longer delay making all things new in the new Jerusalem, where we will sing the song of Moses and of the Lamb.

The Danger of Delay in Taking Possession of God's Promises

Trading places! The casting of lots and the division of territorial plots for Judah, Ephraim, and western Manasseh took place at Israel's camp in Gilgal. Now the Israelites assemble to hear about the distribution of the remainder of the land to the final seven tribes. This must be exciting. The seven tribes will learn where they will be located, which relatives will be closest, and whether they will have to fight to possess their land. They are at Shiloh, a name that means "tranquil."

Delay Leads to Complacency

The tribes of Judah, Ephraim, and the half tribe of western Manasseh had already received their tribal land allotments. Perhaps Joshua was concerned the other seven tribes were becoming apathetic, indifferent, or lethargic. He asked, "How long will you delay going out to take possession of the land that the LORD, the God of your ancestors, gave you?" (18:3). Are we so bold? Are we willing to admonish our brothers and sisters in Christ even though it can be uncomfortable? Are we willing to take honest assessments of ourselves and face our own spiritual lethargy? The Father has sent his Son into the world to save sinners; therefore, we must not delay in taking possession of the salvation he offers in the gift of the Spirit.

Delay Impacts Others

The two and a half tribes were waiting to go home. How long? The tribes of Reuben, Gad, and the half tribe of eastern Manasseh needed an answer to that burning question because their returning home to be reunited with their families was contingent on that issue. They had made a vow to assist the brothers of the nine and a half tribes in fighting to conquer the land of Canaan and could not return to their families on the east side until there was rest from war. That is, after the nine and a half tribes had taken possession of the land, then the two and a half tribes would cross the Jordan on their way home. The fighting soldiers of the two and a half tribes had missed seven years' worth of family births, deaths, anniversaries, and special days of celebration. Furthermore, there was the ever-present need for them to be "family again" with their loved ones! They must have been saying to those who had not received their land, "Let's get this show on the road!"

The tribes needed to conquer territory so the nation could realize its promise. The promise was given, but the possession had not taken place in relation to the seven tribes who had not received their land inheritance. The seven tribes could not sit and wait for the lands to fall into their hands; they had to actively participate in receiving God's promises. Joshua told each tribe to select three men who would survey the land, divide it into seven parts, and give their report to Joshua so he could cast lots for the seven remaining tribes who had not received their territory.

Casting lots was a type of searching and seeking for the direction and will of God. This is what the apostles did in Acts 1 in their effort to replace Judas, the disciple who had committed suicide. It was a kind of holy dice rolling that would determine the boundaries and the size of the land for the remaining seven tribes. This would not be a selection by luck, chance, or fate; it would be conducted by the guidance of the Lord himself, who knew in advance how the dice would fall. Joshua likely recalled the failure in the Gibeonite deception when he and the leaders did not consult the Lord (Josh 9:14). He asks for guidance now.

Believers must not presume on God as it relates to his will. The Father has sent his Son into the world to save sinners; therefore, we must not delay in taking possession of the salvation he offers in the gift of the Spirit. We must seek his will and carry out his instructions explicitly and completely. We must be determined to obey God!

Even though God had promised the land, these three men from each tribe had to participate in obtaining what God had promised. Surveying the land was not necessary for God; God already knew what they would find in advance. Rather, it was necessary for the men so they could see the grace of God with their own eyes and the potential the land held for their dwelling and future development. They were to return to Joshua upon the completion of this assignment. This sending of spies and investigators is a thread running throughout the fabric of Israel's history. Spies and investigators were sent out, not to inform God but to see what God had already promised. God had already promised they would inherit a land flowing with milk and honey. Their position was to be that of worshipers who would give praise to God prior to the possession of the land. They were to count those things that are not yet as though they already were!

This entire process anticipates Acts 6. There the early church was experiencing a conflict. There was a report that special treatment was being given to the Hebraic widows over the Greek-speaking widows with regard to the distribution of charitable goods and services. The apostles did not attempt to manage the crisis unilaterally. Like Joshua, they let the congregation become involved. They admonished the congregation to select seven men who had the essential spiritual characteristics to handle and resolve this conflict so the apostles could keep their focus on prayer and the ministry of the Word.

These seven tribes are less prominent in size and require less land and territory, unlike the three previous tribes of Judah, Ephraim, and western Manasseh. However, these seven tribes are just as important as Judah, Ephraim, and Manasseh in the land of Canaan. In the body of Christ, likewise, the church has level ground at the foot of the cross and in the eschaton (Rev 5:9).

The first of the seven remaining tribes to receive its land allotment is Benjamin. The tribe of Benjamin, with Judah, would comprise the southern tribes that remained with Yahweh after the north abandoned him. The borders of the tribe of Benjamin are identified. Our omniscient God already knew how much territory the tribe of Benjamin needed before the territory was allotted to him. This brings to my mind the great New Testament truth, "My God will supply all your needs according to his riches in glory in Christ Jesus" (Phil 4:19).

He knows how much we need to conquer the territory we are assigned to take. He knows how much we need to take every thought captive to the lordship of Christ. He knows how much we need to turn our lives over to the King of kings and Lord of lords. He knows how much we need to make disciples and be disciples. The Father knows and has sent his Son into the world to save sinners; therefore, we must not delay in taking possession of the salvation he offers in the gift of the Spirit.

Delay Leads to Sin

Faith helps us participate in possessing what God has given. Roberta Martin's gospel song, "Even Me," could express the sentiment of the six remaining tribes after Benjamin received its land allotment. Next discussed is Simeon's inheritance. It will be located within the territorial realm of Judah. Judah had more land than it needed and, being unselfish, was willing to share with Simeon.

Simeon had a violent past. He and his brother Levi almost completely eliminated the family of Hamor because Shechem, the son of Hamor, raped Dinah, the sister of Simeon and Levi. This made Jacob and his sons odious to the surrounding nations. However, by God's grace Simeon still receives a land allotment. Grace is giving us what we don't deserve, and mercy is withholding from us what we do deserve.

Simeon is representative of all of humanity. All of humanity has sinned and fallen short of the glory of God (Rom 3:23). Yet Isaiah says, "But He was pierced because of our transgressions, crushed because of our iniquities; punishment for our peace was on Him, and we are healed by His wounds" (Isa 53:5 HCSB). Simeon needed to learn from the benevolent and magnanimous act of Judah, who was willing to give a portion of its own land to the undeserving tribe of Simeon.

This is a picture that ought to reside within the life of the church and its community. Freely we have received, and freely we must give. The spirits of greed, selfishness, and covetousness must not mark the church. Believers must remember that we are stewards, or trustees, of the manifold grace of God. We own nothing—not even ourselves. Paul tells us we are not our own but are bought with a price; therefore, we should glorify God with our spirits and our bodies, which are God's (1 Cor 6:19-20).

Christ is the ultimate example of the spirit of Judah. He came from Judah, in fact. He was born in Bethlehem within the territory of Judah. Christ not only gave up something in order to supply our needs; he gave up everything. In fact, he gave himself.

The borders of the tribe of Simeon are recorded in the book of the survey of the land of Canaan (Josh 19:2-8).

The third of these seven remaining tribes to receive its land inheritance is Zebulun. It is a small tribe, yet significant enough in God's purview to be mentioned. While not as prominent as the tribes of Judah, Ephraim, or Manasseh, it is significant enough to be mentioned in Holy Writ. Within the economy of God there is no such thing as personal obscurity. God sees all his creation and loves his creation—human, animal, and nature. The borders of the tribe of Zebulun are recorded in the book of the survey of the land of Canaan (19:10-15).

The fourth of these seven remaining tribes to receive its land inheritance is Issachar. Issachar, older than Zebulun, is thus another tribe that receives its allotment out of the usual inheritance order. The borders of the tribe of Issachar are recorded in the book of the survey of the land of Canaan (19:18-22).

The fifth of these remaining tribes to receive its land inheritance is Asher. Asher's farmland inheritance matches his blessing in Genesis 49:20: "Asher's food will be rich." The borders of the tribe of Asher are recorded in the book of the survey of the land of Canaan (19:25-30).

The sixth of these seven remaining tribes to receive its inheritance is Naphtali. The borders of the tribe of Naphtali are recorded in the book of the survey of the land of Canaan (19:33-38).

Lack of faith makes us want more or strive for less than what God has promised. The seventh and final of these remaining tribes to receive its inheritance is Dan. But the warriors of Dan failed to conquer the land assigned to them; it "slipped out of their control" (19:47; Judg 18:1). Therefore, they later went north, fought the inhabitants of Leshem, took possession of that territory, and set up residence in it (Judg 18). They changed its name from Leshem to Dan, after their progenitor, Jacob's son.

Salvation Is in Christ

Finally, all of the tribes had their land inheritance. The two tribes of Reuben and Gad and the half-tribe of eastern Manasseh would live on the east side of the Jordan River. The nine and a half tribes of Judah, Ephraim, western Manasseh, Benjamin, Simeon, Zebulun, Issachar, Asher, Naphtali, and Dan would all live on the west side of the Jordan River. There was only one thing lacking before the curtain could be dropped on the distribution of land to the proper recipients. The leader, Joshua, who had supervised and served as the overseer of this entire distribution process, had not received his land inheritance. The one who is the leader and gives the first of the plots to Caleb and then distributes the plots to the remaining nine and a half tribes is willing to receive his own inheritance last! What a mark of a great leader.

It was not unusual in the African-American home of yesteryear for the mother to cook the food, set the table, and then serve her husband the food, as well as the small children, before she would eat. Like Joshua, she led by example. Joshua is anticipating the principle of Jesus as relates to leadership: "If anyone wants to be first, he must be last and servant of all" (Mark 9:35). Joshua is not operating on entitlement like the tribes of Ephraim and Manasseh. He is recognizing leadership is a privilege and not a license for dictatorship.

Possess It

In the text, we finally have some exciting and engaging activity after a seemingly unending list of borders and boundaries for nine and a half tribes. Joshua's land was the territory of Timnath-serah within the vicinity of his own tribe, Ephraim. Joshua received what was in the will of God. "By the LORD's command, they gave him the city Timnath-serah in the hill country of Ephraim, which he requested" (19:50). However, Joshua would go beyond merely receiving Timnath-serah. He improved it by building up that territory.

Live in It

How appropriate it is to have the two faithful spies bookend these land allotments. In the land they spied out as young men, they start and finish the distributions as older statesmen, wise and discerning. The IREC (Israel Real Estate Committee) is now disbanded, for its assignment has been completed, and the information has been entered in the survey book—the historical archives of Israel. Now there is rest from war.

The Father has sent his Son into the world to save sinners; therefore, we must not delay in taking possession of the salvation he offers in the gift of the Spirit. The greater Joshua also finished his work, ascended to heaven, and sits at the right hand of the throne of his Father. There he lives to ever intercede for us.

Reflections

The Christological Highway to Jesus

Seven tribes had not received their territorial allotment. Joshua asked, "How long will you delay going out to take possession of the land that the LORD, the God of your ancestors, gave you?" (Josh 18:3). This question of how long resounds through the corridors of Israel's history.

The Jews had been asking the same question regarding the coming of the Messiah: "How long?" Christ would come after forty-two generations (Matt 1:17). The question looms large for Christians today: How long will it be before Christ returns? Christ will come again; however, the timing cannot be predicted, for even the angels do not know. As he came the first time according to the kairotic moment, he will likewise come again when the hour has come according to God's timing.

Intratrinitarian Presence

Lots were cast to determine the land boundaries. They were also cast in Acts 1 to determine who would fill Judas's vacant apostolic seat prior to the descent of the Holy Spirit. When the Spirit came, he would lead and guide the followers of Christ into all truth (John 16:13). The Spirit designated Matthias to replace Judas in the apostolic ministry.

The Whole Counsel of God

The entire process of assigning land allotments to each tribe mirrors the congregational involvement in Acts 6. The apostles did not make a unilateral decision in resolving the conflict between the Hebraic widows and the Greek-speaking widows in the matter of the daily distribution of commodities. The apostles involved the congregation. The church is an organism and not an organization—it has life within itself. The congregation must be involved in ministry. Just as the apostles would not be one-man ministers apart from the involvement of the church, so Joshua was not a one-man ministry. Joshua said to the congregation, "Appoint for yourselves three men from each tribe, and I will send them out" (Josh 18:4). Similarly, the apostles said to the Jerusalem congregation, "Select from among you seven men . . . whom we may appoint to this duty" (Acts 6:3).

Reflect and Discuss

1. What promises have been given to believers that we have yet to possess?
2. How important is the practice of worshiping God prior to receiving a blessing from him? How can this influence the way we train our children?
3. What was the purpose of casting lots in the Bible? How can contemporary believers discern God's will?
4. Joshua's confidence was not in the dice but in deity. How often do you consult the Lord in your decision making? What does your frequency or infrequency say about your dependence on deity?
5. What does it mean to presume on God's will?
6. How would you describe Jacob's son Simeon (see Gen 34)? What is unique about Simeon's inheritance?
7. In what ways are the tribes' inheritances tied to the blessings Jacob bestows in Genesis 49?
8. Joshua 19:47 tells us Dan's territory slipped out of their control. Does this negate God's promises to the Israelites?
9. Why do you think Joshua received his territory last? What kind of leadership has Joshua shown throughout the book?
10. We must remember the priest, Eleazar, played an important role in the land distribution. When have you consulted a pastor's wisdom when making a big decision? How was it helpful?

A Refuge for Sinners

JOSHUA 20

Main Idea: The Spirit of God who convicts sinners of their sin convinces them to run to Christ for refuge from eternal damnation.

I. **Cities of Refuge**
   A. Killers face the threat of death.
   B. Killers must hastily run to its gates and testify.
   C. Killers have six places of refuge.
   D. Killers can reach the cities.
   E. Killers must remain there until the high priest dies.
   F. Killers must be accepted.
II. **Churches of Refuge**
   A. Sinners face the threat of death.
   B. Sinners must be quick to run to Christ and repent.
   C. Sinners have one place of refuge.
   D. Sinners can see Christ.
   E. Sinners obtain liberty in the death of Christ.
   F. Sinners who repent will be accepted.

The Big Ten

Text: Joshua 20
Title: A Refuge for Sinners
New Testament Companion: Hebrews 8:11-16
Fallen Condition Focus: Humanity seeks to find refuge and security in persons, places, and possessions instead of in Christ alone. Peter reminds us salvation is in Jesus alone: "There is salvation in no one else, for there is no other name under heaven given to people by which we must be saved" (Acts 4:12).
The Whole Counsel of God: As the six cities of refuge were accessible from both sides of the Jordan, so the Spirit of God draws the unbeliever to Christ who gives people access to the Father in whom one finds eternal refuge without the possibility of being lost (John 10:28-29).

The Christological Highway to Jesus: Cities of refuge only protected an individual who was not guilty of premeditated murder. Christ, who was innocent, became guilty so that we, who were guilty, could be declared guiltless (2 Cor 5:21). Therefore, sinners must urgently come to Christ as their only refuge from eternal damnation.

Intratrinitarian Presence: The gracious Father who assured asylum for the innocent in cities of refuge sends his Son to assure asylum for the guilty. The Father and Son do not leave us to our own sinful devices but send the Spirit of God, who enables us to overcome sin and pursue righteousness. The Father enables us to come to the Son, our sacred refuge, for asylum.

Proposition: The Spirit of God who convicts sinners of their sin convinces them to run to Christ for refuge from eternal damnation.

Behavioral Response: Believers must not run from God as they battle sin but rather run to him, for Christ remains our only refuge and welcomes us with open arms.

Future Condition Focus (Sermonic Eschatonics): The heavenly city is the ultimate city of refuge, where believers will be near to Christ, and sin and death will be no more.

Cities of Refuge

After the land distribution was done, these questions may have claimed the Israelites' attention: "Where do we go from here?" or "What do we do when the conquest is over?" or "Is it over?"

Good leaders make thorough preparations for the leaders who will succeed them. Moses was that kind of leader. Moses's instructions prepared Joshua to effectively handle the request of the daughters of Zelophehad for an inheritance (Num 27:7; Josh 17:3-4) and set up the process for judicially addressing the matter of unintentional manslaughter (Num 35:9-34). The successor of a good leader executes a good plan left by his or her predecessor. This is the case of the Deuteronomic directions in Deuteronomy 34:9: "And Joshua the son of Nun was full of the spirit of wisdom, for Moses had laid his hands on him" (ESV). The omniscient Lord directed Moses to set up a judicial system that would address cases of unpremeditated killing. Just as there was no sacrifice for intentional sin, there was no refuge for intentional homicide.

Killers Face the Threat of Death

If someone killed another person on purpose, the law said a member of the family of the victim could avenge the death by executing the murderer (Num 35:19,21). If someone accidentally knocked a person over or dropped something on a person and he or she died (Num 35:22-23), then, there was a danger that an enraged avenger would execute the killer before a trial could take place.

Killers Must Hastily Run to Its Gates and Testify

In the case of unintentional killing, the offender could flee to the nearest of the six cities of refuge, state his purpose at the gate—where business transactions and judicial discourse took place—and request permission to enter the city by pleading his case to the elders. The elders, after listening to the testimony of the accidental killer, were to weigh its sincerity and truthfulness. If they determined the killing was unintentional, they would admit the offender into the city and provide him a place to live.

If, on the other hand, the elders determined that the killing had been committed out of hate and therefore was intentional or premeditated, they would not admit him to the city. The avenger of blood could thus take revenge on the slayer and be exonerated. The avenger's homicide would be justified.

Killers Have Six Places of Refuge

On the west side, there were three cities located in the mountainous areas. They aligned themselves with the topographical features of the area:

- Kedesh in the hill country of Naphtali (Josh 20:7)
- Shechem in the mountains of Ephraim (20:7)
- Kiriath-arba (Hebron) in the hill country of Judah (20:7)

The other three cites of refuge were located on the east side of the Jordan, the wilderness side. These three cities were in line with the topographical features of that area:

- Bezer in the wilderness on the plateau, from the tribe of Reuben (20:8)
- Ramoth in Gilead, from the tribe of Gad (20:8)

- Golan in Bashan, from the tribe of Manasseh (20:8)

Killers Can Reach the Cities

The six cities of refuge were conveniently located for the two and a half tribes east of the Jordan and the nine and a half tribes west of the Jordan. The cities were elevated and easy for the fleeing spiller of blood to locate and reach.

Killers Must Remain There until the High Priest Dies

Once receiving the favor of the elders of the city of refuge, the offender would be put under protective custody for as long as the offender remained there. There was only one way the offender could leave the city safely: when the current high priest over Israel died, then the slayer could return home without jeopardizing his life. However, if the offender left the city while the current high priest was alive, even if he only did so for a short period of time, the avenger of blood was within his rights to slay that offender.

Killers Must Be Accepted

It took a great deal of faith for those who lived in these cities to admit offenders. Though the citizens had not committed any crimes, they had to be willing to accept killers as neighbors. That was an act of grace.

Churches of Refuge

Sinners Face the Threat of Death

The cities of refuge have strong Christological connections and symbolism. Just as the killer faced the threat of death at the hand of the avenger without them, the sinner faces the threat of spiritual death in the final judgment. Because of our sin, we deserve to die and be separated from God. All human beings have sinned, whether premeditatively or unintentionally. In fact, David says in Psalm 51:5, "Indeed, I was guilty when I was born; I was sinful when my mother conceived me." Sin came through one man, Adam. Christ, the second Adam, came to become sin in order to take the penalty of sin—death—which humanity should have received (2 Cor 5:21; Rom 5:15).

Sinners Must Be Quick to Run to Christ and Repent

There is urgency in this matter. The slayer was not to be casual or nonchalant in seeking asylum from the avenger of blood. The slayer was to flee at once. The same is true for the sinner. Sin is a serious matter. Repentance for sin must be immediately employed lest physical death claim life and close the door on the opportunity for salvation. The author of the book of Hebrews said, "It is appointed for people to die once—and after this, judgment" (Heb 9:27).

Sinners Have One Place of Refuge

There were only six designated cities in which protective rules could be employed and enforced for a person who had accidentally killed an individual. If the slayer ran to a city not listed in the "Cities of Refuge Directory," the slayer would have no protection from the avenger of blood. Likewise, the only protection a person has from eternal damnation and separation from God is in Christ. Jesus said, "I am the way, the truth, and the life. No one comes to the Father except through me" (John 14:6). The proclamation of the gospel must always include the exclusivity of Christ, or it is not the gospel.

Sinners Can See Christ

Just as the six cities of refuge were conveniently located, reachable, and easy to get to, the cross of Mount Calvary is visible from the Orient to the Occident. Jesus said, "Just as Moses lifted up the snake in the wilderness, so the Son of Man must be lifted up," and "As for me, if I am lifted up from the earth I will draw all people to myself" (John 3:14; 12:32). Look and live, my brother or sister; look to Jesus Christ and live! Christ is convenient and available all over the world through the gospel as the spoken Word, the Bible as the written Word, and Christ as the revealed Word.

Sinners Obtain Liberty in the Death of Christ

As the death of the high priest over Israel announced freedom for the slayer to officially leave without penalty of death, so the death of Christ, our high priest, brought life and liberty to sinners. Not only did Christ, our high priest, die in our place through the act of substitutionary atonement (Isa 53:5) as our kinsman redeemer (Heb 2:17); he also rose from the dead for our justification (Rom 4:25). God's justice required perfection, which sinners could not produce. As a result, we receive the death penalty: "For the wages of sin is death, but the gift of God is eternal life in Christ Jesus our Lord" (Rom 6:23). Herein lies the redemptive reversal: Christ paid our wages (death), and we received his gift (eternal life) simply by trusting in him.

Sinners Who Repent Will Be Accepted

The cities of refuge were places of inclusivity for all accidental offenders who lived in the Israelite community: Hebrews, the mixed multitude who came out of the exodus with Israel, strangers and foreigners like Rahab and her family who were spared at Jericho, and the Gibeonites who were also spared due to an oath made in God's name. Schaeffer notes,

> This was entirely new to the heathen world. Here was real justice—a universal civil code that pertained equally to the citizen and the stranger. This justice was not rooted in the notion of a superior people, but in the character of God. (*Joshua and the Flow*, 199)

Cities of refuge are a picture of the church. Churches should be welcoming. Too often the church is guilty of scrutinizing certain individuals in their midst. However, Jesus called his disciples to be fishers of men. Oftentimes, we as disciples try to clean the fish before we catch them. We question their backgrounds, investigate their friends, and police their clothes when they apply for membership within the local church. We categorize them by what others say of them or of what we might know of them. We forget to apply the same grace of which we are beneficiaries. We forget that the church is a hospital for the sick. We forget our duty to disciple, not to disgrace or disqualify.

Remembering this was even difficult for the early church, who hesitated to accept the apostle Paul. Even Ananias questioned God when the Lord sent him to Straight Street in Damascus to minister to him. Later, Barnabas would have to speak up for the man and vouch for him before the other apostles would accept him at Jerusalem.

Jesus died to save sinners—regardless of their ethnicities, creeds, or colors. The eschatological kingdom mirrors the picture of soteriological inclusion. John reports, "I looked, and there was a vast multitude from every nation, tribe, people, and language, which no one could number, standing before the throne and before the Lamb" (Rev 7:9).

Reflections

The Christological Highway to Jesus

As it was necessary for the high priest to die before the manslayer could go free from a city of refuge, so Jesus our high priest had to die in order for us to be free from the wages of sin, which is death (Rom 6:23). Jesus said, "So if the Son sets you free, you really will be free" (John 8:36). We are all guilty of sin—intentionally and unintentionally. As a result, justice demands our death. Ezekiel makes this announcement: "The person who sins is the one who will die" (Ezek 18:4). However, before justice could catch us believers, we made our way to the only place of refuge, in Christ Jesus who took our penalty of sin and died, rose, and ascended to heaven, thus transferring eternal life to those who trust in him. Just as the cities were elevated and were thus places of great visibility for the spillers of blood, so the hill of Calvary is visible—even if it must be revealed by dream—from any place on this terrestrial globe.

Future Condition Focus

Just as the cities of refuge were places of diversity and inclusivity for all who lived in the Israelite community (including the mixed multitude who came out of Egypt, Rahab and her family who were spared in Jericho, and the Gibeonites), so salvation is offered to all who will believe in Christ (John 3:16; Rev 7:9).

Reflect and Discuss

1. God purposely commanded the designation of cities of refuge in his law. What does this tell us about him?
2. What does this practice tell us about humanity?
3. Compare and contrast Jesus with the avenger of blood.
4. How is Jesus like a city of refuge?
5. How is Jesus like the human high priest? How is he different?
6. What do the cities of refuge teach us about grace?
7. How can you help ensure your church is a welcoming city of refuge for sinners?

8. In what ways can church ministries help ensure the church is a safe place in which to live and grow?
9. Why was it important that the cities of refuge be easily accessible from anywhere in Israel?
10. How can one navigate the tension between grace and justice for the dignity of human life? Is one more important than the other?

Standing on the Promises of God

JOSHUA 21

Main Idea: Through the death of Christ our high priest, believers receive the promised Holy Spirit, who is the deposit guaranteeing their spiritual inheritance from God the Father.

I.   **The Lord Gives Israel the Land.**
    A. He keeps his promise.
    B. They take possession of the land.
II. **A Tribe Remembers God's Promises to Their Ancestors.**
    A. He keeps his promise.
    B. They claim their territory.
    C. Believers must do the same.
III. **The Lord Gives Rest.**
    A. To Israel
    B. To Believers

The Big Ten

Text: Joshua 21
Title: Standing on the Promises of God
New Testament Companion: Ephesians 1:13-14
Fallen Condition Focus: The tribe of Levi did not receive a land inheritance. God was their inheritance (Josh 13:33). God was enough. The formula for effectiveness in ministry for some Christian leaders is God plus something else equals success. Paul said, however, "Our adequacy is from God" (2 Cor 3:5).
The Whole Counsel of God: The God of veracity made a promise after the fall of Adam that the seed of the woman (that is, Jesus) will bruise the head of the seed of the serpent (Satan). Jesus came through Abraham, who was promised a great family, a great name, and a great land. In this chapter, God has kept his promise and given the tribe of Judah the land inheritance in which Jesus, the Son of God, will be conceived by the Spirit of God and be

born in Bethlehem as the Savior of the world. All the promises of God are "Yes" and "Amen" in Christ (2 Cor 1:20).

The Christological Highway to Jesus: The many promises God has made in the Law and the Prophets find their resounding *yes* in Christ (2 Cor 1:20), who before the foundation of the world was predestined to save us, becoming in the incarnation what he was not—human—yet remaining who he is—God.

Intratrinitarian Presence: God the Father has sent his Son as the propitiation for our sins so all who repent may inherit eternal life and receive the Holy Spirit, our down payment of that inheritance.

Proposition: Through the death of Christ our high priest, believers receive the promised Holy Spirit, who is the deposit guaranteeing their spiritual inheritance from God the Father.

Behavioral Response: Believers are to review God's faithfulness in the past to renew their faith in his faithfulness for the present and the future. In Christ the victory is already won!

Future Condition Focus (Sermonic Eschatonics): The inheritance of the priestly tribe of Levi was not cattle, land, or possessions but rather God. The future inheritance for believers who are members of the royal priesthood is God, who will dwell in the midst of his people in eternity (Rev 21:3).

Introduction

The verses in this chapter could well be resequenced to achieve greater literary clarity. It could begin with verse 43:

> So the LORD gave Israel all the land he had sworn to give their ancestors, and they took possession of it and settled there.

It could then transition to verses 1 and 2:

> The Levite family heads approached the priest Eleazar, Joshua son of Nun, and the family heads of the Israelite tribes. At Shiloh, in the land of Canaan, they told them, "The LORD commanded through Moses that we be given cities to live in, with their pasturelands for our livestock."

Finally, it could conclude with verses 44-45:

> The LORD gave them rest on every side according to all he had sworn to their ancestors. None of their enemies were able to stand against them,

for the LORD handed over all their enemies to them. None of the good
promises the LORD had made to the house of Israel failed. Everything
was fulfilled.

This reordering sequence emphasizes the practice of beginning with
the end in mind.

The Lord Gives Israel the Land

He Keeps His Promises

More than five hundred years prior to the time of Joshua 21, God had
promised Abraham and his descendants the acquisition of the promised
land (Gen 15:18). God had written a blank check to Joshua and the
Israelites before they crossed the Jordan River and made their entrance
into the promised land of Canaan. The Lord had told Joshua,

> *I have given you every place where the sole of your foot treads, just*
> *as I promised Moses. Your territory will be from the wilderness and*
> *Lebanon to the great river, the Euphrates River—all the land of the*
> *Hittites—and west to the Mediterranean Sea.* (Josh 1:3-4)

They Take Possession of the Land

It had taken Joshua and Israel seven years to conquer the seven nations
of Canaan. They fought and won all their battles except the first fight
against Ai, and even that one was won later. Now the land of Canaan was
their possession. The blank check the Lord had written Israel cleared
the Royal Bank of Heaven. God kept his promise he had made to Joshua
and the Israelites at the outset of their seven-year campaign.

A Tribe Remembers God's Promises to Their Ancestors

He Keeps His Promise

God is the God of enough! Unlike the two and a half tribes east of the
Jordan and the nine and a half tribes west of the Jordan, the Levites did not
receive a land inheritance. God was their inheritance, and God is enough!

Later, the Lord told the apostle Paul in the light of his excruciat-
ingly painful thorn, "My grace is sufficient for you, for my power is
perfected in weakness" (2 Cor 12:9). Through the death of Christ our

high priest, we believers receive the promised Holy Spirit, who is the deposit guaranteeing our spiritual inheritance from God the Father. This is especially significant in light of the fact that the Levites got to know and experience a precursor of what believers would know and experience. God has not overlooked them in the distribution of territorial allotments (Num 35:1-8). God provides for all his people. So, the Levitical tribe will receive forty-eight cities. All priests came from the tribe of Levi. However, all Levites were not priests.

Christians, like the Levites, do not have an earthly inheritance but rather a heavenly one. The Lord is their inheritance, for all believers are "a royal priesthood" (1 Pet 2:9).

They Claim Their Territory

The head of the Levite family approached Eleazar the high priest, Joshua son of Nun, and the heads of the other tribal families of Israel. They had come to Shiloh, the place of worship, and reminded the leaders of what Moses had said about granting towns as residential areas for the Levites and pasturelands for their livestock.

In Scripture, God repeatedly admonishes his people to remember not to forget. In the book of Joshua, remembering is extremely important. What God said through Moses is always recalled so the promises might be executed and completed within the present time of the Israelite occupation. So Joshua and these leaders will obey Moses, who had received the commandments and directions from the Lord.

History must always be an accounting and recounting of his-story. As believers we are granted roles in his-story by grace. Through the death of Christ our high priest, believers receive the promised Holy Spirit, who is the deposit guaranteeing our spiritual inheritance from God the Father.

This arrangement for the Levites was executed without rancor or selfishness. From the larger tribes like Judah and Ephraim to the smaller tribes of Asher and Naphtali, cities were granted to the Levites. Every tribe contributed to the needs of the Levitical tribe.

Believers Must Do the Same

Believers are called to care for one another's needs as well. In the New Testament church, everyone must contribute to the needs of the ministry and of the saints of the congregation regardless of congregational demographics. Paul instructed the members of the Corinthian church to conduct themselves in the following manner regarding giving:

> Now about the collection for the saints: Do the same as I instructed the Galatian churches. On the first day of the week, each of you is to set something aside and save in keeping with how he is prospering, so that no collections will need to be made when I come. (1 Cor 16:1-2)

Just as the tribes gave some of their allotments to the Levites, believers must be willing to share with those in need, especially those of the household of faith.

During the first hasty battle with Ai, the city appeared to have stood before Israel. Didn't the men of Ai fight the Israelites and kill thirty-six of them, thus putting them to flight and retreat? The problem was not in the men of Ai standing before the Israelites; it was in the Israelites' failure to stand before God. Believers can learn much about daily failures and successes. Our calling is to come and stand before our Father in the name of Jesus the Christ in the power of the Holy Spirit with every issue or concern in our lives. When we fail to stand before God like children before a loving, omniscient, omnipotent, and omnipresent Father, then we invite the inability to stand to attend our way. Through the death of Christ our high priest, believers receive the promised Holy Spirit, who is the deposit guaranteeing our spiritual inheritance from God the Father.

The Lord Gives Rest

To Israel

This chapter concludes on an affirming note—not one from a minor chord but from a major chord. After seven years of continuous military combat in Canaan, there was finally rest and victory for the Israelites. The victory and rest came as a result of God's fulfilling the promise he made to his people, Israel. Verse 45 provides us with one of the great texts in the whole the book of Joshua, and, in fact, the entire Bible. Not one word failed! How could a word fail coming from the one who said, "Heaven and earth will pass away, but my words will never pass away" (Matt 24:35)?

To Believers

Our God is faithful, and as Paul spoke to Titus, our God is a God "who cannot lie" (Titus 1:2). We have confidence in our inheritance because the guarantor created and owns all that is, has been, and will ever be! Through the death of Christ our high priest, we receive the promised Holy Spirit, who is the deposit guaranteeing our spiritual inheritance from God the Father.

God's promises must come to pass. As we look at our own lives, we are able to reflect on the promises of God and can testify that God has been faithful and has fulfilled every one of his promises thus far. God's faithfulness in the past gives us assurance for his faithfulness in the future. We, like the Levites, can rest knowing every need will be met. We can stand on the promises of God.

Reflections

The Christological Highway to Jesus

About five hundred years prior to the time of Joshua, God made Abraham the promise of a great land (Gen 12:1)—the land of Canaan, to which the Messiah would come. Although the family of Abraham would experience a four-hundred-year delay in captivity in Egypt and forty years of wilderness wandering, God would give them the promised land by fighting for them. Fourteen hundred years after that, Jesus would be born in Bethlehem of Judea in the former land of Canaan (Matt 2:1; Gal 4:4). No wonder the author of Joshua could declare, "None of the good promises the LORD had made to the house of Israel failed. Everything was fulfilled" (Josh 21:45).

Future Condition Focus

The Levites were the tribe from which the priests emerged. The tribe of Levi did not have a land inheritance; God was their inheritance. Believers in Christ are "a royal priesthood" (1 Pet 2:9). God is our inheritance, too, and we will live with him in the eternal homeland of the soul (Rev 21:1-3).

Reflect and Discuss

1. What was the role of the Levitical priesthood?
2. How is the priesthood fulfilled in Christ?
3. What are the implications of Messiah not having a place to lay his head as our great high priest, since the Levites were not given

an allotment as the family of priests? Is there a relationship between the two?

4. What does the Levitical inheritance teach us about God's provision?

5. Discuss other Old Testament passages in which remembering is important.

6. Discuss New Testament passages in which memory impacts the outcome for the body of Christ.

7. How should Joshua 21:44 encourage and admonish us today?

8. What does it mean to have rest on every side? How is this a reliable expectation for believers?

9. What is the difference between a contract and a covenant?

10. On this side of salvation history, how can we better appreciate verse 45?

I Don't Want No Trouble at the River

JOSHUA 22

Main Idea: Believers who are reconciled to God through the Spirit of Christ, the perfect example of how to live peaceably with one another, are given a ministry of reconciliation to others.

I. **A Crisis at the River**
    A. A pledge leads to service.
    B. Misunderstanding leads to strife.
II. **Respond Responsibly.**
    A. Never compromise convictions.
    B. Participate in collaboration.
    C. Admit culpability.
III. **Interact seeking peace.**
    A. Seek to understand.
    B. Live with one another as one body in Christ.

The Big Ten

Text: Joshua 22
Title: I Don't Want No Trouble at the River
New Testament Companion: 2 Corinthians 5:18-19
Fallen Condition Focus: The congregational life of believers is often disrupted because of a misunderstanding of intentions, which can only be clarified through honest conversation and mutual acceptance.
The Whole Counsel of God: Adam's sin brought enmity between God and humanity and among humanity itself. Jesus the Son of God brought reconciliation through his abandonment by God in order that sinners might be convicted of their sins by the power of the Holy Spirit and be brought into fellowship with God and one another.
The Christological Highway to Jesus: Since Christ who is our peace has reconciled us to himself and to God, believers are given the ministry of reconciliation made possible by the one who is the reconciler (2 Cor 5:18-19).

Intratrinitarian Presence: Because the Father sent the Son to reconcile sinful humanity to himself, one can only show grace and peace through the Spirit of Christ who is our reconciler.

Proposition: Believers who are reconciled to God through the Spirit of Christ, the perfect example of how to live peaceably with one another, are given a ministry of reconciliation to others.

Behavioral Response: Through the power of the Spirit, believers are to execute a ministry of reconciliation by refusing to rebuild the dividing wall of hostility (Eph 2:14).

Future Condition Focus (Sermonic Eschatonics): In the land where there will be no longer any sea (Rev 21:1) or river that divides or signals trouble, believers will live eternally in perfect peace with the Prince of peace in their midst.

Introduction

Nineteenth-century African American abolitionist and statesman Frederick Douglass asserted there is no progress without a struggle. He compared those who want progress without a struggle to those who want crops but do not want to plow the ground, those who want the ocean without the sound of its waves, or those who want the sky without the roar of its thunder.

In *The Reformed Pastor*, Richard Baxter asserted, "In things that are **essential**, there must be unity" (Schaff, *History*, 7:650–53). For instance, Isaiah 40:8 announces, "The grass withers, the flowers fade, but the word of our God remains forever." Holding to God's Word as our infallible truth source is a church essential. But Baxter reasons, "In things that are **non-essential**, there must be liberty." The apostle Paul gets at this idea in Romans 14:5: "Let each one be fully convinced in his own mind." Not every issue is one of right and wrong, and we must allow for that within the church family. Finally, Baxter posits, "In **all things**, there must be charity." In agreement with that, in Ephesians 4:15 Paul encourages Christians to speak the truth in love when there is a point of conflict to be addressed. When these three elements—unity, liberty, and charity—are missing in any church or religious organization, a crisis is inevitable. And it won't be fixed without a struggle. I contend believers who are reconciled to God through the Spirit of Christ, the perfect example of how to live peaceably with one another, are given a ministry of reconciliation to others.

A Crisis at the River

A Pledge Leads to Service

A crisis occurred in the twenty-second chapter of Joshua. The day began on a celebratory note. After seven years of combat in Canaan, the twelve tribes of Israel had conquered the nations in the promised land. Joshua 12 lists thirty-one nations defeated by Israel because God fought for her. The military personnel of the two tribes of Reuben and Gad and half the tribe of Manasseh who decided to set up residence on the east side of the Jordan River in the wilderness were now returning to the east side, the wilderness section of the promised land, to rejoin their families.

In Numbers 32 the two and a half tribes had made a pledge to Moses. Their military personnel would fight alongside the military personnel of the nine and a half tribes until they had gained control of the land of Canaan by conquest. These two and a half tribes had kept their word and fought alongside the nine and a half tribes for seven years. Because of their faithfulness, Joshua was sending them back to their families with valuable articles, including gold gained through the conquest of their enemies. They had been absent from their families for seven years. These men of the two and a half tribes had been away from their wives for that long period and had been absent from funerals of close loved ones and so prevented from witnessing the great accomplishments of others. Now that the battle had been fought, the victory had been won, and the territorial allotments had been assigned to the nine and a half tribes on the west side of the Jordan, these men were returning home to their families on the east side of the Jordan.

Misunderstanding Leads to Strife

The military personnel of the two and a half tribes built an impressive altar at Geliloth (i.e., Gilgal) on the Jordan River (v. 10). When Joshua and the Israelites of the nine and a half tribes heard about this, they were ready to go to war against the two and a half tribes. For seven years, the latter's military personnel had fought alongside the military personnel of the nine and a half tribes, helping them fight the Canaanite warriors. In fact, the text describes these men as brothers (vv. 3-4,7-8). Yet there was a move from celebration to what would appear to be a civil war all because the nine and a half tribes *heard* that the two and a half's military tribal leaders had built an idolatrous altar. Apparently, Joshua and the people of the nine and a half tribes thought the tribes of Reuben, Gad, and the half-tribe of eastern Manasseh built this impressive altar to offer sacrifices on it. Verse 11 says, "The Israelites heard." As a result of reports that the military personnel of the two and a half tribes and their leaders had done something against the law of Moses, the nine and a half tribes were preparing to go to war against them (v. 12). Think of it: this was a move from celebration to civil war.

Respond Responsibly

Joshua appointed Phineas the son of Eleazar the high priest to oversee an investigative committee, which consisted of a tribal leader from each of the nine full tribes and one from the half tribe of western Manasseh on the west side of the Jordan. They received their mission—a not-so-secret mission: interrogate the military personnel of Reuben, Gad, and the half tribe of eastern Manasseh who were at Geliloth where they had built the impressive altar.

Never Compromise Convictions

When the committee arrived at Geliloth, they held a tribunal and indicted the military personnel of the two and a half tribes. They accused them of being ungrateful to God who had watched over their families on the wilderness side of the Jordan for seven years. They censured them for not showing gratitude for God's protection of their families and his provision for them.

They also indicted them for building an altar to make sacrifices at a place not designated by God, in direct violation of Deuteronomy 12:5-7. Sacrifices were only to be offered at the place God had designated. In this time period, sacrifices could only be offered to him at the tabernacle at Shiloh. This committee also indicted the military personnel of the two and a half tribes for dishonoring their own place in Israelite history by failing to remain faithful even after seeing God fight for them in combat. The two and a half tribes had a sterling record but, at the end of the seven-year conquest, appeared to have forgotten their covenant and were on the verge of bringing God's wrath down on all Israel.

This passage revisits Numbers 24, where the Moabite women seduced the Israelite men, and eventually the Israelite men worshiped the false gods of Moab. As a result, God killed twenty-four thousand Israelite men (Num 24:9). Israel, in fact, was still feeling the effect of that judgment. The leaders of the nine and a half tribes reminded the two and a half tribes of Achan's sin in taking the valuables upon the fall of the city of Jericho, too, which caused God to tell Joshua that Israel lost the battle at Ai because one man had sinned. One man's sin affected the whole nation. Similarly, the action of the two and a half tribes might lead to God's judgment against the entire nation of Israel. The nine and a half tribes were afraid enough to try to protect God's name by defending his honor.

Participate in Collaboration

The delegation or committee permitted the leaders of the two and a half tribes to respond to the indictments and accusations made against them. The scene is a reminder that we should not assume the motives of our brothers and sisters before speaking with them. Believers who are reconciled to God through the Spirit of Christ, the perfect example of how to live peaceably with one another, are given a ministry of reconciliation to others. The two and a half tribes explained their actions. They had not sinned against God through ingratitude, disloyalty, or idolatry. They had not brought God's judgment against Israel by building an idolatrous altar for sacrifice. They built the altar as a memorial, in part because they knew their brothers. Their action and the reaction to it actually exposed how fickle and forgetful the Israelites were.

The two and a half tribes had enough time away from their families to see what was habitual of their nation. Earlier, for a similar reason, Joshua had ordered an altar of stones to be built once the children of Israel had crossed over the Jordan River and camped at Gilgal on the Canaan side. Joshua had instructed a man from each of the twelve tribes of Israel to go into the Jordan River that God had dammed, gather a stone, carry it to Gilgal, and pile up the stones as a memorial so when future generations of children asked, "What do these stones mean?", the response of the adults would be, "These stones were drawn out of the Jordan River to help illustrate the story of God's drying up the Jordan River and bringing the children of Israel safely to the other side."

These stones would tell the story of the history of Israel. She had succeeded because God had fought for her. The delegation of the military personnel of the two and a half tribes built an altar so the stones could communicate an important message, too: "The memorial we built at Geliloth is to recall our history so our descendants will know Canaan was conquered because we participated with the nine and a half tribes—it was a united effort." Their youngest children, after all, had never crossed the Jordan River. They could not testify to the grapes, the Jericho walls, the giants, or the hidden treasures. They were not there and could not give a first-hand testimony. These men likely recalled how terrible things had gotten when a pharaoh arose who did not know their great leader, Joseph (Exod 1:8).

Admit Culpability

The people were prone to forget. The military leaders of the two and a half tribes did not want to be written out of Jewish history. Their children in future generations might be discouraged by their distance from the western tribes and be tempted to serve other gods. Unfortunately, history would prove this a valid fear, for in a future time Israel would not know the Lord or what the Lord had done for them (Judg 2:10).

Stones have a story to tell. In Luke 19 Jesus enters the city of Jerusalem on Palm Sunday riding on a donkey. His followers cry out, "Blessed is the King who comes in the name of the Lord. Peace in heaven and glory in the highest heaven!" (v. 38). But some of the religious leaders demanded, "Teacher, rebuke your disciples" (v. 39). Jesus replied, "If they were to keep silent, the stones would cry out" (v. 40). In other words, earth itself would protest. Rocks would stop being what they were, silent witnesses, to tell what had to be known. Stones have a story to tell.

When the delegation sent by Joshua to interrogate the military personnel of the two and a half tribes heard their rationale for building this huge and impressive altar, they were pleased and satisfied (v. 30) and no longer talked about going to war against their brothers (v. 33). These certainly were national brothers, and some of them were even closer brothers. There were probably men from the half tribe of Manasseh on the east side of Jordan (wilderness) who were literal, first-generation brothers with people on the west side of Jordan (Canaan). What a tragedy it would have been for those who had been fighting side by side for seven years to now turn on each other and fight face-to-face.

Later, in Judges 20, this happened: eleven of the tribes of Israel planned to exterminate one of the tribes of Israel, Benjamin, because of a despicable event that had taken place. A concubine of a Levite was gang raped and died. The Levite cut her body into pieces and sent the bloody pieces to the tribes of Israel. Eleven of the tribes were going to wipe out the guilty tribe of Benjamin. If this had been carried to completion, then Saul would have never been the first king of Israel, and Paul would have never been the apostle to the Gentiles who wrote much of the New Testament. Both Saul and Paul were from Benjamin. How sad it would have been to have the story without their part in history. All that potential would not have been realized, for there would have been no tribe named Benjamin out of which they could be born.

A similar thing happened in our own nation during the Civil War when brothers from the north and south fought until their blood stained the battlefields of our nation and their swollen corpses covered the ground. Today we are experiencing intense idealogical battles among brothers and sisters in our churches, in our religious institutions, and in our denominational governments. This must break the heart of God. His Son died on the cross that we might live, and we are killing each other reputationally, carrying out character assassination within our associations. Can we not remember Christ's prayer in John 17:11, "Holy Father, protect them by your name . . . , so that they may be one as we are one"? First Timothy 2:5 says, "There is one God and one mediator between God and mankind, the man Christ Jesus." Believers who are reconciled to God through the Spirit of Christ, the perfect example of how to live peaceably with one another, are given a ministry of reconciliation to others. It is ours to unite with one another through listening and speaking the truth in love. It is ours to seek God for direction, not to lean on our own understanding. It is ours to seek reconciliation as recipients of the same grace through Jesus Christ our Lord!

In review, this historical narrative from Joshua 22 offers the following reflective lessons:

We are never to compromise the **convictions** we have, which are based on the full counsel of Scripture. Those scriptural convictions are essentials and not nonessentials. The church is not to engage in an effort to be politically or societally correct. For the church, the Bible transcends the Bill of Rights. Calvary's hill transcends Capitol Hill. The cross transcends the flag. God transcends our government. And the right house, "my Father's house," transcends the White House.

The church and Christian organizations must participate in **collaboration**. The delegates of the nine and a half tribes and those of the two and a half tribes collaborated. They talked even if the topics were sensitive and the matters difficult. We can no longer accept monologues—we must participate in dialogues. Although diagnoses are significant, in order to treat and transform our ailments and illnesses, we must have prescriptions.

The leaders of the two and a half tribes as well as the leaders of the nine and a half tribes were both **culpable** in some way. If the leaders of the two and a half tribes had informed Joshua and his leaders before leaving for home on the east side of the Jordan that they were going to build this impressive altar at Geliloth for the purpose of a memorial and not for a sacrifice, then Joshua and Israel would have no reason to plan to go to war against them. On the other hand, if Joshua and his leaders had inquired of the Lord in order to discern from God why the leaders of the two and a half tribes had built this altar, then they would have put themselves in position to have God reveal to them that the leaders of the two and a half tribes had built the altar for a worthy and noble purpose—that of remembrance.

The Gibeonites had been able to deceive Joshua and his leaders as to who they actually were—not people from a faraway land with moldy bread and cracked wineskins but their neighbors. Joshua 9:14 declares the Gibeonites were able to deceive them because Joshua and his leaders "did not seek the LORD's decision." Leaders of churches and Christian organizations must be willing to acknowledge their own culpability in the problems they face and not simply play the blame game. Of course, Adam was the first one to do this when he blamed God for giving him Eve and blamed Eve for giving him the fruit from the tree of knowledge of good and evil instead of blaming himself. Eve blamed the serpent for deceiving her.

Interact Seeking Peace

Seek to Understand

In Dr. Timothy George's book *Amazing Grace*, he notes that George Whitefield and John Wesley were friends yet had great doctrinal differences. Whitefield was a Calvinist who believed in limited atonement, irresistible grace, and perseverance of the saints. John Wesley believed in Christian perfection and discounted Whitefield's doctrinal postulations. However, they agreed on the importance of preaching the gospel to the lost so the lost would be saved. Their ministry made a significant impact during the First Great Awakening in America. Both decided that when one died before the other, the survivor would give a eulogy at the funeral. Whitefield died first, and Wesley gave a sterling eulogy at the funeral of his friend (George, *Amazing Grace*, 73–75).

Is it possible today for leaders of churches and religious organizations to come together and agree on matters of the highest importance when it comes to eternity while their time-related differences remain in a subordinate position? Yes, because believers who are reconciled to God through the Spirit of Christ, the perfect example of how to live peaceably with one another, are given a ministry of reconciliation to others.

Live with One Another as One Body in Christ

Rod Carew was a Major League Baseball player who played for the Minnesota Twins and the Los Angeles Angels for a combined eighteen years. He wore number twenty-nine on his jersey for both teams. In his first year in the American League, he was voted Rookie of the Year. He won seven batting championships. He appeared in eighteen consecutive All-Star Games. He won the Most Valuable Player award once and was eventually voted into the Hall of Fame. He was a great baseball player. However, in July 2016, he had a massive heart attack while playing golf. He was rushed to the hospital and revived, and his life was spared. However, his heart was damaged to the point he would need a new heart if he was to live much longer. Number twenty-nine had to wait for a heart. What a position to be in—to know you could only get a new heart and a new life through the death of someone else.

A young man by the name of Konrad Reuland played in the NFL for a few years. One day he had an aneurysm and was rushed to the hospital, only to linger in a coma for a few days. His mother Mary climbed up into his bed and laid her ear on his chest all day long because she wanted to memorize his heartbeat. She wanted to recognize his heartbeat. She wanted to know his heartbeat.

Konrad soon died. As an organ donor he had requested that his vital organs be given to an individual who was in need. Konrad was twenty-nine years old. The twenty-nine-year-old NFL football player's heart was given to number twenty-nine, Rod Carew, the Major League Baseball player. The surgery would take thirteen hours. It was successful. Rod Carew had a new heart and with it a new life. He was grateful.

After several months of recovery, he and his wife, Rhonda, would visit Mary and Ralph Reuland's home to express their appreciation for the gift of life that had come at the expense of the life of their son Konrad. Upon entering the house, Rod, an African American, married to Rhonda, a white woman, would hug Mary and Ralph, a white couple, the parents of Konrad. Rod would give Ralph a stethoscope, which Ralph immediately placed on Rod Carew's chest. He heard the heartbeat of his son, the heartbeat of a white man, in the chest of a black man. Rod Carew then gave the stethoscope to Mary, Ralph's wife and Konrad's mother. When she placed the stethoscope on Rod Carew's chest, she immediately recognized the heartbeat because she had memorized the heartbeat so she would know it when she heard it again. She knew that this was her son's heart. Emotions swelled up in her (Waleik, "MLB Legend").

One heart can join two families together for life. Two families who were different were now one. Believers who are reconciled to God through the Spirit of Christ, the perfect example of how to live peaceably with one another, are given a ministry of reconciliation to others.

This is a great story, but there is a greater story. A crisis occurred in the garden of Eden. **The reason for the crisis?** Sin! Adam and Eve sinned. **The results of the crisis?** Adam and Eve were evicted from the garden of Eden. **The responsible decision in relation to the crisis?** God would send his Son, Jesus, as the incarnate one. John 1:14 declares, "The Word became flesh and dwelt among us. We observed his glory, the glory as the one and only Son from the Father, full of grace and truth." **The redemption from the crisis?** Christ would not only come in the incarnation; he would die on the cross during the crucifixion and be raised from the dead in the resurrection. He would restore unity.

Reflections

The Christological Highway to Jesus

The memorial altar built by the two and a half tribes of the east side is called "Witness." This altar served as a symbol of the unity between the two and a half tribes on the east side and the nine and a half tribes on the west side. It represented the unity both groups had with God and with one another. This altar finds its fullest expression in Christ, whose body was broken and blood was shed to bring us into unity with himself and one another. Regarding the Lord's Supper, he said, "Do this in remembrance of me" (Luke 22:19).

Future Condition Focus

Upon completion of their promise and assignment, the military from the two and a half tribes returned to their territories on the east side of the Jordan after a seven-year hiatus from their families. They were separated from their families for a long time. But in the eternal city, there will be no more sea of separation (Rev 21:1), and there will no longer be a broken unity (divided community).

Reflect and Discuss

1. How would you describe the character of the two and a half eastern tribes?
2. How are Joshua's commands in verse 5 (love and serve God, walk in his ways, keep his commands, and remain loyal) connected to one another?
3. What are some of the essential scriptural convictions on which believers must not compromise? What are the supporting scriptural texts?
4. What are some nonessentials of the faith we can handle with liberty?
5. What does this chapter teach us about church discipline?
6. Have you had to confront a fellow believer about his or her sin? How did you do it? What was the result?
7. Why are dialogues more important than monologues?
8. How may we better foster Christian friendships across denominational lines?
9. How can you be quicker to accept culpability rather than play the blame game? Why is this important?
10. How can the church safeguard itself from terrible misunderstandings like the one in Joshua 22?

Not in Part, but the Whole

JOSHUA 23

Main Idea: Believers can trust in the promises of God because of the trustworthiness of the God who fulfilled his greatest promise in sending Christ the Messiah, who sent believers the Holy Spirit to abide in them.

I. **Joshua's Life in the Rearview Mirror**
   A. He reminds Israel about their God.
   B. He admonishes Israel to obey their God.
II. **Work from Salvation, Not for Salvation.**

The Big Ten

Text: Joshua 23
Title: Not in Part, but the Whole
New Testament Companion: 2 Corinthians 1:18-20
Fallen Condition Focus: Believers are inclined to be selective about the promises of God that cannot fail. They tend to affirm the promises that carry blessings accompanying obedience and dismiss the promises announcing curses as a result of disobedience.
The Whole Counsel of God: God kept his promise to Abraham by bringing his descendants to the land of Canaan and fighting for them until they possessed the land. God also kept his promise by sending his Son, who by substitutionary atonement purchased our salvation. The Son of God kept his promise by sending the Holy Spirit, who is the guarantee of our eternal inheritance. In the eschaton, the Son of God will appear riding a white horse and will be called "Faithful and True" (Rev 19:11).
The Christological Highway to Jesus: Christ who is the personification of truth (John 14:6) exemplifies the trustworthiness of the triune God who can never lie (Titus 1:2). Believers can stand on the promises of God in Christ because God's promises are reliable for time and eternity.
Intratrinitarian Presence: Christ is the Word who was with God and is God. All God's words are true and his promises sure. We know

228

this because the Holy Spirit illuminates Scripture to confirm in us that these words are from God (1 Cor 2:12).

Proposition: Believers can trust in the promises of God because of the trustworthiness of the God who fulfilled his greatest promise in sending Christ the Messiah, who sent believers the Holy Spirit to abide in them.

Behavioral Response: In times of harvest and famine, we are to study God's Word and remember that everything he promised has come to pass or will come to pass. Because of God's past reliability in keeping his promises, we can have present confidence in his Word.

Future Condition Focus (Sermonic Eschatonics): Christ is pictured in the eschaton as the rider on a white horse who is called "Faithful and True." So his promises can be trusted both now and when time will be no more.

Joshua's Life in the Rearview Mirror

The countdown is on. Joshua is facing the final curtain and is preparing to sing the ancient Near Eastern version of "Auld Lang Syne" with the Israelite congregation. The clock is ready to strike midnight on his service to the Hebrew nation. It is time for Joshua to say goodbye. Joshua has, in the words of the apostle Paul, fought the good fight, finished the race, and kept the faith (2 Tim 4:7).

Old age can be a blessing if the former years have been productive and fruitful and if the time has been used constructively and productively. A feeling of consolation pervades the heart and mind when one can look back and see a life lived in the service of the Lord and people. This was the case for Joshua. He has had an illustrious military career tainted only by a loss during the first battle at Ai and the deception by the Gibeonites. The war was over, and the land had rest from the fighting of battles. He had supervised the distribution of the territory of Hebron, given what was promised to Caleb, and allotted the territorial inheritances of the nine and a half tribes on the west side of the Jordan River. He had supervised the selection of the six cities of refuge and oversaw the process of choosing the land allotments for the forty-eight Levitical cities. He had organized a commission to investigate the possibility of an idolatrous act by the army of the two and a half tribes as they returned home to the east side of the Jordan River. Joshua had received his territorial plot, Timnath-serah, developed the land, and built a retirement home in the mountains of Ephraim. He has had a fruitful life and a fulfilling ministry. Joshua 11:15 provides a concise and authentic description of his ministry to Israel: "Just as the LORD had commanded his servant Moses, Moses commanded Joshua. That is what Joshua did, leaving nothing undone of all that the LORD had commanded Moses."

He Reminds Israel about Their God

There was only one thing left for Joshua to do before he transitioned from time to eternity: rehearse the history of what the Lord had done for Israel from the days of Abraham to Israel's present state as a nation carrying the ownership deed of Canaan. Joshua needed to remind Israel of their need for continued faithfulness to God.

Last words are to be heeded intensely. If people are ever truthful, they are most likely to be truthful when they are knowingly giving their last words. Parents will often give their last words tearfully yet with a sense of hope as they admonish their children to avoid pitfalls and to seek that which really matters in life. This is what Joshua does.

Joshua is not just old. He is very old. He is "advanced in age" (v. 1). He was born in Egypt as a slave and experienced the Egyptian bondage. He heard the whips of the pharaoh's taskmasters on the backs of his people. He also saw the great wonders of God. God opened the Red Sea and the Israelites crossed on dry ground into the wilderness on the other side. He saw Pharaoh's pursuing army drown. He witnessed God's taking the waters of Marah, which were unfit for human consumption, and making them sweet when Moses threw a tree into those waters. He observed God's delivering quail into snatching distance so the children of Israel could have not only manna but also meat. He could testify of the power of God executed in the defeat of the Israelites' enemies, the Amorites, during their trek in the wilderness. He attended the memorial service of Moses when God buried Moses in an unmarked tomb. He had heard this announcement from the lips of God: "Moses my servant is dead" (1:2). He had received the commission following Moses's death to lead the people across the Jordan River to possess the land God had promised to their ancestors, Abraham, Isaac, and Jacob. He was probably also an octogenarian at the time of Caleb's request and proclamation: "Here I am today, eighty-five years old. . . . Now give me this hill country the LORD promised me on that day" (14:10,12). Joshua will die at age 110 (24:29). So here Joshua calls a leadership meeting of all Israel ("all Israel" is likely a representative group of the congregation): elders, tribal heads, judges, and officers (23:2).

Joshua reviews Israel's history as their national leader by giving an account of his stewardship among them. Reflection can have a redemptive trajectory. It enables one to look back productively so one can look forward redemptively. It suggests that the God who has been faithful in the past is faithful in the present and will be faithful in the future. Therefore, he can be trusted and must be praised. Joshua is not bragging or expressing arrogance when he says, "See, I have allotted these remaining nations to you as an inheritance for your tribes, including all the nations I have destroyed, from the Jordan westward to the Mediterranean Sea" (v. 4).

These personal expressions follow what God had done to make Joshua's leadership and Israel's success possible: "Because it was the LORD your God who was fighting for you" (v. 3). There were still people groups Israel had not expelled, yet Joshua was so confident in the God who fights for Israel that he divided the land for Israelite possession even before those nations were expelled from Canaan (v. 4). Joshua speaks out of his faith in God who said to him,

Now you and all the people prepare to cross over the Jordan to the land I am giving the Israelites. I have given you every place where the sole of your foot treads, just as I promised Moses. (1:2-3)

Remember, believers can trust in the promises of God because of the trustworthiness of the God who fulfilled his greatest promise in sending Christ the Messiah, who sent believers the Holy Spirit to abide in them.

He Admonishes Israel to Obey Their God

Joshua rehearses in the Israelites' hearing the imperative God gave to him during the day of his calling: "Be very strong and continue obeying all that is written in the book of the law of Moses, so that you do not turn from it to the right or left" (23:6; see 1:6-7). Joshua knows Israel had a propensity toward idolatry. He could never forget the day when Israel, who had miraculously been delivered from four hundred years of Egyptian bondage by the Lord, danced around a golden calf constructed by Aaron the priest while Moses was communing with God on Mount Sinai.

Joshua understands the alluring potential the nations surrounding
Israel can have on them to dislodge them from their faithfulness to God.
The surrounding peoples were committed to polytheism; they believed
in many gods. Joshua thus reminds Israel what Moses said to Israel and
what God had said to Moses: "Do not have other gods besides me. . . .
Do not bow in worship to them, and do not serve them" (Exod 20:3,5;
Deut 5:7,9). They were not even to associate with these nations because
these nations would have the tendency to draw them away from God.
They were to be a witness to the nations without fraternizing with the
nations because light has no relationship with darkness. This was especially pertinent because Israel had failed to drive all the pagan locals
from their midst.

Joshua admonishes his nation not to invoke the names of foreign
gods or to swear by their gods. They must not serve or bow down to
such gods. One Hebrew word for *idol* means "no thing" or "worthless"
(Lev 19:4). It would be ludicrous to bow down to a nothing god who had
hands but could not rescue, feet but could not run or walk to anyone in
order to deliver them, ears but could not hear the plea of the worshiper,
or eyes but could not see the plight of the servant (Ps 115:4-8; Isa 45:20-
22). The God of Abraham, Isaac, and Jacob, however, could hear, see,
and rescue them from any situation. He had already proven this.

Joshua warns the Israelites that God's continued fighting for them is
contingent on their continued obedience to him. If Israel intermarries
with the idolatrous nations who remain in the land, the Lord will no
longer expel those peoples but will allow them to bring incredible pain
and discomfort to Israel. God will turn the tables on Israel, so they are
evicted from their promised homeland in Canaan (v. 14).

You and I need to hear the same admonition as the Israelites. We
live as the light in darkness. Darkness must not snuff out our light;
therefore, we should not fraternize with those likely to lead us astray.
Believers can trust in the promises of God because of the trustworthiness of the God who fulfilled his greatest promise in sending Christ the
Messiah, who sent believers the Holy Spirit to abide in them. Believers
must make the decision to obey God and abandon all imposters.

Work from Salvation, Not for Salvation

Obedience to the Lord is not to be a laborious effort but rather a loving service (v. 11). In light of what God had done for Israel, Joshua

implores Israel to be careful to love the Lord their God. This is a challenge intended to move Israel to love God beyond duty so they love him out of delight, beyond a job so they love him out of joy, and beyond a burden so they love him out of a sense of blessing. The proper response to God for all he has done is to love him. This is not love coerced or even demanded. It is love that willingly, gratefully submits. It is love like a spontaneous reaction to the grace of God.

Joshua stands as a character witness for God (not that God needs one). Joshua, as he is "going the way of all the earth" (v. 14), reminds the leaders of the truth they already know: everything God has spoken regarding the nation of Israel has come to pass. Not one word spoken by the divine was left unfulfilled. Once again, knowing Israel was at high risk of contracting amnesia or, at best, had a short memory, Joshua calls to their attention the fact that God not only deposits to their account, but he can also withdraw from it. He owns the bank. God's Word in Hebrews 12:4-11 tells us he chastises us, his children by faith in Christ, because he loves us. He does not love to chastise us, but his love for us obliges him to discipline us. He blesses us and punishes us just like the good Father he is. God gives Israel the land, but he will permit them to be destroyed in the land if they disobey (Josh 23:15). Of course, that happens in 587 BC during the destruction of the temple in Jerusalem and the deportation of its people to a seventy-year exile in Babylon. Abandoning the covenant of God would result in the God of the covenant abandoning them. Fourteen hundred years after Joshua, Paul would write an appropriate word for the church: "Don't be deceived: God is not mocked. For whatever a person sows he will also reap" (Gal 6:7).

In the final analysis, even though Israel disobeyed and was eventually evicted from the promised land, God would not ultimately destroy them completely because he promised salvation would come out of the tribe of Judah. Exiles from Judah, along with others, finally came out of Babylonian captivity and reentered the promised land. About five hundred years later, a baby was born in Bethlehem of Judah who would be the Savior of the world. God saved Judah in order to keep the promise he had made about two millennia earlier.

However, we must not presume on the covenantal love of God. Salvation should produce works; works cannot produce salvation. Therefore, our works of love and service for God must be an expression not of our working *for* salvation but rather working *from* salvation. Our love for God must result in obedience. Believers can trust in the promises of God because of the trustworthiness of the God who fulfilled his greatest promise in sending Christ the Messiah, who sent believers the Holy Spirit to abide in them.

We love him because he first loved us. Joshua says a word the church needs to hear today: there is danger in neglecting God after being blessed by God. Therefore, our lives must scream reminders of the goodness of God. This chapter, in fact, screams of God's goodness. It is full of God. Joshua did not finish the job. Jesus Christ would finish the job (John 19:30). The Holy Spirit empowers the Israelite soldiers so one of them chases a thousand. The Holy Spirit empowers us to do equally great things for God as he reminds us of what God has done for us.

Reflections

The Christological Highway to Jesus

Joshua rehearsed the history of Israel by telling of the mighty works of God done on behalf of Israel to bring them from the time of Abraham, a wandering nomad, to their present residence in Canaan. This is the story of Israel—the story of God fighting for them throughout the times of the patriarchs, judges, kings, and prophets. Similarly, God fought our battles in human history and won through the cross of Christ.

Future Condition Focus (Sermonic Eschatonics)

Heaven will be about the story of the Lamb who receives glory because he was crucified on our behalf and is worthy of praise, for he is not only the lamb who was slain but also the lion of the tribe of Judah who conquered.

Reflect and Discuss

1. What is the purpose of a farewell address?
2. What are your favorite famous last words? What are your favorite last words in Scripture? Why?
3. How can reflection be redemptive? Have you experienced redemptive reflection?
4. Compare and contrast Joshua 23 with Joshua 1. How has Joshua changed? How has God remained the same?

5. What or who are today's believers tempted to make into gods and worship? How can believers avoid this great sin?
6. What is the difference between loving God out of joy and loving God out of obligation?
7. God's promises not only include blessings but also curses. What is Joshua's purpose in verse 16?
8. Does sin still bring consequences even if one is a believer? Why or why not?
9. How does it make you feel to know not one word spoken by God will be left unfulfilled?
10. How can the church proactively prevent herself from neglecting God's instructions?

Lest I Forget

JOSHUA 24

Main Idea: Jesus the greater Joshua calls believers to a renewal of worship and service to God through the power of the Holy Spirit.

I. **Shift When God Moves.**
   A. From Shiloh to Shechem
   B. From peace to war
   C. From war to peace
II. **Trust God's Plan.**
   A. Joshua recounts God's faithfulness to Israel.
   B. Israel presents herself to God.
   C. Joshua warns Israel to eradicate idol gods.
III. **Carefully Consider Your Response.**
   A. Israel's response
   B. Believer's response
   C. To Christ our Prophet, Priest, and King
   D. Look forward to living at peace with the King of glory.

The Big Ten

Text: Joshua 24
Title: Lest I Forget
New Testament Companion: Revelation 2:1-7
Fallen Condition Focus: Believers have a disposition toward seeking to worship and serve the Lord half-heartedly instead of completely like Joshua did (Josh 14:8,9,14). God will not tolerate neutrality (Rev 3:16). We must choose to serve the one who has chosen us or choose not to serve him. There is no middle ground.
The Whole Counsel of God: Because of sin, we are not able to serve God in our own strength. Therefore, in the incarnation, God in Christ had to become sin so that we as sinners might become the righteousness of God (2 Cor 5:21) and be empowered by the Spirit to worship and serve God in sincerity and truth.

The Christological Highway to Jesus: Christ, who is our greater Joshua, was anointed by the Holy Spirit to faithfully serve his Father. In fact, the first recorded words of Christ at age twelve are, "Didn't you know that it was necessary for me to be in my Father's house?" (Luke 2:49). Among his last words on the cross were, "It is finished" (John 19:30).

Intratrinitarian Presence: We can only worship and serve the Father through faith in the Son by the sanctifying power of the Spirit.

Proposition: Jesus the greater Joshua calls believers to a renewal of worship and service to God through the power of the Holy Spirit.

Behavioral Response: Christians are to live in sold-out service to the Lord. God commands us not to serve other gods but rather to daily choose to worship and serve the One who has chosen us.

Future Condition Focus (Sermonic Eschatonics): Believers who have faithfully served our Lord on earth will faithfully serve and worship him in heaven (Rev 7:14-15).

Shift When God Moves

From Shiloh to Shechem

There has been a shift. The venue has shifted from Shiloh to Shechem. Joshua gives his State of the Union address to the representatives of Israel's tribes and the leaders of the nation. Shechem holds a great deal of historical significance for Israel. It was the first place in Canaan where Abraham arrived after his long journey from Mesopotamia. At Shechem, Abraham built an altar. At Shechem, Joshua held a covenant renewal ceremony for Israel after their rebound from a previous loss to Ai. Now Joshua gathers the congregation en masse along with its leaders to give his parting words, his farewell address, at Shechem.

Joshua and the congregation presented themselves before God (v. 1). Joshua reiterated Israel's history and connected it to their destiny. He knew the history well. He is not merely reading a historical book or document. They *are* their history, and they have been living in his-story. Joshua cannot be recounting boring facts, dates, and names. He is a walking historical vault. He is not a secondhand reporter of their history. He and Caleb serve as eyewitnesses from their past to the present grace of God in their story. He did not need to say, "I heard." He can say,

"I know; I was there." God had granted Joshua and Caleb life when their contemporaries died in the wilderness. They lived to tell the story, and Joshua, the people's leader, reminds them, once again, of their need to remember.

Believers must be eyewitnesses who tell the stories of what God has done in their lives. Believers must not rely on Mama's story or Daddy's story. They cannot rely on Grandmother's story or Grandfather's testimony. God does not offer a salvation family plan, and he has no grandchildren—only children. Each believer must know God personally and individually for himself or herself.

Hearing their history must have been like walking through the annals of time for Israel. The middle-aged and senior adults would have been familiar with this story Joshua tells. The older male adults would have been less than twenty years old when they reached the promised land. The youth and young adults needed to become more intimately acquainted with their national history.

Joshua reminds all assembled at Shechem that Israel's history did not begin with monotheism but with a polytheistic man—Abraham, the son of Terah, the idolator. Abraham received his divine call out of that at Ur of the Chaldeans in Mesopotamia. He immediately answered the call and traveled to Canaan. Abraham, the father of our faith, too, is known for his immediate obedience. What a fitting way to root the family story! Abraham would have a son of promise, Isaac. Out of Isaac came Jacob. That man's descendants journeyed from Canaan to Egypt. The presence and prominence of Joseph, son of Jacob, as the vice-regent of Egypt sustained the Egyptians during a devastating famine. In the end, Joseph enabled his own family to survive as well.

From Peace to War

At the end of four hundred years of Hebrew slavery in Egypt, God used Moses of the tribe of Levi to lead Israel from Egyptian bondage through the miraculous highway God formed by parting the waters of the Red Sea. Joshua, who succeeded Moses, caused Israel to remember how God protected them against the prophet Balaam's attempt to destroy them. Balaam had been hired by King Balak of Moab to curse them. Instead, Balaam blessed Israel.

When making note of the crossing of the Jordan River and the battle at Jericho, Joshua is too modest to include his name in these two historical moments. He simply says, "*You* then crossed the Jordan and came to Jericho. The people of Jericho . . . fought against *you*" (v. 11 HCSB; emphasis added). Joshua lists the Israelite opposition in the promised land: the Amorites, Perizzites, Canaanites, Hethites, Girgashites, Hivites, and Jebusites. He lists the two Amorite kings on the wilderness side of the Jordan River who strove against Israel: Sihon and Og.

From War to Peace

Joshua ends the necessary and nostalgic historical journey with a heart-throbbing and emotionally engaging conclusion designed to move both head and heart. Speaking for God, he says, "I gave you a land" (v. 13).

Trust God's Plan

Joshua Recounts God's Faithfulness to Israel

Joshua's brief summary of Israel's history served one dominating purpose: to showcase from Israel's history the sovereignty of God that brought them to their destiny! Joshua uses the first-person singular pronoun *I* for God as he explains Israel's past deliverance and present placement (emphasis added throughout):

- "*I* took your father Abraham from the region beyond the Euphrates" (v. 3).
- "To Isaac *I* gave Jacob and Esau" (v. 4).
- "*I* gave the hill country of Seir to Esau as a possession" (v. 4).
- "*I* sent Moses and Aaron" (v. 5).
- "*I* defeated Egypt by what *I* did within it" (v. 5).
- "Afterward *I* brought you out" (v. 5).
- "When *I* brought your ancestors out of Egypt" (v. 6).
- "Your own eyes saw what *I* did to Egypt" (v. 7).
- "*I* brought you to the land of the Amorites" (v. 8).
- "*I* handed them over to you" (v. 8).
- "*I* annihilated them before you" (v. 8).
- "*I* would not listen to Balaam" (v. 10).
- "*I* rescued you from him" (v. 10).
- "*I* handed them over to you" (v. 11).
- "*I* sent hornets ahead of you" (v. 12).

And, finally, verse 13 says, "*I* gave you a land you did not labor for, and cities you did not build, though you live in them; you are eating from vineyards and olive groves you did not plant" (emphasis added).

Paul echoes this sentiment in 1 Corinthians 4:7. As commanded by God, he asks the sobering questions, "For who makes you so superior? What do you have that you didn't receive? If, in fact, you did receive it, why do you boast as if you hadn't received it?"

Verse 13 provides the reason for Israel's present and future prominence: God! Israel can't take any credit for their ascent from Ur of the Chaldees to Canaan. God and God alone accomplished it.

Israel Presents Herself to God

Israel received the gift of *chesed*—God's unconditional, loyal, covenant love. Israel's response to *chesed* must be obedience. So, Joshua said, literally, "And now" (v. 14). This is the phrase Joshua heard from God after Israel mourned the death of Moses for thirty days (Deut 34:8). Then the Lord said to Joshua, the newly appointed leader, "Now you and all the people prepare to cross over the Jordan to the land I am giving the Israelites" (Josh 1:2). God calls his people to respond to his *chesed*, or grace, through the "now" of obedience in unquestioned and unambiguous sincerity and truth. Such devotion to God would be indicated by the putting away of the gods that Abraham's birth family served on the other side of the Euphrates River as well as the idol gods Israel served in Egypt.

Joshua Warns Israel to Eradicate Idol Gods

It is evident some Israelites were still attached to these idol gods because Joshua had to tell them, "Get rid of the gods your ancestors worshiped" (v. 14). Why were they still transporting idol gods? The Lord prohibited idol gods in the Decalogue:

> Do not have other gods besides me. Do not make an idol for yourself, whether in the shape of anything in the heavens above or on the earth below or in the waters under the earth. Do not bow in worship to them, and do not serve them; for I, the LORD your God, am a jealous God. (Exod 20:3-5)

In the light of all God had done in Israel's history to get them to their present destiny, their idolatry was a slap in the face of the sovereign

One. In fact, experience should have made them destroy any idol gods their fathers served on the other side of the Euphrates River and in Egypt. At the foot of Mount Sinai, Aaron, the first high priest, fashioned the golden calf from the earrings of the Israelites. This golden calf was an Egyptian idol. Aaron said to them, "Israel, these are your gods, who brought you up from the land of Egypt!" (Exod 32:4). Punishment fell swiftly. They should have learned.

Carefully Consider Your Response

Joshua presented a ludicrous proposition to Israel. He said, "If you think it is evil or the improper choice to serve the Lord, I have this alternative for you: choose today to either serve the idol gods your fathers served in Mesopotamia or the idol gods of the Amorites in the land where you are now dwelling" (author's translation). The choice must be an immediate one—the idolatry issue will not go away, and there is no time to mull it over. "Today" foreshadows the sentiments of the author of Hebrews: "Today, if you hear [God's] voice, do not harden your hearts" (3:15). Joshua is postulating that Israel's history clearly demonstrates that neither the gods of Ur of the Chaldeans nor the gods of Canaan are able to defend themselves against the God of Israel. Certainly, they were incapable of defending the Israelites against God. They couldn't even defend the Israelites against other nations. To choose either group of idols over Israel's God would be to choose certain loss and failure.

Joshua now transitions from the national to the personal: "But as for me and my house, we will serve the LORD" (v. 15 ESV). In modern days, this statement is etched in wood, written on the finest of paper, and hung as placards and posters on the walls of homes. But these words are meant to express the heartfelt conviction of true believers who are fully surrendered to serving the Lord. The Hebrew word translated "serve" or "worship," in fact, is the pulsating heartbeat of this passage. It is found sixteen times in this chapter: in verses 2, 14a, 14b, 14c, 15a, 15b, 15c, 15d, 16, 18, 19, 20, 21, 22, 24, and 31.

Israel's Response

The Israelites considered it nonsense to even suggest a possibility of their returning to idolatry and abandoning their service to the Lord. God was their deliverer from Egyptian bondage, sustainer, preserver, and miracle worker through their trek in the wilderness to the promised land. To paraphrase their answer to Joshua, "Don't even give a single thought to us not serving the Lord but serving idols instead. We will stand firm and sure in obedience!"

Joshua responds with a seemingly inappropriate and inaccurate statement about God's character and action. God is a God of long-suffering, mercy, and second chances. Israel's history has proven this. Throughout their history, Israel has been the beneficiary of God's benevolence, forgiveness, and restoration. But Joshua tells them they will not be able to serve the Lord! He even tells them God will not forgive their sins and transgressions, though God has forgiven them for past generations. Hadn't he just told the story?

However, Joshua was not talking about permissibility. He was talking about the nature of God and the nature of this people. God would not tolerate unholiness and insincerity because he is a holy and jealous God. Holiness is the essence of who God is. God is wholly other, righteous and just. He is wholly other, merciful and mighty. He is wholly other, forgiving and punishing. God is set apart from everything unholy, because he cannot tolerate sin. Joshua aims to prevent Israel from making an emotionally charged decision. Joshua knows how fickle Israel has been through the years. He is telling their story, his story, as a crucial part of his-story, and their past failure to obey and their failure to rid themselves of idols do not bode well for their future obedience.

After the deaths of Joshua and the elders who survived him, another generation will arise that does not know the Lord or what he has done for his people. They will resort to worshiping idol gods (see Judg 2:10-11). Joshua knew his people. Joshua knew Israel's repentance would not be sincere and their service to God would not be genuine.

The people of Israel continued to contend with him. "No, but we will serve the Lord" (v. 21 ESV). Joshua eventually acquiesces and says, "You are witnesses against yourselves that you have chosen the Lord, to serve him" (v. 22 ESV). Joshua challenges them to remember they heard themselves with their own ears and would be prosecutors of themselves if they did not live out their commitment to worship and serve the Lord! Vows are not meant to be broken; vows are meant to be kept. God even says in Ecclesiastes 5:5 it is best not to make a vow if one is not going to keep it.

Knowing Israel's history, Joshua's warning, and the people's response, one cannot help but wonder how Israel soon forgets the loving-kindnesses and tender mercies of her God and falls into diverse temptations and idolatry. Israel's future will be filled with disobedience and a refusal to serve the Lord. She is an unfaithful bride to a perfect husband. She is an ungrateful child to a faithful parent. She is an obstinate participant in God's holy plan.

Believer's Response

God knows the hearts of his people and knows we can be sincere in what we say when the threatening moment is not near. However, when the tension has mounted and the threat is standing before us believers, we become like Peter, who in the safety of the upper room made the great commitment never to deny the Lord but weakened in that commitment when he stood in the courtyard of the high priest's residence. Peter denied the Lord three times because of the possibility of human punishment he would receive if he confessed his relationship to Jesus.

Believers typically do not have the greatest track records of keeping our commitments to God when the pressure is on and temptation is before us. Thank God for making a way of reconciliation! Jesus the greater Joshua calls believers to a renewal of worship and service to God through the power of the Holy Spirit. The Israelites would have been better served if they had said, "*As the Lord helps us*, we will worship the Lord." So will we; however, we have the Holy Spirit and must cultivate obedience from hearts of love and gratitude. Good intentions are not good enough. We need to be—and we have been—empowered with strength that is beyond our strength.

The Israelites accept Joshua's sobering warning. Once again, Joshua tells them to put away their foreign gods, which were presently among them, and draw near to their God, the God of their fathers Abraham, Isaac, and Jacob. They were not perfect, but their hearts were faithful. They put off sin, struggled with sin, and put on obedience through faith.

This is Pauline language. Paul will admonish the Roman Christians in Romans 13:11-13 to put off darkness and put on light: "The night is nearly over, and the day is near; so let us discard the deeds of darkness and put on the armor of light" (Rom 13:12). There is no room for compromise in Christian living (see Rev 3:14-19). God chose lowly Israel and is faithful to her as he blesses all nations through her. He expects similar dedication, determination, and attestation from believers. We must put away sin and put on righteousness.

Jesus tells the story of a house inhabited by a demon. The demon was evicted, and the house was cleaned and garnished. However, the house remained empty with no occupant. The evil spirit, after staying in the dry places, sought residence back in the empty house and brought seven more demons to reside in it. The last state of the house was worse than the first (Matt 12:43-45). Putting away idol gods must be accompanied by putting on faithfulness and service to the Lord. It cannot be a mere act; it must be true worship.

The congregation finally understood how worshiping and serving the Lord are inextricably connected to obeying the Lord: "So the people said to Joshua, 'We will worship the LORD our God and obey him'" (v. 24). They committed to keep on obeying and to keep on worshiping and serving. Believers do not give their right hands of fellowship to the preacher and then go sit down and wait for glory. No! We work while it is day because the night will come. Joshua drew up a covenant, a statute, and an ordinance with Israel at historic Shechem. He wrote the words of their commitment in the book of the law of God. He took a large stone along and placed it and the written document under the oak tree by the sanctuary of the Lord. (This was probably a well-known tree in Shechem with significant historic value.) The stone would serve as "state's evidence" or a prosecuting attorney against Israel in the future if and when Israel denied their God and turned to serve idol gods.

Stones are significant in the history of Israel and even of the church. Jesus is the stone that the builders rejected and that became the chosen and honored cornerstone. The stone at the garden tomb in Jerusalem was rolled away, revealing the empty borrowed tomb, for Jesus is our risen Savior.

After this ceremony, Joshua pronounced the benediction, and the people departed to the places of their inheritance.

This chapter is filled with funerals. The book of Joshua, in fact, opens with death: "After the death of Moses the LORD's servant, the LORD spoke to Joshua son of Nun, Moses's assistant" (1:1). It also concludes with death. Joshua, the successor of Moses, dies at age 110. He began his career as "Moses's assistant" (1:1), but Joshua ends his ministry with the designation "the LORD's servant" (24:29). This designation is eternally attached to Joshua. It transitions from time to eternity. Being Moses's assistant is a time-conditioned designation that has an expiration date. Being the Lord's servant carries with it a timeless declaration, for the Lord will say to those who have been faithful in service, "Well done, good and faithful servant!" (Matt 25:21).

Joshua is buried on his homestead of Timnath-serah, the place of his inheritance. Israel was faithful to serving God throughout all the years of Joshua's leadership (v. 31). There was not one incident of Israel breaking its covenant with God through an idolatrous act. Furthermore, Joshua's leadership influenced Israel even after his death. Israel continued to remain faithful throughout the administrative leadership of the elders who had served with Joshua and who witnessed the mighty works of God done on Israel's behalf.

To Christ Our Prophet, Priest, and King

There is a trinity of deaths in this chapter that approximate in three persons what Christ simultaneously embodies within himself—the roles of prophet, priest, and king. The book of Joshua is the first of the Former Prophets. As such, Joshua can be seen as a prophet. He dies at 110 years of age in this chapter. Like Joshua, Jesus can be seen as a prophet. Human prophets only speak the word of God; however, Jesus is the Word of God.

In this chapter Eleazar, the high priest, who was the son of the first high priest, Aaron, dies (v. 33). Like Eleazar, Jesus can be seen as a priest. Human priests bring an offering for the people to God and intercede for the people to God. However, Jesus is the offering for the sacrifice, too. John the Baptist articulates it this way: "Look, the Lamb of God, who takes away the sin of the world" (John 1:29). Additionally, he is our high priest who has ascended into heaven (Heb 4:14-16).

In this chapter Joseph, who died long ago in Egypt, is interred in the promised land (v. 33). He had demanded that his bones would not be left in Egypt but would be carried to and buried in the promised land. Joseph was buried at Shechem. Joseph was second in command in Egypt and rode in the second chariot behind the pharaoh. He was the vice-regent of Egypt. Joseph was a prototype of a king. A king rules and reigns over government. Like Joseph, Jesus can be seen as a ruler within a domain (kingdom). However, Jesus is the King of kings and Lord of lords. He reigns not only on Earth but in heaven and over hell. Isaiah 9:6 says, "And the government will be on his shoulders."

Jesus simultaneously embodies all three of these offices and holds the three offices in tension.

Look Forward to Living at Peace with the King of Glory

One day, Jesus Christ will raise Joshua, a prophet type, Eleazar, a priestly type, and Joseph, a kingly type from the dead, for he is the resurrection who puts death to death. They will be resurrected to worship the one who is the faithful prophet, holiest priest, and King of kings. One day, in the new Jerusalem, they will walk the streets of gold in the homeland of their souls.

One day, in fact, we modern believers will worship with all saints because Jesus the greater Joshua calls believers to a renewal of worship and service to God through the power of the Holy Spirit. Faithful servants will hear, "Well done!" Well done for persevering through the rain. Well done for running on through the rain. Well done for learning and recounting the history of the ancestors of our faith. Well done for studying the Word made understandable through the Spirit. Well done for teaching others the way to the cross! Well done, good and faithful servants, well done! The pronouncement will be made in the Land of No More—no more sorrow, no more pain, no more suffering, no more tears. All God's children will hear, "The kingdom of the world has become the kingdom of our Lord and of his Christ, and he will reign forever and ever" (Rev 11:15). Amen! Amen!

Reflections

The Christological Highway to Jesus

The theocratic offices of Christ—prophet, priest, and king—are reflected in the ministries of Joshua, Eleazar, and Joseph. Joshua is the first book of the Former Prophets in the Hebrew Bible. Therefore, Joshua can be seen in light of a prophet who *speaks* the Word of God while Jesus as a prophet *is* the Word of God. Eleazar is a high priest who brings offerings and sacrifices to God on behalf of the people. Jesus is our great high priest who brings himself as a sacrifice and offering to God as the Lamb of God who is sacrificed on our behalf (John 1:29). Joseph is a kingly figure, having been the vice-regent of Egypt who rode in the second chariot behind Pharaoh, the ruler of Egypt. Jesus was not just a king; rather, he is the King of kings and Lord of lords! Even the government is on his shoulders (Isa 9:6); the kingdoms of this world will become the kingdom of our Lord and of his Christ; and he will reign forever (Rev 11:15). Christ simultaneously holds all three offices. Joshua, Eleazar, and Joseph all died. Christ, prophet, priest, and king, died once but came back to life, never to die again. He reigns forever and ever more.

Reflect and Discuss

1. The book of Joshua begins and ends with the deaths of the faithful. Why is this significant?
2. Why is it appropriate for this farewell address to be given at Shechem?
3. Why is it important to know not only biblical history but church history as well?
4. When have you made verbal promises you intended to keep but found it difficult to do? How did you respond?
5. On what basis is Israel to fear the Lord and worship him? On what basis are we to fear the Lord and worship him?
6. How are we, like the Israelites, unable to worship and serve God?
7. How can we worship and serve God in spite of ourselves?
8. What does it mean that God is jealous?
9. Why the mention of Joseph's bones?
10. How does the book of Joshua challenge your faith? How does it strengthen your faith?

WORKS CITED

Augustine. *Confessions*. Trans. William Watts. Cambridge, MA: Harvard University Press, 1998.

Auld, G. *Joshua, Judges, and Ruth*. Philadelphia, PA: Westminster, 1984.

———. *Joshua Retold: Synoptic Perspectives*. Edinburgh: T & T Clark, 1998.

Babcock, Matlbie D. "This Is My Father's World." Public domain.

Brueggemann, Walter. *Divine Presence Amid Violence: Contextualizing the Book of Joshua*. Eugene, OR: Cascade, 2009.

Campbell, A. F. *Joshua to Chronicles: An Introduction*. Louisville: Westminster John Knox, 2004.

Chapell, Bryan. *Christ-Centered Preaching*. Second ed. Grand Rapids, MI: Baker Academic, 2005.

Colson, Charles W. *Loving God*. Grand Rapids, MI: Zondervan, 2018.

Creach, J. F. D. *Joshua*. Interpretation: A Bible Commentary for Teaching and Preaching. Louisville:Westminster John Knox Press, 2012.

Davis, D. R. *Joshua: No Falling Words*. Fearn, Ross-Shire: Christian Focus, 2012.

Dickens, Charles. *A Tale of Two Cities*. Illustrated by H. Dunn. New York: Cosmopolitan Book Corporation, 1921.

Dixon, Jessy. "The Wicked Shall Cease Their Troubling."

Drummond, Lewis. *Spurgeon: The Prince of Preachers*. Grand Rapids, MI: Kregel, 1992.

Ellsworth, Roger. *Opening Up Joshua*. Leominster, England: Day One, 2008.

George, Timothy. *Amazing Grace: God's Pursuit, Our Response*. Second ed. Wheaton, IL: Crossway, 2011.

Greidanus, S. *Preaching Christ from Ecclesiastes: Foundations for Expository Sermons*. Grand Rapids, MI: Eerdmans, 2010.

Harstad, A. L. *Joshua: A Theological Exposition of Sacred Scripture*. Concordia Commentary. St Louis: Concordia, 2004.

Hawk, L. D. *Every Promise Fulfilled: Contesting Plots in Joshua.* Eugene, OR: Wipf and Stock, 2009.

The Hiding Place. Charlotte, NC: Billy Graham Evangelistic Association, 2006.

Hughes, R. K. *Living on the Cutting Edge: Joshua and the Challenge of Spiritual Leadership.* Wheaton, IL: Good News, 1987.

Hugo, Victor. *The Future of Man.*

Hussey, Jennie E. "Lead Me to Calvary." Public domain.

Jones, Edmund. "The Successful Resolve." Public domain.

King, M. L., Jr. "We Shall Overcome." https://www.smu.edu/News/2014/mlk-at-smu-transcript-17march1966. Accessed August 21, 2022.

Lischer, R. *The End of Words: The Language of Reconciliation in a Culture of Violence.* Grand Rapids, MI: Eerdmans, 2008.

McConville, J. G. *Joshua: Crossing Divides.* Sheffield: Sheffield Phoenix, 2013.

————, and S. N. Williams. *Joshua.* The Two Horizons Old Testament Commentary. Grand Rapids, MI: Eerdmans, 2010.

Miles, C. Austin, "I Was Once a Sinner." Public domain.

Monroe, Harriet, ed. *Poetry: A Magazine of Verse.* Vol. XIX. Chicago: October 1921.

Robinson, Roberts. "Come, Thou Fount of Every Blessing." Public domain.

Sanders, J. O. *Promised Land Living: You Can Be an Overcomer.* Chicago, IL: Moody, 1984.

Santayana, George. *The Life of Reason.* New York: Scribner's Sons, 1905.

Schaeffer, F. A. *Joshua and the Flow of Biblical History.* Wheaton, IL: Crossway, 2003.

Schaff, Philip. *History of the Christian Church.* Reprint ed. Grand Rapids, MI: Eerdmans, 1965.

Smith, Robert, Jr. *The Oasis of God.* Mountain Home, AR: BorderStone, 2014.

Soggin, J. A. *Joshua: A Commentary.* London: SCM, 1988.

Thielicke, Helmut. *Being a Christian When the Chips Are Down.* Trans. H. George Anderson. Philadelphia: Fortress, 1979.

Waleik, Gary. "MLB Legend Rod Carew and the Former NFL Pro Who Gave Him a New Heart." wbur.org. September 28, 2018. https://www.wbur.org/onlyagame/2018/09/28/rod-carew-konrad-reuland-heart-assists. Accessed July 25, 2022.

SCRIPTURE INDEX

22:30 *222*
22:33 *222*
23 *228, 234*
23:1 *230*
23:2 *231*
23:3 *231*
23:4 *231*
23:6 *231*
23:10 *10*
23:11 *232*
23:14 *14, 232–33*
23:15 *233*
23:16 *235*
24 *236*
24:1 *237*
24:2,14-16,18-
  22,24,31 *241*
24:3 *239*
24:4 *239*
24:5 *239*
24:6 *187, 239*
24:7 *239*
24:8 *239*
24:10 *239*
24:11 *239*
24:12 *239*
24:13 *239–40*
24:14 *240*
24:15 *241*
24:21 *242*
24:22 *242*
24:24 *244*
24:29 *10, 13–14,
  160, 191, 231,
  244*
24:31 *74, 245*
24:33 *245*
24:41 *163*

Judges
1:2 *17, 19*
2:8 *13–14*
2:10 *17, 222*
2:10-11 *74, 242*
18 *198*
18:1 *198*
19:12 *182*
20 *222*

1 Samuel
15 *89*
16:17 *132*
31:4 *161*

1 Kings
16:34 *107*

2 Kings
2:6,12 *63*

1 Chronicles
7:20-29 *13*

Nehemiah
7:25 *133*

Job
2:12 *114*
23:10 *59*

Psalms
1:2 *24, 36*
23:4 *25*
27:14 *167*
30:5 *19*
32:1 *110*
34:19 *19*
37:4 *138*
37:23 *141*
51:3 *90*
51:5 *205*

56:8 *157*
103:2 *64*
103:10-12 *43, 80*
115:4-8 *232*
118:22-23 *73*
119:89 *122*
124:1 *76*
150:6 *103*

Proverbs
3:5-6 *129*

Ecclesiastes
5:5 *242*

Isaiah
2:4 *37*
6:7 *63*
9:6 *135, 246*
40:8 *218*
40:31 *171*
45:20-22 *232*
46:10 *99*
49–53 *14*
53:5 *197, 206*
55:8 *158, 177*
65:10 *116*

Jeremiah
8:22 *18*
20:9 *87*
29:11 *23*

Ezekiel
18:4 *208*

Hosea
2:15 *116*
3:1 *121*

Jonah
1:17 *32*